G000066240

PLANNING FOR CRIME PREVENTION

Crime and the fear of crime are issues high in public concern and on political agendas in most developed countries. This book takes these issues and relates them to the contribution that urban planners and participative planning processes can make in response to these problems. Its focus is thus on the extent to which crime opportunities can be prevented or reduced through the design, planning and management of the built environment. The perspective of the book is transatlantic and comparative, not only because ideas and inspiration in this and many other fields increasingly move between countries but also because there is a great deal of relevant theoretical material and practice in both the USA and the UK which has not previously been pulled together in this systematic manner.

The first part of the book looks at the context for understanding ideas and practice in this field. It introduces the key concepts of place-based crime prevention, and explores what we know both about the nature and scale of crime in the two countries and about some of the issues surrounding crime statistics. The second part looks at policy and practice in the USA and the UK, with a full presentation both of how policy issues are perceived and handled nationally and of how this translates into practice on the ground via a series of case studies. The third part of the book makes a more formal comparison between the positions in the USA and the UK as they have been presented, before drawing some ideas and lessons out of this material to point the way forward.

This book is for anyone who wants to know about how planning processes and crime prevention activities can be more effectively integrated. It is essential reading not just for planning students but also for those in many built environment and community disciplines, for practitioners in these fields including police and property development professionals, for politicians interested in this area of public concern and those who advise them.

Richard H. Schneider is Associate Professor of Urban and Regional Planning at the College of Design, Construction and Planning, University of Florida, USA and Graduate Studies Co-ordinator in the Department of Urban and Regional Planning.

Ted Kitchen is Professor of Planning and Urban Regeneration and Director of the School of Environment and Development at Sheffield Hallam University, England.

THE RTPI Library Series

Editors: Cliff Hague, Heriot Watt University, Edinburgh, Scotland
Robin Boyle, Wayne State University, Michigan, USA
Robert Upton, RTPI, London, UK

Published in conjunction with The Royal Town Planning Institute, this series of leading-edge texts looks at all aspects of spatial planning theory and practice from a comparative and international perspective.

The series

- explores the dimensions of spatial planning and urbanism, in relation to people, place, space and environment;

- develops the theoretical and methodological foundations of planning;

- investigates the relationship between theory and practice;

- examines the contribution of planners to resolving social, economic and environmental concerns.

By linking planning to disciplines such as economics, anthropology, sociology, geography, environmental and urban studies, the project's inherent focus on sustainable development places the theoretical and practical relationships between social, economic and environmental issues in their spatial context.

Already published:
Planning in Postmodern Times
Philip Allmendinger, University of Aberdeen, Scotland

Planning for Crime Prevention
Richard Schneider, University of Florida, USA, and Ted Kitchen, Sheffield Hallam University, UK

Forthcoming:
Sustainability, Development and Spatial Planning in Europe
Vincent Nadin, Caroline Brown and Stefanie Duhr, UWE, Bristol, UK

Public Values and Private Interests
Heather Campbell and Robert Marshall

Shadows of Power
Jean Hillier

Planning for Place Identity
Cliff Hague and Paul Jenkins

Urban Planning and Cultural Identity
William J. V. Neill

PLANNING FOR CRIME PREVENTION

A Transatlantic Perspective

RICHARD H. SCHNEIDER and
TED KITCHEN

London and New York

First published 2002 by Routledge, 11 New Fetter Lane, London EC4P 4EE
Simultaneously published in the USA and Canada by Routledge, 29 West 35th Street, New York, NY 10001

Routledge is an imprint of the Taylor & Francis Group

Typeset in 9.5/13.5 Akzidenz Grotesk by Wearset Ltd, Boldon, Tyne and Wear
Printed and bound in Great Britain by Biddles Ltd, Guildford and King's Lynn

British Library Cataloguing in Publication Data
A catalogue record for this book is available from the British Library

Library of Congress Cataloging in Publication Data
Schneider, Richard H. (Richard Harold), 1947–
 Planning for crime prevention : a transatlantic perspective / Richard H. Schneider and Ted Kitchen.
  p. cm. – (The RTPI library series)
 Includes bibliographical references and index.
 ISBN 0-415-24136-7 – ISBN 0-415-24137-5 (pbk.)
 1. Crime prevention–United States. 2. Crime prevention–Great Britain. 3. City planning–United States.
 4. City planning–Great Britain. 5. Crime prevention and architectural design. I. Kitchen, Ted. II. Title.
 III. Series.

HV7431 .S355 2002
364.4'9'0941–dc21

                                                                            2001052000

To Samantha, Joanna, Amanda and Christopher

CONTENTS

LIST OF FIGURES

LIST OF TABLES

FOREWORD

Richard M. Titus, Ph.D.
National Institute of Justice*

The role of place in crime causation and control has in recent years received increasing attention from criminologists: routine activity theory and opportunity theory being two examples. The same can be said for criminal justice practitioners; examples being crime analysis, crime mapping, problem-oriented policing, community policing, Weed and Seed, and COMPASS. The situation with planners and architects is different: as the authors of this text point out, those who create the environments in which we live, work, play, and travel too often seem to be minimally conscious of how their work can affect the safety of those who use these environments. And while avoidance of victimisation may not be uppermost in the minds of those who locate and operate businesses, decide where to live, plan an evening's entertainment, etc., it is a factor in all these decisions.

The authors are not arguing an environmental determinism. While thoughtless planning and architecture can create environments that criminals find to be more congenial, it does not follow that security-conscious design can eliminate the risk to people and their property: the authors point out the need for involvement of the users and managers of these environments, along with public and private security.

The authors are careful to place their recommendations in the context of the available research and evaluation. They point out that this literature is rather scanty. Nonetheless, the burden of the evidence they review is that changes in the environment can lead to reductions in various types of crime. This evidence is difficult to assess: much of it was accumulated during a period when crime rates – at least in the USA – were trending downward. It is tempting to assume that the many environmental crime prevention strategies put in place over the period** may have contributed to this decline, but if not, it remains to be seen how they will perform if crime rates rise again.

* For identification only. The opinions expressed are those of the author and do not represent policy of the National Institute of Justice or the US Department of Justice
** e.g. the placement of security guards or concierges in the lobbies of almost all downtown office buildings.

The authors properly urge the reader's attention to fear as distinct from risk. If the public's mental maps of feared places and situations are not congruent with the actual geographic distribution of risk, planners can analyse the fear as a separate problem to be addressed. But if they are congruent, it would be improper to reduce fear without first reducing risk.

The authors indicate that recommendations must be put in the context of the characteristics of particular settings and actors. If we apply lessons from examples that are not generalisable to the current situation, the results are not likely to be satisfactory. The authors also remind us that environmental strategies must be examined as one of many available strategies. For example, if the crime of concern is burglary, the strategies might include physical modifications, resident organisation, victim-centred policing, anti-fencing programmes, and anti-truancy programmes; all of which have been shown to impact burglary.

Whenever possible we should narrow our focus from 'crime' to the specific crimes of concern at the location of interest. Police crime analysts and crime prevention officers are a resource, but designers can also use available software and crime data to conduct their own analysis. The stranger-nonstranger dimension will be an important element in the analysis. For example, place-centred strategies may have a role to play in the crimes of burglary and domestic violence, but the role is likely to be quite different in the two cases.

The authors point out that fullest use of available technology for surveillance and access control is more likely to be found in private space than in public space – especially in the USA. This gap may well grow larger. For example, parents who work are already using nannycams over the internet to guard their children from the office; they can do the same with their residences, perhaps rotating the assignment among adjacent neighbours, or, paying their retiree neighbours to do it. It will be a continuing challenge to find ways to protect public space with the sophistication that we bring to bear in private space.

I believe that these authors have done an excellent job with a difficult topic. It is to be hoped that their volume will find a large and attentive readership among the intended audiences.

PREFACE

We have chosen to collaborate on this book because we have each seen from our differing starting points the need for something like this in the available planning literature. Richard Schneider comes at this with a long-standing academic interest in crime and environmental design, reinforced by research and practice collaborations with both police and planning professionals in Florida and by a sabbatical period at UMIST in Manchester in 1995/96 looking at British practice in the field. Ted Kitchen comes at it very much from the planning practitioner's perspective, having tried (if such a grand claim can be made) during his time as City Planning Officer of Manchester from 1989 to 1995 to make that City's planning service more community-orientated and discovering as a result that this field was one of considerable concern to local communities, if not typically to planners. Both of us observed from these differing starting points the ways in which these concerns generated considerable controversy and influenced decisions about the approaches adopted to the redevelopment of Hulme in Manchester in the early and mid-1990s, which is one of the case studies in Chapter 8 of this book. And both of us subsequently, in collaborating on common teaching projects at our two universities, where we used email exchanges to swap results between our groups of students, became aware not only of the absence of much useful textual material for students and practitioners but also of the need for improved understanding on both sides of the Atlantic of what was being done and written in the USA and in Britain before its uncritical application. Hence this book.

Transatlantic writing collaborations are not especially common, and they bring some fairly obvious difficulties in their wake. The old saw about 'two nations divided by a common language' certainly applies to an endeavour of this nature, and it was reinforced by an early recognition of the fact that we each had naturally rather different writing styles. Rather than go for some sort of mid-Atlantic compromise (whatever watery solution that might entail), we decided not to worry about that but instead to concentrate on covering the agreed ground, adopting broadly common structures for each chapter, so that at least the approach was common, and then exchanging drafts for comment as critical friends. So, Richard Schneider took the lead in respect of Chapters 1 and 3–6 and Ted Kitchen took the lead in respect of the Introduction and Chapters 2 and 7–10. Ted Kitchen then took responsibility for ensuring that all the text was in British rather than American English, it being the view of all the parties to this endeavour that our readers would benefit from a common approach in these terms. This working method seemed to work well enough for us without (we hope) submerging the differences both of styles and of perspectives that must inevitably be part of a transatlantic cooperation. It is, of course, for our readers to judge whether this book achieves its objectives and provides a product that they find helpful; but we hope that it does.

ACKNOWLEDGEMENTS

Richard Schneider would like to thank Professor George Birrell and Alison Birrell for opening up their home and hearts to him when he came to Britain as a visiting Research Fellow at the University of Manchester Institute of Science and Technology in 1995–1996. Without their guidance and help – including an introduction to his co-author – this work would not have taken place. Pamela Hyde, Management Division Administrator for Civil and Construction Engineering at UMIST, facilitated every stage of this research and, as a gracious host and friend, deserves a great deal of credit. Special thanks are due to Ray Catesby, former Architectural Liaison Officer, Greater Manchester Police, for allowing Richard to accompany him on many site visits throughout the city. He is most appreciative to Ray for his time, effort and endurance in putting up with too many questions. Acknowledgements also are due to Royston K. Smith, UMIST Security and General Services Manager, for assistance at various stages of this work. Richard would also like to thank Officer Sterling Keys, former Crime Prevention Officer with the City of Gainesville, Florida Police Department (presently with Boulder, Colorado's police force) for his interest in and contributions to this work and he also acknowledges the Florida CPTED Network, and in particular Dorinda Howe, for access to its mobile library. Finally but not least, Richard thanks his colleagues at the University of Florida College of Design, Construction and Planning, Department of Urban and Regional Planning, and especially Professors Ernest Bartley, James Nicholas, Earl Starnes, Jay Stein, Ruth Steiner and Paul Zwick for their encouragement and support throughout the course of the research.

Ted Kitchen would like to thank Trish Wood, Faye Revill and Anne Adderley for all their work typing and retyping drafts and experimenting with layouts. Their patience has been inexhaustible, not least with the authors. Trish also did most of the editorial work in the later phases of the process with a cheerfulness and an enthusiasm that would have been hard to match, and her willingness to keep returning to material in the constant search for improvements was a real source of encouragement. Ted would also like to thank his academic colleagues at the School of Environment and Development at Sheffield Hallam University for bearing with him while he tried to balance the task of co-authoring the book against his day-job as School Director. He would also like to thank colleagues at the School of Architecture, Construction and Planning at Curtin University, Perth, Western Australia for providing a stimulating and enjoyable environment for him during a Visiting

Fellowship in the (British) summer of 2000, when Chapters 9 and 10 got drafted and the Australian comparative material that can be found in the text was explored.

Richard and Ted would jointly like to thank Caroline Mallinder and Rebecca Casey at Routledge for their encouragement throughout this project, and for their pithy comments when academics were at some risk of missing the wood for the fascination offered by individual trees. Lesley Ann Staward and Steve Turrington worked closely with us in turning the book from a submitted typescript to a finished product, and asked some pointed questions along the way which undoubtedly helped to improve upon our original efforts. Professor Cliff Hague, as the RTPI's nominated editor for the RTPI Library Series, made some helpful comments on an early working draft and was also encouraging throughout as he travelled the world. Dr Tim Pascoe of the Building Research Establishment commented on our near-final draft, and as well as offering helpful individual comments also reinforced our views about the market that might exist for a book of this nature. Likewise, Dr Richard Titus of the US National Institute of Justice read the near-final draft, gave us his support throughout, and contributed the Foreword, for which we are grateful.

Joseph J. Sabatella contributed the line drawings used in Chapter 3, which give visual expression to the concepts discussed therein and help to make them much more readily understandable, and we would both like to thank him for these. They represent his interpretations of historical artefacts, based upon previous work by Hogg (1975 – Figures 3.1, 3.4 and 3.5), Reps (1965 – Figure 3.2) and Kostof (1992 – Figures 3.3, 3.6 and 3.7). Except where otherwise indicated, the photographs used throughout the book were taken by the authors.

There are also a large number of other people that we have spoken to or otherwise communicated with during the life of this project, who have helped us in many ways with this book without perhaps even being aware of this themselves. We would hope that they can spot something in here which relates to their exchanges with us, and feel good about that contribution. At the end of the day, of course, decisions about what to include and what to exclude were down to us working together, as is responsibility for any errors or omissions.

INTRODUCTION

We have two primary objectives in writing this book. The first is to encourage planners and other professionals to take more seriously the relationship between crime prevention and the design of the built environment in all its aspects. The second is to contribute to moves which are trying to push work in this field towards more evidence-driven approaches, since too often ideas have been promoted loudly but with very little empirical basis, have waxed in the glow of fashion for a short period of time, and have then been replaced by something else with a similar pedigree including the lack of much empirical evidence to support it. Before going on to describe how we set about these tasks through the structure of this book, therefore, we would like to introduce these two primary objectives in a little more detail, because we return to them both on several occasions throughout.

One clearly observable phenomenon from some of the data we will be presenting later is the belief that crime prevention and the fear of crime matter very much to local citizens when they are considering the quality of life available to them in the areas where they live, work, shop, send their children to school and spend their leisure time. We will show how high up scoring systems about public concerns matters of this nature consistently appear in surveys carried out on both sides of the Atlantic. If planning and other related professional activities concerned with the quality of the environment are to substantiate claims about being 'for people', then it seems to us that one of the most basic requirements is that they should address themselves to the concerns of those people in relation to their environments and not just to the concerns and interests of the professionals themselves. And yet, with some clear exceptions, we would assert that the relationships between planning activities, crime prevention, and the design of the built environment have not registered as major concerns of planners and indeed typically do not feature very highly on planning education curricula.

Perhaps one of the reasons for this is that ideas in the field have often been promoted with dogmatic zeal in some quarters and dismissed as 'environmental determinism' with equal fervour in other quarters, leaving the majority of planners both confused and with little reliable guidance about these relationships. Our view is that there is no need to adopt either of these extreme positions to accept that in some situations and in varying degrees the nature and organisation of the built environment both have an effect on perceptions on the part of criminals about the opportunity for crime and on the behaviour of people in the built environment because of their fear of crime. The likelihood is that these relationships are often subtle, complex, and variable both in relation to the huge range of forms taken by the built environment and by the ways in which people perceive and use that environment. That simple observation should of itself be a sufficient warning against hard-sold standardised solutions, since if what it says about observable complexity is true then it is inherently unlikely that externally predetermined common solutions will fit other than a small fraction of situations on the ground. So instead of starting from dogmatic and simplistic views about these relationships (which may indeed be environmentally deterministic), planners and other environmental professionals should study them on the ground, working with local people to find and implement solutions which are carefully monitored and if need be modified in the light of that information. That way, planners and others can make an effective contribution tailored to particular sets of local circumstances to the elimination or reduction of problems that matter a great deal to local people. In so doing, they will almost certainly need to get involved in multi-professional partnerships, including with the police. Police officers have often in the past had to try to work on issues to do with crime and the design of the built environment in the absence of support from other professionals, who do have a considerable amount of knowledge about environmental design issues (far more than the police usually do) but have simply tended not to apply it in relation to crime prevention. Increasingly, on both sides of the Atlantic, there is a growing acceptance, including from many people in the police service, that multi-professional teams are needed in order to tackle this job effectively rather than leaving it to the police, and that is also what local citizens need if their wishes and concerns are to be effectively recognised by professionals. So, we assert that there is both a need and an opportunity for planners and others to take this issue more seriously and that the time is overdue for this to happen.

Our second primary objective, to argue for more evidence and less assertion as the basis for the growth of knowledge and understanding in this field, is in a sense a corollary of the first. If the relationship between crime and the design of the built environment is to rise successfully up the planning agenda, this will be not just because more planners spend more time on the issue, but also because a great deal of collective learning is taking place and is influencing what they are actually doing. Our hope is that this will create a virtuous circle, which will also assist with the problem of getting local people to trust inputs from professionals in that they will see these as empirically based rather than as driven by professional dogma. This is particularly important in cases where professional dogmas are seen by local residents to have been significant contributors to their present problems, for example in relation to the quality of some of the high-rise public housing that has been constructed in the inner city during the past thirty years or so. We say far more about the need for an empirical approach as we go along throughout this book, but the single most important thing that needs to happen in this context is for initiatives to be monitored, appraised and reported on in openly accessible ways. Modern information technology offers more opportunity to do this than has ever been the case before, but the really important need is for this opportunity to be grasped so that we can build up a pool of experiential knowledge of the kind that to a considerable extent cannot yet be said to exist.

This assertion about the current 'state of play' in this field leads us to make one cautionary statement about what this book is not, before we go on to describe its contents. We do not wish to mislead readers into expecting that they will find here a series of 'recipes' in a 'cookbook' that they can simply go out and apply in a given set of circumstances. We do not believe that the state of knowledge in the field at present would support such an approach, even if we felt that it was intellectually justifiable. This may be possible at some time in the future, although we would doubt that there will ever be a substitute for careful immersion in the local circumstances working alongside local people. For the present, however, we conclude this book, on the basis of the material we present throughout, with a set of broad propositions which we hope will help planners and other professionals to begin to think their way into these kinds of situations, but which are not of the 'this is what to do' variety. We believe that this is more helpful to readers in the present state of knowledge than would be an attempt to construct a 'how to do it' manual; and we hope also that it will encourage readers to see the opportunity through their own efforts to attempt and to report upon what may be innovative initiatives which may be both of local value and contribute to the broader growth of experiential knowledge for which we are arguing.

To these ends, this book is divided into three parts, as follows.

PART 1. CONTEXT AND KEY IDEAS

Chapter 1 introduces the relationships between crime, the fear of crime and the organisation and management of the built environment as major matters affecting the quality of life.

Chapter 2 discusses recent crime trends in both the USA and in Britain, not just in terms of overall statistics but also in terms of some of the major distributional issues that these contain.

Chapter 3 looks at the history of how issues of defensible space have been handled in relation to human settlements, making the point that much of our apparently contemporary thinking can actually be found throughout this very long story of human endeavour.

Chapter 4 sets out the major principles, ideas and theories that are to be found in relation to this field.

PART 2. POLICY AND PRACTICE

Chapter 5 looks at policy and practice in the USA, showing the extent to which in that society most of what has been done to date has been a function of local initiative rather than of central direction.

Chapter 6 then looks in more detail at a small number of informative case studies in the USA, to demonstrate something of what has actually been happening on the ground.

Chapter 7 looks at policy and practice in Britain, and in particular at the growth in recent years of a strong central policy direction to work in this field.

Chapter 8 then looks in more detail at a small number of case studies in Britain, again chosen to try to illustrate in some detail something of the range of initiatives taken in recent years.

PART 3. COMPARISONS AND KEY ISSUES

Chapter 9 makes some formal comparisons between the USA and Britain in terms of the matters covered in the previous eight chapters, since a feature of this particular book is that it is strongly transatlantic in its perspectives.

Chapter 10 then draws together some key principles which we believe help to point the way forward in this field, and discusses some of the key research issues that we would wish to see given a degree of priority in the coming years.

The transatlantic perspectives that we have adopted are, we believe, both a distinguishing and an important feature of this book. They are distinguishing in the quite literal sense that it is unusual for American and British academic authors to cooperate on this type of book. And we believe that transatlantic perspectives are important because the literature and the ideas that are used in the field tend to be treated as being common between the two societies, without much acknowledgement both of the similarities and of the differences that ought to be understood if we are to make full and effective use of this heritage. Both societies have also in recent years seen a considerable number of new initiatives, some of which have borrowed from each other without formal attribution or apparent awareness of the contextual differences affecting their application, and we believe that this will only achieve its full potential as a rich learning opportunity if we understand both the similarities and the differences between the two societies before seeking to borrow and apply ideas uncritically. We hope, therefore, that this book makes a worthwhile contribution in these terms, as well as achieving the two objectives we have described in this introduction.

We hope that this approach will mean that a wide range of potential readers will find this book helpful and interesting. Clearly, a book which takes as its title 'Planning for Crime Prevention' is aiming particularly at planning students and planning practitioners, and thus we address much of what we have to say to the planning community. But, to purloin a phrase, planning is far too important to be left just to the planners, and so we hope that many of the professionals in other fields who work with planners or whose activities are affected by the planning process such as architects and civil engineers will also find something here to challenge and stimulate them. In particular, we hope that people in or interested in the police service will find the perspectives presented here of value, not least because we believe that the way forward in this field requires much stronger partnerships between police and built environment professionals based upon mutual respect for each other's contributions. We hope also that participants in the property development process will find useful material in these pages, because their decisions will make a real difference (for good or ill) to outcomes on the ground in many of the areas we discuss. Since much of this is about matters of legitimate public policy concern, we hope that politicians with an interest in this field and those that advise them will find the contents of this book a stimulus to think through the policy frameworks they create or enable that provide the context for action on the ground. And, last but not least, we hope that some community groups and individuals who are interested in crime prevention and other civic improvement initiatives in their localities, and recognise that this will require them to work alongside a range of professionals, will find some help and encouragement in these pages. This is a large and quite diverse potential audience; but then, this is a field in which a lot of people have a part to play.

We wholly accept, of course, that readers from these various audiences will have different reasons for looking at a book of this nature, and will wish to get different things out of this experience. While we hope some readers will stay with us from start to finish, we acknowledge that many will want to read particular chapters for particular purposes and skip material that is of lesser interest to them. We therefore offer the following 'route map', in the hope that this will help readers to find the material in which they are most interested.

Chapter 1 is a general introduction to the key themes of the book, and will be familiar ground to readers already aware of the major relationships at work here.

Chapter 2 goes into a certain amount of detail about crime statistics and trends in the USA and in Britain and can be passed over by those not interested in this issue, but it also contains some important messages about crime data which should be understood by anyone who wishes to make use of this material.

Chapter 3 is an historical chapter, presented at this level of detail partly because it is a fascinating story not usually told like this in the literature, and partly because it demonstrates that many of our contemporary ideas actually have their roots in earlier periods when defending cities from attacks from outside rather than crime from within was the primary concern. Readers not interested in the history of this could skip this chapter.

Chapter 4 in effect brings the story begun in Chapter 3 up to date, by presenting the emergence of ideas in the twentieth century about the relationships between crime prevention and the design and organisation of the built environment. We think that this is a critical chapter to the development of an understanding of the arguments we are presenting in this book.

Chapters 5 and 6 present material on policy and practice in the USA, with the former having more of a broad policy focus and the latter having a case-study focus. Clearly, readers who are particularly interested in US policy and practice can go straight to these pages and those who are not interested in how these issues are tackled in the USA can skip these chapters, but we feel that an understanding of what is happening on the ground is an essential complement to the ideas presented in Chapters 1 and 4. This comment also applies to Chapters 7 and 8, since the USA and the UK are two of the world's leading open societies that are experimenting in this field.

Chapters 7 and 8 present the UK equivalents of the material on the USA in Chapters 5 and 6, and so the same comments *mutatis mutandis* apply here also.

Chapter 9 is a comparison of policy and practice in the USA and the UK organised around key themes, and it is in our judgement essential to developing an understanding of the transatlantic perspective that is a central feature of this book.

Chapter 10 presents what we feel we can say about the way forward with a degree of confidence on the basis of what we currently know, and so we would hope that all readers whatever their interests in previous chapters would look at and reflect on our conclusions.

We hope that this 'route map' demonstrates that there is useful material here for each of the groups we see as being amongst our audience, and that it helps readers to find what they are looking for quickly.

PART 1

CONTEXT AND KEY IDEAS

CHAPTER 1

CRIME, COSTS AND THE QUALITY OF LIFE

INTRODUCTION

For urban planners and designers, police, policy makers and a growing number of citizens, the concept of 'quality of life' has become increasingly important as a defining measure of the health of cities and the societies of which they are a part. In this chapter we discuss crime and the fear of crime as key factors directing the choices that citizens make and as these choices affect the quality of life in Britain and in the United States. Towards that end:

- we explore the implications that basic questions of safety have for ourselves and our families relative to urban places, the fundamental building blocks of British and American cities. We review definitions of the component elements of crime prevention planning, focusing on measures of programme success in reducing crime and the fear of crime.
- we consider the theoretical predicates of crime prevention, through origins in the classical, positivist, sociological and modern schools of criminology. In so doing, we focus particularly on *offender* and *environment-based* approaches as related to traditional and emerging models of crime prevention.
- we review the impacts that crime has had on the quality of life of citizens in Britain and the United States, noting citizens' responses to crime and the fear of crime in residential, shopping, recreational and employment choices. Since crime is a major expense to both nations, we review some of the relative costs of crime as estimated by recent national studies.
- beyond mere statistical measures, we explore the role crime has in driving citizen choices, noting that these have important impacts on the viability and liveability of large metropolitan areas in the United States and Britain. We suggest that a primary role of urban planning is to increase the range of choices available to citizens, while crime and the fear of crime have the opposite effects. Despite that, we note that crime prevention planning has been understated in the traditional planning and urban design literature and in available coursework, even though, as we see in Chapter 2, it is consistently at or near the top of concerns stated by citizens in repeated national polls. We conclude with a summary that attempts to integrate the multiple concepts expressed in this chapter and pave the way for future research and practice.

'IS IT SAFE?'

As every parent knows who has ever sent a child off to live away from home, whether for a day or a semester, the fundamental questions asked are: 'Is it safe where you'll be living? Is the neighbourhood a high crime area? Is there adequate street lighting? Are the doors strong, the windows secure? Will there be parents or guardians to watch over you?' We put such questions to our loved ones (and to ourselves) countless times in our lives. Often, the answers we get flow from gut feelings, from casual observations, from impressions based on newspaper reports, from speaking with friends and relatives, or infrequently, from police statistics or from survey data. While those responses may be sufficient to guide the average citizen's choices in answering the question 'Is it safe?', they are rarely helpful in understanding 'How can we make places *safer*?'

We generally look to the police to make places safe. Until victimised, and perhaps not even after then, most citizens never consider the role that others may play – urban planners and designers, architects, environmental and behavioural scientists – in making places *safer* by preventing future crime. Moreover, most people never consider the linkage between the design and management of the physical environment and crime prevention. But there is a growing body of evidence to show that these are indeed connected. This book explores those connections by reviewing the theory and application of crime prevention planning to places in Britain and in the United States. Our intent is to understand where we are in the struggle to make places safer for ourselves and our loved ones.

We are particularly concerned with how much of what we believe about environmental crime prevention is based upon reasonable empirical research, and the implications of proceeding with crime prevention interventions in the absence of such validation. Our concern therefore is that the development of crime prevention policy be evidence-driven (Van Dijk, 1997), and that planners and other professionals concerned with the urban environment take more of a role in policy making and application processes.

In developing those themes, our first task is to characterise the concepts that we use throughout the book.

DEFINITIONS

The Oxford English Dictionary defines *crime* as 'an act punishable by law, as being forbidden by statute or injurious to the public welfare' (1982, page 603). Recognising that each nation defines crime differently within their criminal codes, we are primarily concerned with those crimes that national surveys in Britain and the United States tell us citizens fear the most: 'stranger to stranger' personal and

Britain and the USA where the marketplace of individual choice-making has been valued for centuries. While British and American cultures have long prized the good sense of ordinary people to make their own judgements – many based on perceptions as distinct from 'reality' – about everything from politics to their own personal safety, such judgements have benefits and costs. The net result of this calculation about the safety of places can mean that individuals may become trapped at home, businesses may fail, neighbourhoods may deteriorate, and entire communities may be consigned to poverty and despair. Just as the separate pieces ultimately combine to complete a puzzle, places matter to the integrity of the city, and perceptions of crime, whether based on real or imagined incidents, affect the value of each place and subsequently, the viability of neighbourhoods, cities and entire societies. Minneapolis–St Paul Metropolitan Council Chair, Curt Johnson says:

> fear of crime is a very real and powerful force. It can shape people's preferences about where they live and work and influence market demand for housing and commercial development. The stakes are high. If we, as a region, fail to address issues related to crime, real and perceived, we will be turning our backs on some of our historically liveable neighbourhoods, and, eventually, putting our region's economy at risk (Minneapolis–St Paul Metropolitan Council, 1997).

The assumption inherent in all this is that people do indeed have a range of options to choose from, as well as the ability actually to make a choice among those options. But we know that options and choice-making abilities are limited for many citizens, and especially for the poor wherever they live and for those in distressed neighbourhoods in urban centres. As the statistics show us in Chapter 2, these are the citizens who tend to have the most to fear from crime. Without wishing to appear elitist, we contend that it is precisely these individuals who are in the greatest need of place-based crime prevention planning and urban design assistance and advice, as the wealthy can and do fend for themselves and are able to create options and decide among them. This makes the roles and responsibilities of planners and urban designers all the more significant, inasmuch as they have a central public-interest role in the creation of safe and liveable urban places for and, most importantly, *with* those citizens who are least prosperous and who may be unwilling or unable to speak for themselves. With this social imperative in mind, the crime prevention planning approaches discussed in this book suggest a range of physical design and management theories and strategies aimed at mitigating real and perceived crime in places – the primary structural elements of our societies.

THEORETICAL PREDICATES OF CRIME PREVENTION:
OFFENDERS AND ENVIRONMENTS

Chapter 7 details British thinking, through the 1990s to now, about the interrelated themes of crime prevention policy centring on *offenders*, *victims*, *environment* and the *community*. The same themes can be said to characterise the range of American policy response to crime prevention across a wide variety of public agencies, as discussed in more detail in Chapters 5 and 6. Historically, in both nations crime prevention policy has flowed from choices among increased *punishments* and/or *treatment* of the offender, treatment of the offender's *social-economic conditions* or *hardening targets* – more locks, stronger windows, doors and other environmental interventions. These choices and the modern themes they have come to represent, can be brought together into two general approaches, one emphasising *offenders* and the other emphasising *environments*. Adopting these approaches is in no way intended to minimise the plight of victims; we suggest rather that there is reasonable empirical justification to suggest that physical environments have a good deal to do with victimisation (Spelman and Eck, 1989; Spelman, 1995), which may properly be considered to fall within the environmental approach, as within sociological, economic or psychological approaches. Indeed, inasmuch as victims can be considered as 'targets' of crime, they are central to the theory and practice of place-based crime prevention.

While the police can be said to have a place in both offender and environmental approaches to crime control, their roles as agents of environmental crime *prevention* have only within the last four decades generally emerged as a central concern in both theory and practice; traditionally far more emphasis has been placed on duties in investigation and apprehension (NCPI, 1986). This trend is demonstrated by recent national legislation in both Britain and the United States, such as the 1994 Crime Act, which created the Community Oriented Policing Services (COPS) programme in the USA, and the 1998 Crime and Disorder Act in Britain, which requires community level partnerships focusing much more attention on the link between policing and local (physical and social) environments than has previously been the case. We therefore include the police within the context of our discussion of contemporary environmental approaches.

While there is evidence to support the use of both offender and environmental approaches in developing strategies to prevent crime, there is also an increased understanding that apparently obvious remedies in both contexts can also produce negative and unintended effects and that new empirically based approaches are essential.

PUNISHMENT OF OFFENDERS AS CRIME PREVENTION

Perhaps the most traditional societal approach to crime prevention is *punishment*. While the biblical injunction prescribing 'an eye for eye, tooth for tooth' (Leviticus, Chapter 24) has long been championed as an effective preventative approach, its true crime deterrent value also has been argued for centuries. For instance, Waller (2000) reports that in the four decades between 1680 and 1720 the number of crimes that warranted the death penalty in England soared from approximately eighty to more than 350. 'Indeed, there are so many that no one can be absolutely sure what you can or cannot be hanged for' (page 309). However,

> No one could have failed to notice that the severity of the law for offences against property was having little effect in stemming the rising tide of crime. As Cesar de Saussere observed: 'Executions are frequent in London ... notwithstanding this, there are in this country a surprising number of robbers. They may be classed in three divisions – highwaymen, foot pads, and pickpockets, all very audacious and bold' (page 315).

These observations were obviously lost on eighteenth century crime theorists of the *classical school,* such as utilitarian philosopher Jeremy Bentham (1962), who argued that the deterrent effect of the fear of punishment was the best crime prevention tool (Hart, 1968). Basic tenets of this conception were that offenders act rationally and out of free will and that punishment was intended to punish the *offence*, rather than the *offender*.[7] Moral and legal principles guided this early branch of criminology in its attempt to protect the rights of the accused and standardise punishments.

Laudable as these sentiments were, the effectiveness of punishment as crime prevention remains questionable. Police Chief of Salt Lake City, Utah, Ruben Ortega, recently noted that 'I have locked up more people than I care to count ... we cannot jail our way out of this' (Calhoun, 2000). This is a common refrain of law enforcement and other public officials across both sides of the Atlantic; and it is made all the more vexing by public attitudes that lay the vast majority of crime prevention responsibility squarely on the abilities of the police to apprehend offenders and on the criminal justice system's role to punish them. A recent United Nations' report notes growing disillusionment with the effectiveness of punitive measures, inasmuch as:

> Recidivist rates of ex-prisoners are almost universally very high (above fifty per cent). In many parts of the world crime rates have continued to go up since the sixties ... in spite of considerable extra investments in law enforcement,

prosecution, courts and prisons. This situation has led to a world-wide search for innovative, alternative approaches (UN Commission on Crime Prevention and Criminal Justice, 1999, pages 5–6).

Environmental design and related place-based crime prevention approaches are among those innovative strategies that are being increasingly 'discovered' as cost-effective and practical answers. They are receiving more attention since they are generally politically neutral, divert potential offenders away from the formal criminal justice apparatus, and tend to emphasise 'self-help' strategies that do not necessarily rely on governmental intervention or resources. However, they are not nearly as dramatic to the media and political opportunists as locking up criminals, or as personally emphatic as bolting the doors or windows shut. Moreover, environmental design does not pretend to treat what many conceive as the 'root' causes of crime – offenders' psychological temperament or socio-economic conditions.

TREATMENT AS CRIME PREVENTION

The concept of treatment as crime prevention flows out of the *positivist* school of criminology which developed in the early 1800s and became rooted in British empiricism, Darwinian determinism and Comte's sociological determinism (Jeffrey, 1977). It focused not on the legal and moral aspects of crime and punishment – which the positivists rejected out of hand – but on sociological, psychological and biological aspects of crime. It was, in short, a 'scientific' approach to crime control. Proponents of this approach concentrated on the *offender*, not on the *offence*, hoping that treatment would rehabilitate him. Under this scheme, crime could best be addressed by 'healing' the criminal, rather than punishing him; this ultimately gave rise to the modern concept of the correctional system. Its guidance as to crime prevention is thus primarily directed to causes *within* the individual and to his treatment and ultimate redemption through rehabilitation.

This theory indirectly influenced the *sociological* school of criminology that developed in the United States in the 1920s, which also suggested that crime prevention was best achieved through treatment rather than punishment. However, in this model, largely developed by theorists at the University of Chicago, it was the offenders' *sociological* and *economic* environments that required treatment, since the 'root causes' of crime were seen to stem from inadequacies in these. Although its adherents used such spatial and ecological terms as city 'sectors, rings and zones' (Park *et al.*, 1925; Shaw, 1969), it is clear that this school of thought was concerned with the social and economic fabric of crime rather than its physical environment (Michelson, 1976).

In that light, emphasis was directed away from punishment or rehabilitation as crime prevention and toward the repair of underlying social ills, such as the lack of employment or the negative influences of juvenile gangs in the neighbourhood. While these strategies are used in Britain and the United States today, they are seen as part and parcel of a wider package of crime prevention measures, none of which monopolise public funding or academic research to the exclusion of the others. Indeed, the growing trend toward crime prevention *partnerships* at local levels among a variety of agencies, from the police to health services, employing a range of approaches demonstrates the attraction of this multi-faceted strategy in present day Britain and the United States.

However, in its heyday during the 1930s–1950s, public remedies to crime suggested by the sociological theorists tended to drive out other strategies, especially in the United States. At the core of this conception was an urban form shaped by competition for space, with resulting ecological zones carved out by various economic and social groups. Within each niche one could ostensibly predict individual and group behaviours, and thus the propensity toward crime as a function of the social organisation (and disorganisation) found therein. While research on the uneven spatial distribution of crime in England had been charted since the rookeries were documented by Mayhew in the 1860s, the social ecologists went well beyond descriptive statistics and maps, and their views became the prevailing paradigm in academia and in government circles. For the most part, however, these theories remain controversial, especially when applied to small areas within American cities. The zonal hypotheses also proved particularly problematic in predicting patterns of criminal residence in England, where large-scale public housing projects redistributed en masse the populations from which offenders were more likely to come from city centres to city outskirts (Brantingham and Brantingham, 1981).

TARGET TREATMENT AS CRIME PREVENTION

Target hardening treats the *place* where crime occurs as opposed to the offender or their socio-economic surroundings. As such it is both a forerunner and component of contemporary environmental crime prevention planning. Target hardening increases the efforts that offenders must expend to reach their intended rewards by making them more difficult to attain. As a long-established approach to crime prevention, its development can be traced back to the beginnings of civilisation, as we discuss in Chapter 3, and may be found across a wide range of applications, from the construction of *communal* devices such as city walls and gates to the strengthening of entryways by *individual* property owners. In both Britain and the

United States, target hardening has been time-honoured advice given out by police agencies, and a wealth of standards for locks, doors and window fittings have been produced to guide builders and residents in implementing it.

While studies support its effectiveness as a crime prevention tool, target hardening can create counterintuitive results, as when designers fortify structures inspiring fear and repulsion which counterbalance security intents. A recent example of this is the problem of hardening embassies against terrorist attacks. A *Los Angeles Times* article notes that newly fortified and remotely located American embassies 'were forbidding to foreign residents and that the precautions prevented US diplomats from coming into contact with the citizens of the countries they were supposed to be observing' (Kempster and Meisler, 1998). This is clearly not the message that open societies want to convey to the rest of the world. Another example, offered by Tim Pascoe (from the UK's Building Research Establishment) in the course of commenting on an earlier draft of this book, is of the resident who, disturbed by the possibility of burglary, fits new but inappropriate locks to his front door, thereby structurally weakening it. The end result is to enhance rather than diminish the likelihood of a burglar's success, certainly a counterintuitive effect.

In Britain, target hardening of individual properties has been one of the major criteria that police use in presenting 'Secure By Design Awards' to residential and commercial estates. However, British research on offenders' decision making has shown that the choice of which residences to burgle is largely based on environmental cues gathered from the periphery of the target area (e.g. at the entrance to the neighbourhood), as distinct from the target itself, no matter how well fortified it was (Pascoe, 1993a). In the United States, other studies have provided only limited confirmation that protective devices and target hardening are important in protecting properties from burglaries (DeFrances and Titus, 1993). Moreover, there is evidence that builders are concerned that target hardening may in fact lessen the attractiveness and marketability of developments (Hoare, 1995). Target hardening strategies, as part and parcel of environmental crime prevention generally, also have been criticised as encouraging crime *displacement* rather than actual crime *prevention*, a subject we shall return to in Chapter 4.

All the above approaches are streams flowing out of traditional approaches to crime prevention that, while variably effective, have demonstrable shortcomings in modern application. They illustrate the point that no matter how obvious the solutions may appear to be, there are no simple answers to problems as complex as crime prevention. This has become increasingly clear as theory and practice have moved from a priori reasoning to empirical testing over the last three hundred years and have adapted modern technological and analysis techniques to crime and crime prevention.[8]

ENVIRONMENTS: CONTEMPORARY PLACE-BASED CRIME PREVENTION

Contemporary place-based crime prevention planning owes debts to both traditional punishment and target hardening conceptions described above, and – despite the protestations of some criminologists (Jeffrey, 1977) – to the social ecologists as well. Punishment, though debatable as to effect, makes the core assumption that potential offenders make rational choices; target hardening extends that logic by suggesting that increasing the efforts required to reach a reward will deter offenders, who are presumed to be rational. Although they dominated the crime prevention debate for years, social ecologists helped stir interest during the 1960s and 1970s in geographical themes relative to socio-pathologies and spin-off theories that stressed spatial variables, and ultimately the physical environment in which crime occurs.

As one result, physical *places* started to become important in and of themselves, and not merely as receptacles of socio-economic variables. Moreover, besides their physical design, attention also became focused on how places were used and managed, so that modern crime prevention theory has come to incorporate holistic conceptions about opportunity, risk, efforts and reward as part of the overall picture of the *situational* nature of the criminal event (Clarke, 1997).

Writings of social critics, and research conducted by behavioural scientists (and especially early environment-behaviour scientists), architects and criminologists provided positive, though not unquestioned, support for the concept that the physical environment influenced human behaviour generally and could be a 'criminogenic' (crime-causing) factor in particular (Hall, 1959; Lynch, 1960; Jacobs, 1961; Newman, 1973; Jeffrey, 1977; Brantingham and Brantingham, 1981; Sommer, 1983; Coleman, 1990; Clarke, 1997). We discuss some of their specific contributions relative to the development of place-based crime prevention in Chapter 4, but suffice to say for now that, because of their pioneering work, crime prevention interventions into the design and management of the physical environment have been largely legitimised.

Indeed, one such place-based approach – Crime Prevention Through Environmental Design (CPTED) – is now widely accepted by police agencies in the United States and Britain as a crime prevention strategy, even though it is much less well known among or applied by planners and urban designers. Its advocates hold that 'the physical environment can be manipulated to produce behavioural effects that will reduce the incidence and fear of crime, thereby improving the quality of life' (Crowe, 2000, page 34). Although implicit in the long history of target hardening, this connection is, as we have seen, relatively new to criminology and to applied crime prevention. Recognition of explicit and systematic linkages among environment, behaviours, crime and the quality of life are also relatively recent phenomena in academic and government circles.

CRIME AND THE QUALITY OF LIFE IN BRITAIN AND THE UNITED STATES

Systematic British assessments of the quality of life in cities are probably traceable to Booth's survey of East London in the 1880s, one of the earliest social surveys (Booth, 1888). A range of societal health indicators has been in wide usage in the United States since the 1930s when Baltimore journalist H. L. Mencken published a series of articles ranking the quality of life in American cities and states based on, among other variables, infant mortality, house price, crime rates, education and income levels. Since these early efforts British and American social scientists and pollsters have developed many such measures to produce 'community bench-marks', 'sustainability indicators' or 'quality of life indices'. In particular, the elabora-tion of indicators owes a large debt to advocates of sustainable development (and lifestyles) who have made this an art and science over the past decade (Brugmann, 1999). Indeed, the notion of sustainability – defined as 'development that meets the needs of the present without compromising the ability of future generations to meet their own needs' (UN Commission on Environment and Development, 1987, page 1) – is highly compatible with place-crime prevention planning. The latter is presumed to enhance community stability, by helping discourage among other things crime-generated urban out-migration and related economic and social dis-order, while improving overall life quality for present and future residents.

Communities throughout the United States and Britain use quality-of-life indicators, derived from a variety of government statistics and citizen surveys, as a means of identifying social well being at any point of time and of gauging it against past status. The range of indicators employed is extraordinary and often tailored to the unique character of the community's problems, needs and opportunities. For example, counties in California's Sierra Nevada range measure the rate of old growth timber harvests as a quality of life indicator, while Seattle counts wild salmon in the Cedar River. Communities in the Connecticut River Valley tally the number of new developments in the floodplain as a measure of quality of life, whilst cities in South Florida measure the number of tourists who visit each year. In Britain, Devon County Council employs fourteen general headings, including resources, pollution, bio-diversity and public safety, under which are grouped more than sixty subheadings of quality-of-life indicators.

No matter how diverse the communities, almost all have one indicator, or family of indicators, in common – 'public safety' – of which crime and the fear of crime are key components. The reason for this is simply that crime and perceptions of crime are quality-of-life factors that affect citizens' abilities to make seemingly trivial choices such as ordering pizza delivery at home as well as basic life decisions, such as where to live, work or send their children to school. Grayson and Young (1994) report that in the United Kingdom, citizens have identified crime and healthcare as issues that have the most significant impacts on their quality of life. When questioned in more detail, respondents to the 2000 British Crime Survey report that they are most worried about burglary, thefts of and from cars, credit card fraud, mugging and physical attack (Home Office, 2000b).

There are convincing arguments that quality-of-life measures ought to reflect changes in common everyday activities that people identify with, as a complement to impersonal government statistics. Calhoun (2000) has identified several examples of this approach collected in communities across the United States, including: the restoration of pizza delivery to certain neighbourhoods in Columbia, South Carolina, holding dances at formerly problematic neighbourhood schools in Richmond, California, the construction of new homes on the sites of former "crack houses" in San Antonio, Texas, and the ability of citizens to take a late bus to work in the evening without danger in many cities. Answers to these queries amplify responses to the more direct questions on surveys, such as 'Do you think your area has become safer over the last three years?' as asked of residents in fifteen different areas of Greater Manchester, Merseyside and Tyne and Wear, and reported in Chapter 7 (Robson et al., 1994).

Devon County Council in south-west England uses sustainability as a guiding philosophy,[9] within which its notion of 'public safety' is couched. Specific definitions of public safety focus on levels of crime and fear of crime, including fear of burglary and fear of being physically assaulted, two of the crimes that the British public in general fears the most (Devon County Council, 2000). In northern England, Bradford Metropolitan District Council recently conducted its first crime audit, a quality-of-life survey that all local authorities in Britain are now required to carry out in accordance with the provisions of the Crime and Disorder Act, 1998. The audit was undertaken in cooperation with the District's twenty-four partnership agencies. The results were used to develop multi-agency strategies to combat crime and diminish fear of crime, two of the intents of the Act. In Bradford, as in other British communities carrying out the new auditing process, community views on crime were assessed by wide-ranging community consultation; this uncovered responses that typify crime fears in both the United States and Britain, as the statistics presented in Chapter 2 bear out. A further discussion of the general requirements of the Crime and Disorder Act of 1998 is presented in Chapter 7, and the Salford case study in Chapter 8 provides a detailed example of local strategies used to implement them.

A fundamental question is: 'What do people do as a response to crime or to the fear of crime?' One response is to move away from the problem area, which as comparative statistics tell us in Chapter 2, is often the central city. At the national level in the United States new studies have added to the existing knowledge about urban flight. While there are certainly other reasons why people leave cities, there is a body of research showing that crime is an important factor driving people out of large American cities (Sampson and Wooldredge, 1986; Marshall and O'Flaherty, 1987), although British cities are also affected by this phenomenon. In so doing, crime and the fear of crime add to urban sprawl, which has affected the costs and quality of life of almost every American wherever they live; the consequences of sprawl for sustainability have been a major focus of urban planners, designers and social critics for the last decade (see, for example, Kunstler, 1998). A recent study by Cullen and Levitt (1996) demonstrates that *rising* crime rates (as distinct from high crime levels) are indeed correlated with the depopulation of large American cities, especially their central cores, and that Americans are so sensitive to upward movements in crime rates that 'each additional crime is associated with a one-person decline in city residents'.

Those people most likely to move are the more affluent and those with children. People also tend to change work venues because of particular types of crime, a 'hidden' cost of crime and certainly a diminution of choice, which no doubt affects the quality of life. For instance, a 1998 study of the 'timing' of work concluded that since 1973 higher homicide rates have reduced the propensity of people to work evenings and nights in large metropolitan areas. The study estimates that this has cost the American economy between $4 and $10 billion (thousand million) a year (Hamermesh, 1998). The practical impact of these residential and work choices that people make in response to crime and the fear of crime is that those most able to support city services leave behind those who need the services the most, but are least able to support them. Demands for police, public hospitalisation, education, social services and public transportation are intensified by the remaining urban poor, who have little recourse to private institutions to protect, heal, educate or house them.

At a different administrative level in Britain, a significant proportion of the population – in this case over a third of those questioned in the Bradford District – have changed small-scale place-related behaviours. The Bradford audit notes that:

> The most common places that people avoid after dark are town/city centres (36%), poorly lit areas (16%), secluded/quiet streets (15%) and parks/woods (13%). The locations most commonly mentioned as places that are avoided during the day are secluded/quiet streets (23%), subways (21%) and parks/woods (20%) (Bradford Metropolitan District Council, 2000).

The clear implication, although the question is not directly asked in the Bradford case, is that people avoid these environments because of crime or the perception of criminal activity.[10] Recent national estimates reported by the 2000 British Crime Survey suggest that about a quarter of the citizens surveyed report that they 'never walked alone in their local areas after dark' or did so less than once a month and, of those, 19 per cent said the reason was 'fear of crime' (Home Office, 2000b). This closely corresponds to the results of a nation-wide survey that about 20 per cent of Americans (38 million people) had 'reduced their activities' due to the fear of crime over the previous year (NCPC, 1999).

In both nations, women and especially elderly women, were more likely than men to restrict their activities because of crime or the fear of crime. Women's heightened fear of crime and their likelihood to change shopping, recreational, and entertainment-related behaviours, especially after dark, are borne out by research conducted across a range of different sized urban and suburban areas, and across income groups (Valentine, 1991; Pettersson, 1997). This lends credence to Whyte's notion that women are more sensitive to environmental socio-pathologies such as crime than men; and to his claim that the deserting of urban places by women is an urgent distress signal (Whyte, 1980).

In Britain those individuals most likely to report that the *fear* of crime has affected their quality of life are older women (over sixty years), minorities, those with physical disabilities, the impoverished, those living in council or housing association housing, and people living within areas of high levels of physical disorder (Home Office, 2000b). As in the United States, where the list is generally comparable, we find that those who have traditionally been the most vulnerable to pervasive social and economic discrimination are also those whose quality of life is further undermined by the direct and indirect effects of crime and the fear of crime. Quality-of-life impacts are therefore unequally distributed, despite the fact that all citizens are affected in one manner or another.

THE COSTS OF CRIME AS A QUALITY-OF-LIFE ISSUE

The financial burden of crime is a key element in its effects on quality of life and, as demonstrated by recent studies undertaken by private and public agencies across the English speaking world, that burden is enormous. In one research effort, the Association of British Insurers (1998) estimated that the total cost of crime to the British economy exceeded £35 billion a year, with the average cost amounting to £31 per household each week. This figure included the costs of police services, prosecutions, prisons, insured and uninsured losses, fraud and prevention costs. A more recent study by the Home Office almost doubled that estimate, putting the cost of crime in England and Wales at approximately £60 billion for 1999–2000 (Brand and Price, 2000). Moreover, the study emphasises that the figure is far from comprehensive in that it does not count fear of crime or its effects on the quality of life. Computer theft and damage alone was estimated in 1996 to cost British businesses more than £1.5 billion (Nando, 1996). An example at the local level in Britain comes from the London Borough of Hammersmith and Fulham, which estimated that the cost of domestic burglaries to victims was almost £2 million for 1997–1998, not counting police costs and other indirect expenses. The Borough uses these figures in developing its audit of local crime, pursuant to the Crime and Disorder Act of 1998 (London Borough of Hammersmith and Fulham website at http://lbht.gov.uk/OurBorough/Reduction/thecostsofcrime.html).

In what was billed as the most comprehensive study of its type ever undertaken, researchers for the United States Department of Justice estimated that crime costs the American economy at least $450 billion a year. That study was controversial in that it included for the first time the costs of child abuse, domestic violence, mental healthcare costs and estimated reduced quality-of-life costs for crime victims, along with more direct and traditional costs of crimes such as murder, rape and robbery (National Institute of Justice, 1996). In comparison, the United States Department of Defense spends about *half* that amount each year. A 1999 study by economist David Anderson put the US costs of crime at over one trillion (thousand billion) dollars, calling it the 'single most expensive – and wasteful – aspect of life in America'. Anderson's research added in 'hidden' costs of crime, such as lost wages, personal anguish, and the costs of protective devices. He concluded that strategic planning in local communities, among other cost effective approaches, should be used in place of many current and ineffective crime deterrence practices (Anderson, 1999).

Recent Canadian estimates put the cost of crime there at about 46 billion Canadian dollars a year, including physical and mental health costs and lost productivity (Department of Justice, Canada, 1998), and in Australia researchers have suggested that crime costs at least 18 billion Australian dollars a year, which equates to $A2,800 per household, or more than 4 per cent of that country's gross domestic product (Walker, 1997).

Because different crimes and costs are assessed differently in each of these nations it is generally impossible to compare them. However, recent efforts to estimate the costs of crime in Britain, the USA, Canada and Australia are alike in that they have become more inclusive, calculating a host of secondary and tertiary impacts that have not been previously considered, such as the reduced quality of life of victims. Consequently it has become apparent, even to the most inattentive citizen, that crime is a monumental depletion of national economies, with wide reaching impacts on communities, as well as on individual victims and their families. Many cities, especially in the USA, have been left with declining tax bases in their central cores while their more affluent citizens migrate outwards into sprawling suburban rings, thus creating a disturbing downward spiral. The general decline in national crime rates over the past decade in the United States has not reversed this trend: crime thus has a pernicious poisonous residual effect that is hard to shake off – another hidden cost.

GOVERNMENTAL CRIME PREVENTION RESPONSES

What are the responses of governments to the assaults on quality of life and personal finances made by crime and the fear of crime? A recent United Nations report suggests that although 'prevention of crime is far more effective than paying for the processing of offenders through the criminal justice system', governments are much more likely to make rhetorical statements on the need for and value of crime prevention than to provide the resources to make it a priority (Newman, 1999). The same study estimates that for industrialised nations such as Britain and the United States, investment in crime prevention amounts to less than one per cent of all criminal justice system expenditures, while in developing and transitional counties there is virtually no investment in it at all. In fact, while theories about crime prevention have been discussed for centuries, actual resource expenditures by governments in this area are quite new, dating in both Britain and the United States from the 1960s, when a variety of government initiatives were launched in both nations.

We present a more detailed discussion of crime prevention policy and application in the United States and in Britain in Chapters 5–8, but we can say here that approaches over the past four decades in both nations have generally been characterised by attempts to move national crime prevention agendas down to local levels; this has been accompanied by increased research and training support and by either providing *incentives* for local agencies to cooperate (as in the grants approach favoured in the United States, and exemplified by 'Community Oriented Policing' programmes) or *mandating* that local agencies form partnerships (as in Britain and exemplified by the Crime and Disorder Act 1998). These ambitious undertakings require the coordination of many bureaucracies struggling with an intractable and volatile problem, which has not escaped the attention of politicians at both ends of the liberal-conservative spectrum in both nations. The problem is also one of balancing national agendas with regional and local concerns, for in truth they often do not match up very well at all.

Despite that, the perseverance of both nations toward multi-party, multi-level responses recognises an increasingly sophisticated view that crime prevention is a complex issue beyond the command of law enforcement alone and that it involves interventions with *offenders*, *victims*, *environments* (as a physical entity) and the *community* (as a social-economic entity) in some mix that we do not completely understand. This has come to characterise much of the modern organisational reaction to crime prevention in Britain and the United States although, as some commentators note, there are inherent difficulties in multi-party crime prevention efforts, however well intentioned they are.[11]

Nevertheless, there is clear evidence that national policies in both nations are directing more and more attention to communities generally and to environmental and place-based crime prevention responses in particular. Examples of these efforts include 'Safe Cities' and 'Safer By Design' initiatives, experiments with 'Problem and Community Oriented Policing' and the adoption and support of crime mapping using geographic information systems (GIS) technology. One of the key questions that emerges from many of these efforts is how to set national directives strong enough to guide local action effectively, while ensuring that they are flexible enough to account for local variations.[12] Chapters 5–8 provide some insights as to how this is playing out in Britain and the United States relative to crime prevention applications and policy. Much of the new responsibility for carrying forward national initiatives at the local level within the context of place-based crime prevention has been assigned to law enforcement agencies, an ironical situation since, while they have historically had the most responsibility for ensuring that places are safe, they have had the least control over the design and construction of the built environment (Kitchen and Schneider, 2000).

RESPONSES, RESPONSIBILITIES AND OPPORTUNITIES OF PLANNING AND URBAN DESIGN IN PLACE-BASED CRIME PREVENTION PLANNING

Given the fundamental significance of crime impacts and costs to urban liveability in Britain and the United States, it is extraordinary how peripheral a role urban planners and designers have played in place-based crime prevention. Among the variety of reasons for this are: the fact that 'crime prevention as a form of public policy is in many respects in its infancy' (UN Commission on Crime Prevention and Criminal Justice, 1999); the fact that the field of environment-behaviour research is still emerging; the fact that the police have traditionally been given the role to make society *safe* and have also been presumed to be the lead agencies to make it *safer*; the fact that historically there has been little *compulsion*, especially in the United States, whether through ordinance, public policy or client demand, for planners to become involved; and to the fact that planning and design literature and curricula have devoted so little attention to crime prevention planning. In the latter context, even a casual review of most current planning and design texts reveals few, if any, references to place-based crime prevention planning strategies such as defensible space, CPTED, situational crime prevention, or environmental criminology. Rather, most such works are full of descriptions of the design and comprehensive planning processes, with land development codes and regulatory practices, with portrayals of planning politics, with housing, regeneration, ecological issues or with grieving the lack of 'smart growth' policies or 'sustainable' communities – all topics certainly worthy of attention but which have tended vastly to overshadow crime prevention planning. The neglect of crime as a fundamental planning and design issue is also evidenced by the paucity of attention it is accorded within American and British planning school curricula and research agendas, and what we perceive to be its near absence as a design topic within architecture schools, and within the mainstream of the professional community.

A review of resources, for example, listed in the (American) National Crime Prevention Council's handbook on 'Designing Safer Communities' (1997), identifies fourteen university-based 'Researchers and Other Experts,' only two of whom are located at an architectural or planning college (the same one). Most of those listed represented schools of criminal justice or social science. While we in no way wish to belittle the important contributions of the latter researchers, and while we are aware that this cannot be a comprehensive list, we believe that it is nevertheless representative of the lack of attention that the planning and design disciplines have traditionally afforded crime and the fear of crime. A similar review of the articles included in *Planning* newspaper (a weekly professional journal for British planners published in conjunction with the Royal Town Planning Institute) for 2000 reveals not a single article dealing with crime prevention planning, although there are contributions on everything from 'Planning for Protected Species' to 'Tourism and Conservation Planning' (RTPI Website at http://www.rtpi.org.uk/).

This is an odd response to one of the most significant forces driving *up* the costs of life and driving *down* its quality. Perhaps the focus on sprawl as the bête noire of modern urban planning and design, particularly in the United States and less so in Britain, has so dominated the attention of planners and related professionals that they have been blinded to the reasons (crime among many) for why people have 'voted with their feet' to escape to suburbia. An easy target in this regard has been transport policy and practice. Based on the evidence, however, it seems just as likely that the transportation systems that have funnelled millions out to the suburbs have facilitated – not caused – the choices that people have made to escape large urban cores.[13] In this context, crime and the fear of crime have limited the menu of choices that citizens in the United States and Britain have had to choose from.

If planning is about anything, it is about increasing the choices available to citizens. The evidence suggests that as places actually become and are perceived to be safer by citizens, citizens' choices are given freer reign to play out among a wide spectrum of living, work, and related options. And, while the police have an undeniable role in making places safe, planners, designers and associated professionals have public interest missions that are as intimately connected to safety as are those of law enforcement, and are conceivably more important in efforts to make places *safer*. Recent research in the USA points toward how place-based crime prevention can be incorporated in the day-to-day responsibilities of planners and designers, in spite of Zahm's point (1998) that American land use and development codes were not originally framed with safety from crime as their basic intents.

Thus, for example, planners have a great deal of influence in shaping comprehensive plans which lay out long-term community visions and in developing land use regulations, including *zoning*,[14] *subdivision regulations*, *landscaping ordinances* and *design guidelines* that make the comprehensive plan vision come alive. In the US planning system zoning, for instance, regulates a variety of spatial attributes including the type of land uses permitted, the density of development allowed, building height, mass and bulk, lot sizes and dimensions, setbacks for yards, allowable open space, and parking requirements. In Britain, contemporary development plans tend not to use the concept of zoning, but include policies and proposals that address the same general elements. Each of these elements in turn has crime prevention strategies or issues potentially associated with them. Thus, lot sizes, dimension and yard setbacks relate directly to CPTED principles dealing with surveillance, territorial perceptions and public–private space definitions (discussed in Chapter 4).

Subdivision regulations also determine lot sizes and dimensions, as well as specifying street right-of-way locations and dimensions, sidewalk construction and the locations of utilities. Each of these relate to defensible space and CPTED crime prevention strategies including activity generation, access control, and the delineation of public and private space. Finally, planners and designers typically have a great deal of input into the development and enforcement of landscape regulations and design guidelines. These determine such spatial elements as wall locations and dimensions, plant materials, site layouts, and the design and placement of buildings, footpaths, roads, and car parks. Place-based crime prevention principles and issues inherent in these spatial considerations include concern that offenders have increased (or diminished) opportunities for concealment, for open sight lines across property, for territorial definition, for maintenance to diminish perceptions of abandonment, for access control and for increased place legibility and wayfinding.

By influencing day-to-day strategic decisions in these very specific place making processes and by moulding long-term visions through comprehensive (or master) planning, planners and designers have an enormous potential to make places safer for citizens. Our view is that there is scant evidence to date that they have indeed realised this potential, much to the detriment of public choice making generally, and for those of us in particular who ask our children, 'is it safe where you'll be living?'

CONCLUSIONS

Crime and the fear of crime are major issues in British and American societies that help mould our cities and influence the qualities of life in both nations. Crime affects a wide range of choices such as where we will live, where and when we will work, whether or not to take a stroll in the park downtown, or whether we can order pizza delivery to our home. We think about crime when our children leave our care for even a short period of time. For many, these concerns constrain choices and the liveability of our cities and societies. This is demonstrable not only in what we do or refrain from doing but is registered on surveys and quality-of-life benchmarks, from the local to national levels in both the United States and Britain. Both crime prevention and planning seek to improve the quality of life and to broaden choices.

Though employed for millennia through self-help target hardening and offender-oriented punishment approaches, systematic crime prevention policy and practice is only a relatively recent development across the globe generally, and in Britain and the United States in particular, arising in response to rising crime rates in the 1960s in both nations. While some crime prevention approaches have focused primarily on healing offenders or the socio-economic conditions in which they reside, contemporary crime prevention suggests a more holistic approach that includes the environment in which the targets of crime are found, and a focus on strategies that manipulate the design and management of places – the relatively small-scale physical locations from bus stops to neighbourhoods that comprise cities – where crime is likely. In both the United States and Britain, such strategies increasingly involve partnerships between a range of local agencies guided by national objectives in efforts to decrease opportunities and rewards for offenders while increasing the risks and effort required to commit crimes. In both nations the credibility of crime prevention has been subject to attack because programme results often have not matched or been measured against advertised objectives, and because many strategies have not been vindicated by objective empirical testing.

Even though their expertise and responsibilities provide them unique access to regulatory arenas that influence the design and management of places, planners and urban designers have taken much less of a lead in the area of crime prevention than their public interest missions would suggest, often leaving crime prevention to traditional approaches and to other actors. This neglect ignores a growing body of evidence that crime prevention approaches can be effectively employed at places, although there is still considerable debate as to the measurable results of interventions and the body of empirical evidence to support those results. We suggest, therefore, that there is both room and cause to increase the role of planners and urban designers in place-based crime prevention efforts in Britain and the United States, and the following chapters of this book expand upon that view.

NOTES

1 For example, a review of 266 'suspect actions' from an American police crime analysis unit reveals forty-six that are clearly or likely place or spatially-based. The latter category includes such crimes as all types of burglary (business, conveyance, residential), drug dealing, graffiti, home invasions, prowling, peeking in windows, business, residential and strong arm robberies, purse snatching, vandalism and trespassing. The former – non-spatial – category includes such offences as possession of child pornography, exposed sexual organs, homosexual acts, harassing and obscene phone calls, stalking, making threats, resisting arrest, making racial slurs, and being under the influence of drugs (Crime Analysis Unit, City of Gainesville, Florida, 2001).

2 Sherman *et al.* describe seven major institutional settings in which much of the existing crime prevention literature fits, including communities, families, schools, labour markets, places, police agencies, and other criminal justice agencies (Sherman *et al.*, 1998).

3 Modern 'white collar' crime can take place in cyberspace locations, and there is evidence from the 2000 British Crime Survey that this type of crime concerns citizens a great deal. However, citizens in both Britain and the United States still fear violent stranger-to-stranger encounters and property crimes more.

4 An excellent discussion of the linkage of places to crime employing ecological psychology and spatial epidemiology perspectives can be found in Taylor (1998).

5 This definition roughly follows John Friedmann's broad conception of planning as the 'attempt to link scientific and technical knowledge to actions in the public domain' (Friedmann, 1987). The issue of definitions is a central concern of planning, both as an academic discipline and a profession. An excellent discussion of planning definitions can be found in Chapter 4 of Alexander (1992).

6 This is not intended to slight other nations, such as the Netherlands, Canada, Australia, Japan and France which have provided support at national and regional levels to environmental crime prevention research.

7 This is in contrast to retribution theory which holds that:

   • The criminal act must be a voluntary and morally wrong act;
   • Punishment must fit the offence;

- Punishment must represent the return of suffering to the wrong-doer for his morally wrong act (Jeffrey, 1977).

As a 'backward-looking' process that punishes past acts and ignores future ones, Jeffrey and others do not consider retribution to be a legitimate part of crime prevention or control.

8 See, for example Pascoe and Harrison's paper (1997) on the combined use of statistical techniques, geographic information systems (GIS) technology, and situational crime prevention theory in predicting the risk of domestic burglary among different neighbourhoods in Britain.

9 Devon County Council notes that 'a sustainable community would be one in which people live without fear of crime, or persecution on account of their race, gender, sexuality or beliefs' (Devon County Council, 2000).

10 That the Bradford statistics are relatively high when compared to the 2000 British Crime Survey (BCS) statistics may be due to the winnowing effect of asking people 'why' they avoid certain places. Thus, as the BCS suggests, there are many reasons why people may avoid certain areas after dark, among them that they simply did not want to walk there (Home Office, 2000b).

11 Liddle and Gelsthorpe (1994) note in relation to interagency cooperation in Britain that 'relations between particular agencies involved in crime prevention are highly complicated, seldom static and influenced by a variety of institutional, individual and local/historical factors' (page 26). The same can be said to be no less true of relationships among such agencies in the United States.

12 For instance, referring to the implementation of Britain's social exclusion policies, RTPI Planning Policy Officer David Barraclough says:

> The SEU sees the key issues for neighbourhood regeneration as employment, health, crime and education and, while the Institute would want to see these at the heart of the Urban White Paper, it is extremely uncomfortable with the idea that national templates can be devised and applied to all deprived neighbourhoods (*Planning newspaper*, 13 October 2000, page 22).

13 This is particularly ironic since 'murder rates in [American] cities are lower than traffic fatality rates in exurban areas' (Lucy, 2000).

14 Zoning is a particularly important planning tool in the United States and is sometimes confused with planning itself, although it is only one means to *implement* planning. Zoning has developed since the early part of the twentieth century as a legal device to stabilise and preserve private property values (and hence is status quo oriented) and is a means of 'insuring that the land uses of a community are properly situated in relation to one another, providing adequate space for each type of development' (Goodman and Freund, 1968, page 403). Although zoning ordinances vary from one community to another in the United States, they generally control or direct such elements as special districts (e.g. historic or business improvement districts), development density, and the overall regulation of nuisances. Zoning is the primary planning tool used to publicly manage *private* property in the United States.

CHAPTER 2

CRIME TRENDS IN THE USA AND IN BRITAIN

INTRODUCTION

In this chapter we look at what has been happening to crime in the USA and in Britain, both in an overall sense and in terms of trends in relation to different types of crime. As part of this process, we comment in passing on what we know about fear of crime in those societies, because fear of crime can be as serious a problem as crime itself. We also consider the demography and the broad geography of crime, because these factors have major effects on its place-specific elements which are also the main focus of the relationship between crime and the design of the built environment. It is necessary to undertake a breakdown of this nature in any event, because overall crime figures mask very significant spatial differences.

This chapter therefore has four sections:

* a general cautionary introduction to the use of crime statistics;
* an examination of crime trends in the USA;
* an examination of crime trends in Britain;
* comparison and conclusions.

CRIME STATISTICS

There are two common sources of crime statistics. The first is data on crimes recorded by the police; these tend to be the easiest to use, since they are readily available, and they have an apparent consistency to them, since they are published annually and thus invite comparisons with what happened in previous years. They are often used in the absence of available alternatives, as we will do for this reason in this book; but there are some very important cautionary notes that need to be entered about data of this kind which must never be forgotten when they are used. We set these out below. The second major source is periodic surveys, either of victims of crime or of the population at large, which are usually done on a sample basis. This means, of course, that they are subject to all the problems usually associated with sample surveys, plus some particular difficulties which arise from the nature of their subject matter. Again, therefore, we set these difficulties out below, and we also look at what can be learned about the reliability of these data sources when they are compared with each other.

There are four main difficulties with police data on reported crimes.

REPORTING

The willingness on the part of victims to report crime to the police is very variable. There is no doubt that it is affected by a variety of factors, including whether people think the police will actually do anything to catch the offender or get stolen belongings returned, whether insurance claims are likely to follow which will require some sort of police corroboration, the general level of trust in the police in the community or by individuals, or whether in relation to some crimes (for example, rape) victims think they will get a sympathetic hearing from the police or will simply be adding to the ordeal they have already experienced. Table 2.1 shows for the USA and for England and Wales some estimated reporting rates based upon survey information for 1981 and 1995.

Table 2.1 shows very clearly that there are differences in reporting rates for the same crime over time within countries, for the same crime between countries, and between different types of crime. The highest reporting rates are for motor vehicle theft, which is regarded as being related to subsequent insurance claims. The lowest reporting rates are for burglary (in the USA) and for assault (in England and Wales), which may respectively be related to whether the scale of what has been lost is seen to be worth the effort and whether people regard (at any rate minor) assault as a matter for the police at all, as compared with something to be sorted out between individuals. However, the four types of crime recorded in Table 2.1 do not represent the full range of crime; Table 2.2 by way of example shows for England and Wales the broader pattern of willingness to report crime when this range is widened. To put this in context, the overall average in England and Wales is that about 40 per cent of all crimes get reported; this result was repeated in the 2000 British Crime Survey, which showed that in the year 1999, on the basis of the most up-to-date view about the comparability of police records and British Crime Survey results, 41 per cent of crimes were reported to the police (Home Office, 2000b, Table 2.1, page 6).

Table 2.1 Percentage of crimes reported to the police, 1981 and 1995

	USA		England and Wales	
Crime	1981	1995	1981	1995
Robbery	56.0	55.0	46.5	56.6
Assault	46.7	54.0	40.2	40.0
Burglary	49.0	50.0	66.2	66.3
Motor vehicle theft	87.0	88.8	94.9	97.5

Source: Langan and Farrington (1998) pages 10 and 69

Table 2.2 Percentage of crimes in England and Wales estimated to have been reported to the police in 1997 in rank order

1. Theft of vehicle	96.5
2. Burglary with loss	85.0
3. Burglary with entry	79.0
4. Bicycle theft	63.6
5. Robbery	56.8
6. Mugging	55.3
7. Attempted burglary without loss	50.2
8. Snatch theft from a person	50.0
9. Wounding	45.3
10. Theft from a vehicle	43.1
11. Household theft	32.9
12. Domestic violence	26.4
13. Vandalism	26.3

Source: Home Office (1998) Table A4.1, page 51. The categories have been selected from this table to illustrate the range it contains

THE PROCESSES IN PRACTICE

Reporting processes are themselves problematic: they can be seen by people as difficult and complex; they change over time, thus making trend statistics difficult to establish; they may vary between police forces, thus making comparison difficult; and there can be major difficulties with the classification of crimes, both because classifications themselves change over time and because individual judgement determines to which category a crime is assigned (often with rather imperfect information) at the time it is reported. This is a particular difficulty when attempting to make cross-national comparisons using data of this nature; for example, assault is defined differently in the USA and in Britain. A further potential difficulty is that whether or not something is formally reported depends upon the judgement of the individual police officer at the first point of contact with the public, and then upon the diligence of officers in contributing reports to statistical records. Without in any way intending this last comment as a sweeping criticism of the police, it is probably fair to say that we are dealing with a wide range of performance simply because of the different characteristics of the individuals involved.

RECORDING

There is clear evidence of an important distinction between *reported* crime and *recorded* crime. Some of this is undoubtedly entirely legitimate. For example, if it becomes clear upon subsequent investigation that no crime was in fact committed, it would be wholly appropriate not to record that report as if it constituted a criminal incident. There is also the likelihood that relatively minor crimes get weeded out, although clearly this is a more contentious practice. However, this does not explain either the scale of non-recording in Britain that has been reported in a recent study (Povey, 2000) or the degree of variation found between individual police forces. Inevitably, this may lead to more cynical interpretations, such as the suggestion that the police have a vested interest in not recording crimes because this makes their clear-up rate look better. Povey concluded that in Britain some 25 per cent of reported crimes are not recorded, and the evidence presented in Table 2.3 suggests that this may be an underestimate, at any rate for some types of crimes. It was (perhaps inevitably) this more cynical explanation that was latched onto by the press when reporting this study; *The Independent*'s front-page headline on 1 August 2000 of 'Crime figures sham as police fail to report 1.4m offences' is a typical example. Langan and Farrington (1998, page 11) show that this is more of a problem in England and Wales than it is in the USA (see Table 2.3). They also suggest that the trends towards higher recording rates over the period 1981–1995 (but not for England and Wales in respect of burglary and of motor vehicle theft) can be attributed to changes in policing practice.

Langan and Farrington (1998, page 11) offer five reasons for the trend towards recording a growing fraction of reported violent crimes by the police:

- The police are becoming more professional.
- Police operations have become more computerised.
- Electronic recording of calls to the police creates an audit trail.
- The police are responding to public expectations that domestic violence will be handled more formally and treated more seriously; for example, a growing number of states in the USA now mandate arrests in all domestic assaults.
- Society is arguably becoming more litigious (perhaps particularly in the USA), and this has resulted in more 'defensive policing' which defines rules about when and how officers must act and as a consequence reduces police discretion.

Table 2.3 Recording of reported crimes by the police in 1995 in the USA and in England and Wales (%)

Crime	USA	England and Wales
Robbery	78.4	34.7
Assault	100.0	52.7
Burglary	72.1	55.3
Motor vehicle theft	100.0	82.6

Source: Langan and Farrington (1998) pages 10 and 70

POLICE OPERATIONS

There is inevitably a self-fulfilling component in police statistics of recorded crimes deriving from the nature of police operations. To take an obvious example, it might be decided because of public complaint to target a particular type of illegal activity (for example, car parking in an area where it is banned or restricted, or an intensification of shoplifting in a shopping centre). The inevitable consequence of a police operation aimed at clamping down on such activities – assuming that in its own terms it is successful – will be an increase in the numbers of recorded crimes under these headings. This is not necessarily a measure of relative crime rates (although of course it could be, in the sense that what triggered the operation in the first place may have been a belief that a particular type of crime in a particular locality was on the increase and needed to be tackled more intensively), as much as a reflection of a change in police operational practices. This can have a particular effect on the crime figures for a particular locality, sometimes in a direct sense, as in the examples quoted above, and sometimes in an indirect sense. An example of an indirect effect, which we discuss in more detail in Chapter 6, would be the introduction of closed-circuit television (CCTV) cameras into a shopping centre deflecting certain types of crime into other areas which did not have cameras (Dawson, 1994). It is important, therefore, when looking at crime figures for individual small areas based upon police records, to try to understand whether any significant changes in police operations affecting that area in recent times might have had an effect of this nature.

These four difficulties, although clearly serious, do not mean that police crime statistics should never be used, but they do suggest that they should be used with considerable care and with an awareness that they can carry these sorts of difficulties with them. One of the most important reasons why we do not suggest that police crime statistics should not be used is because they are the most common currency in the field, and indeed are often the only data available in cases where specific surveys have not been carried out. To take the view that they are so unreliable as to be able to contribute nothing to discussion and debate would often be to condemn study of those activities to the absence of any sort of factual basis whatsoever, and we think there is enough difficulty of this sort in the field as it is without adding to it by taking up such an extreme position. In particular, we think that such data can be useful both as a means of providing some sort of scale for crime problems in an area and for relatively short-term comparison within the same area,[1] provided in this latter case that no obvious intervening variables, such as significant changes in police operations, affect the area in the meantime. We do think, however, that the health warnings deriving from this explanation of the difficulties associated with police crime statistics mean that they should always be used with care. Readers who want to follow up these matters and the issues surrounding them in more detail can do so by referring to Walker (1995) and Coleman and Moynihan (1996).

As far as *survey data* generated either from victim surveys or from surveys of the general population are concerned, the main difficulties are as follows:

(1)   The usual problems of any sample survey around its reliability, deriving from the size of the sample and its structure and from the nature of the questions asked, apply here also.

(2)   In addition, some of the issues that are dealt with in surveys of this nature are very sensitive and personal; this raises concerns about whether victims of crime are prepared to talk about their experiences with interviewers or, indeed, whether the questions asked are sufficiently sensitive to those experiences (Pain, 2000, page 368). There must also be some doubt about whether in all cases memories of such events are wholly reliable. There can also be an exaggerated response, where people for whatever reason embroider their experiences in various ways, including perhaps in instances where an inflated insurance claim has already been made. We do not wish to imply that for the most part people in responding to surveys of this nature do anything other than tell the truth. But surveys are totally dependent upon what people say in these terms, because it is rarely possible for there to be any sort of independent check on answers given; and even leaving aside deliberate distortion, it needs to be understood that people's recall is fallible, perhaps particularly when they have found a particular event psychologically distressing.

(3)   Surveys tend to provide fragmentary evidence, in that they occur only at particular points in time. So, for example, Langan and Farrington (1998), when comparing statistics on crime victimisation from surveys in the USA and in England and Wales over the period 1981–1996, had annual results from the US National Crime Victimisation Survey, but the British Crime Survey was undertaken only six times during the period in question in England and Wales (1981, 1983, 1987, 1991, 1993 and 1995). Undertaking surveys is, of course, expensive and generally speaking the cost (as well as the reliability) rises with the size of the sample; it may be this factor which very often determines what an organisation is actually able to do, irrespective of views about the inherent desirability of regular survey work.

(4)   Comparison between surveys can be particularly difficult, because of the uncertainty surrounding whether or not like is being precisely compared with like. For example, surveys which ask slightly different questions may result in

slightly different answers, so it is important to be clear about whether apparently similar data do emanate from processes that are likely to make the data inherently comparable.

In the light of the preceding discussion, our preference, where both police crime data and survey data are available, would be to regard the survey data as probably more reliable, although we acknowledge that there is a debate about whether *any* of the data in this field can be regarded as wholly reliable (Pain, 2000). As we have already noted, however, we would not go so far as to discard the police data, and would suggest that using the two in tandem can have certain advantages. A simple illustration will make this last point. It can scarcely be regarded as being desirable that, for certain types of crimes and in certain localities, reporting rates to the police are very low; one of the objectives behind a local initiative might well be to improve reporting rates as part of a process of tackling local crime more effectively. Without comparing survey data with police figures, it is impossible to know what the relationship is between someone regarding themselves as the victim of a crime and that crime eventually emerging as part of police records. The police vested interest will almost certainly be not merely in improving crime reporting but also in improving their clear-up rate, because if the former rises and the latter remains static police performance, according to the statistics that result, will actually be deteriorating. Equally, local people are more likely to be willing to report certain types of crime if they believe that something will be done about that crime as a result, and if they have confidence in the police in the locality; and these things too are likely to be parts of local initiatives. Thus, survey information and police records taken together are likely to be able to paint the best available picture both of the patterns of crime in the area and of public reactions to these activities, both as victims and in terms of their perceptions of crime as a factor affecting their quality of life.

There are some large-scale differences between what the two sources tell us about levels of crime, however, and this point should help to reinforce the messages set out above about the available data and how they should be used. Table 2.4 illustrates these differences by using 1995 police and survey statistics for both the USA and England and Wales for selected types of crimes.

Table 2.4 shows that, except for motor vehicle theft, the scale of crime as recorded in police data is usually well below (and in the cases of robbery and assault, less than half) that recorded by surveys. Survey data also show England and Wales to have higher crime levels than the USA in all four of the categories used for Table 2.4, whereas police records show the rates for robbery and for assault in England and Wales to be lower than those in the USA; thus choice of data in this case would lead to completely different conclusions being drawn from

Table 2.4 Crime rates per 1,000 population according to police records and to surveys, USA and England and Wales, 1995

Crime	USA		England and Wales	
	Survey data	Police records	Survey data	Police records
Robbery	5.3	2.2	7.6	1.3
Assault	8.8	4.2	20.0	3.9
Burglary[1]	18.3	9.9	33.8	23.9
Motor vehicle theft[1,2]	4.2	5.6	9.6	9.8

Source: Langan and Farrington (1998) pages 67 and 68

Notes:
1 To make survey data compatible with police records in these cases, it has been necessary to convert the survey data from 'per 1,000 households' to 'per 1,000 population'. This has been done by dividing the survey data figures by the average household sizes for the USA and for England and Wales, which in 1995 were respectively 2.59 and 2.45.
2 The more conventional method of recording rates for this type of crime would be per 1,000 vehicles rather than per 1,000 population, because comparisons over time are affected by growing vehicle ownership rates. The method that has been used here, which is for a single year, has been chosen to facilitate comparisons between types of crime.

a comparative study. We comment later in this chapter on the different rates of crime and the different trends in the two countries, but we close this section by reiterating a point that we have already made. Generally, we believe survey information to be more reliable than police records, and so for the remainder of this chapter we will base our discussion of crime trends in the USA and in Britain on survey data, unless we indicate otherwise in a particular instance.

CRIME TRENDS IN THE USA

The headline figures in relation to crime in the USA can be summarised as follows (Langan and Farrington, 1998):

*   The broad pattern over the period 1981–1996 has been one of crime rates falling in the early 1980s, then rising until about 1993, and then falling again, a process which has continued subsequently.
*   *Robbery* rates have fallen from just under 7.5 per 1,000 population in 1981 to just over 5 per 1,000 population in 1996.
*   *Assault* rates have fallen from around 12 per 1,000 people in 1981 to just under 9 per 1,000 people in 1996.

Table 2.5 Key statistics on crime trends, USA, 1981–1996

Type of crime	1981	1986	1991	1996
Robbery (rate per 1,000 population)[1]	7.4	5.1	5.9	5.2
Assault (rate per 1,000 population)[1]	12.0	9.8	9.9	8.8
Burglary (rate per 1,000 households)[1]	105.9	73.8	64.6	47.2
Motor vehicle theft (rate per 1,000 households)[1]	10.6	9.7	14.2	9.1
Murder (rate per 1,000 people)[2]	0.10	0.09	0.10	0.07
Rape (rate per 1,000 females)[2]	0.70	0.74	0.83	0.71

Source: Langan and Farrington (1998) pages 68 and 69

Notes:
1 These data come from the annual National Crime Victimization Survey (NCVS).
2 These data come from police records. The data for rape may be unreliable because of the particular problem of the unwillingness of women to report this crime to the police, given their often low expectations of how they will be treated or whether they will even be believed. Survey information, such as that contained within the NCVS, may be more reliable than police records, therefore, but Langan and Farrington use this latter source because their focus is on achieving comparability with the situation in England and Wales (see Table 2.18).

- *Burglary* rates have fallen from about 105 per 1,000 households in 1981 to under 50 per 1,000 households in 1996.
- *Motor vehicle theft* was at a fairly constant rate of just over 10 per 1,000 households at each end of the 1981–1996 period, although there were some fluctuations between these two dates. It should be noted, however, that vehicle ownership rates in the USA rose substantially over this period.
- The *murder* rate in the USA was 9.8 per 100,000 people in 1981 and had fallen to 7.4 per 100,000 people in 1996, which equates to 0.10 per 1,000 people in 1981 and 0.07 per 1,000 people in 1996.
- The *rape* rate in the USA was around 0.7 per 1,000 females at each end of the 1981–1996 period, although it rose between these two dates (but see the qualifying note 2 to Table 2.5).
- According to 1996 police statistics, *firearms* were used in 68 per cent of USA murders in that year and in 41 per cent of robberies.

Table 2.5 provides more detail in support of these headline figures. This overall pattern, of a fall over the 1981–1996 period and in some cases (most notably motor vehicle theft) of a steep fall in the 1990s, clearly represents an inherently desirable trend. It is not our purpose in a book of this nature to attempt to say why this has happened; in any event we suspect that there is no single answer to this (despite what many protagonists of particular viewpoints may claim) but that it is a complex amalgam of a range of causes. For example, after examining a broad range of explanations, ostensibly accounting for the twenty-five year decline in burglary rates in the USA (including increased risk and severity of punishment, national economic trends, greater stability of institutions, migration out of cities, demographic changes and changes in the portability of consumer electronics), Titus (1999) concludes that while there may be some truth to all the reasons offered, none of them alone accounts for this extraordinary phenomenon, which has not received the attention it merits in the literature.

It is important not to conclude from this, however, that crime is no longer a problem in the USA, and that there is no need as a consequence to continue thinking about ways in which crime can be prevented. Crime clearly remains a problem for those who are on its receiving end, and in an absolute sense many of the levels of crime reported in Table 2.5 do not represent grounds for complacency in society, even though in a relative sense they are improving. That the trajectory here is a positive one may mean that the pressures on the political process, and hence on the professionals who advise the politicians, to find new answers to the problems of crime in society are less than they would have been if the trajectory had been negative. On the other hand, evidence from the USA suggests that people's fears of crime are not diminishing simply because the crime statistics are improving, and fear of crime in its own way can be just as serious a problem in society as crime itself (and can lead to very similar pressures on the political process for action), especially when it leads people to change their behaviour.

The importance that people attach to crime as an issue of concern to them in the USA is emphasised by the data summarised in Table 2.6. This reports the results of a CBS News public survey conducted by telephone in the USA in October 1999, when just over 1,000 voters were asked what they felt would be the most important problem facing the USA in the twenty-first century. The answers, which put crime at the top of a pile of really major issues, demonstrate clearly that the mere fact that crime rates have been falling in the USA for several years has not of itself removed concern about crime from the public agenda; although it is of course possible to argue (as some would) that the gap between crime and the next highest item on the list in Table 2.6 would have been still greater if crime figures in the USA had been worsening rather than improving.

This conclusion is in terms reinforced by the headlines from the findings of the 1999 National Crime Prevention Survey in the USA, which were as follows:

- One in eight Americans said they were more fearful of walking in their neighbourhoods this year than last.
- One in five people said that to varying degrees they had curbed their activities out of fear of crime over the past year.

Table 2.6 Public views about the most important problem facing the USA in the twenty-first century

8%	crime
7%	moral values
5%	healthcare, poverty
4%	economy, education, environment, drugs, jobs and employment, overpopulation, war
3%	racism/race relations, technology/computers
2%	social issues, terrorism

Source: *Public Agenda Online* http:///www.publicagenda.org/issues/pcc

Note: the figures relate only to respondents to the survey who gave specific answers, and thus cover 63 per cent of the total response. Since the question that was asked was about 'the most important problem', respondents could only give one answer. The balance consists of other answers, don't know's, and those who gave no answer. Where more than one subject is listed against a particular score, each subject in the list achieved that score; so, for example, seven subjects each scored 4 per cent.

- Three in ten survey participants said that to varying degrees violence was a problem in the neighbourhoods where they live, work and shop.
  (Source: *National Crime Prevention*, http://www.ncpc.org/rwesafe3.htm)

All of this reminds us that in many ways we are dealing with two distinct problems – crime, and the fear of crime – where the relationship between the two is by no means as straightforward as it may appear to be. Indeed, a recent review of the literature (Pain, 2000) has concluded that 'fear of crime' is an elusive concept with a range of meanings that is probably best understood in the context of place, community, social relations and experience, within which environment might be a relatively small component; whereas we believe that the relationship between environment and some types of criminal activity is inherently more straightforward.

National crime statistics obscure a great deal of important information about the demography and the geography of crime. At the local level too, it is not what the national statistics say that matters to people; it is what is happening in their locality. So the remainder of this section looks at some of the key indicators of the demography and the geography of crime in the USA. The headline point is that these crime statistics both reflect and act as contributors to the social polarisation that is a characteristic of many American cities (see, for example, Kelso, 1994; also Logan, in Marcuse and van Kempen, 2000). Table 2.7 pulls out some of the key statistics from the USA National Crime Victimization Survey for 1998 (US Department of Justice, 2000) by reference to different sizes of core cities in Metropolitan Statistical Areas.

Table 2.7 shows that the residents of core cities in metropolitan statistical areas are much more likely to be on the receiving end both of crimes against the

Table 2.7 Crime risks by size of urban areas, USA, 1998

Type of crime	Population of core city in metropolitan statistical area				Rural areas
	50,000– 249,999	250,000– 499,999	500,000– 999,999	1,000,000 or more	
Crimes against the person[1]	44.4	47.9	56.1	48.1	28.2
Property crimes[2]	280.2	289.2	285.1	254.6	173.5

Source: US Department of Justice (2000) Tables 52 and 53

Notes:
1 These figures relate to the number of victims per 1,000 people aged 12 and over.
2 These figures relate to the number of victims per 1,000 households.

person and of property crimes than are residents of rural areas. It also shows that crimes against the person grow in frequency with city size until the core city's population size is 1 million or more, and although this broad relationship also holds for property crimes in respect of the largest cities, the differences between property crime rates for the various categories of smaller cities are not particularly significant. This relationship can be taken further from the available tables by making a more straightforward distinction between urban areas (the equivalent of the core cities in Table 2.7), suburban areas, and rural areas. Table 2.8 looks at some of the key variables in this context.

Table 2.8 shows that, in all the four cases it includes, there is a clear gradient down from urban to suburban to rural, with crime rates lessening the further down the gradient one goes. In all categories, the distinctions between urban, suburban and rural areas are also quite marked; the differences between them are not marginal. Table 2.8 also shows that there is a clear relationship between crime patterns and tenure, with rented property being much more likely to be targeted than

Table 2.8 Crime rates by type of area, USA, 1998

Type of crime	Urban	Sub-urban	Rural	US average
Crimes against the person[1]	48.7	36.7	28.2	37.9
Property crimes[2]	274.2	204.5	173.5	217.4
Property crimes, property owned/being bought[2]	256.2	181.8	149.9	221.5
Property crimes, property being rented[2]	291.9	262.9	237.6	272.0

Source: US Department of Justice (2000) Tables 52, 53 and 56

Notes:
1 These figures relate to the number of victims per 1,000 people aged 12 and over.
2 These figures relate to the number of victims per 1,000 households.

property which is owned or being bought; and the differences between these two categories in these terms are much more marked in suburban and rural areas than they are in urban areas. So crime (at least when measured in terms of crimes against the person and property crimes) is clearly a much more marked phenomenon in urban areas in the USA than it is in suburban and rural areas. There are important regional variations within this pattern of urban concentration, with urban dwellers in the west of the USA being nearly twice as likely as urban dwellers in its north-east to be on the receiving end of property crime (US Department of Justice (2000) Table 58). This also has a considerable effect on the overall US average figure, which in all the cases in Table 2.8 is somewhere between the urban and the suburban figures.

Family income is also a key differentiator of risk of being on the receiving end of crime in the USA, although this is much more marked for some types of crime than it is for others. Table 2.9 draws together some of the key indicators in these terms, taking the lowest and the highest annual income categories in the Department of Justice tables and a representative middle income bracket ($35,000–$49,999 was chosen for these purposes, because it contains the largest population aged 12 and over and the largest number of households). Table 2.9 shows that the poorest people in the USA are virtually twice as likely to be on the receiving end of crimes against the person than are people who are in the higher income brackets, although the differences between middle and higher incomes in these terms are not particularly significant. For property crime, the likelihood of being a victim rises with income; the rate of risk illustrated by the figures in Table 2.9 is about 20 per cent greater in these terms for the highest income band than it is for those in the lowest income band.

There is also a racial dimension to these statistics; Table 2.10 looks at this in more detail by race (defined for these purposes in terms of 'black' or 'white' with

Table 2.9 Crime rates by selected family income ranges, USA, 1998

Type of crime	Less than $7,500	$35,000– $49,999	$75,000 or more
All personal crimes[1]	65.5	33.3	34.1
Property crimes[2]	209.0	221.7	248.6
Population aged 12 and over in this income range	11,724,160	34,039,640	29,414,500

Source: US Department of Justice (2000) Tables 14 and 20

Notes:
1 These figures relate to the number of victims per 1,000 people aged 12 and over.
2 These figures relate to the number of victims per 1,000 households.

Table 2.10 Crime victim rates by income and by race, USA, 1998

Type of crime	Less than $7,500		$35,000–$49,999		$75,000 or more	
	White	Black	White	Black	White	Black
Crimes of violence[1]	66.0	63.4	32.0	33.4	33.1	50.3
Household burglary[2]	53.6	61.6	32.3	42.1	27.2	50.5
Theft[2]	146.7	133.1	175.0	194.6	209.5	253.2
Theft of motor vehicle[2]	6.6	20.6	8.5	30.4	11.6	13.2

Source: US Department of Justice (2000) Tables 15, 21–23

Notes:
1 These figures relate to the number of victims per 1,000 people aged 12 and over.
2 These figures relate to the number of victims per 1,000 households.

'other' excluded) and by income band. This shows that black people are usually more likely to be the victims of the specified crimes than are white people (this is true in 10 out of the 12 cases cited in Table 2.10), sometimes markedly more so, and that these differences also vary with income levels. So, for example, the poorest black people are actually slightly less likely to be on the receiving end of crimes of violence than are the poorest white people; but by the time that the comparison is with the wealthiest people (although the overall risk has decreased) the differential has changed markedly, such that the wealthiest black people are approximately 50 per cent more likely to be the victims of crimes of violence than are the wealthiest white people. A broadly similar pattern emerges for household burglary and for theft, with in both cases a markedly higher risk for the wealthiest black people than for the wealthiest white people, and it is only in relation to the theft of a motor vehicle that this particular differential is not so marked. In this latter case, however, there are very large differences in risk at the lower levels of income, with the poorest black people being more than three times more likely to be the victims of theft of a motor vehicle than the poorest white people, with this differential jumping to nearly four times for middle income people. There is also evidence to suggest that as well as being differentially more likely to be the victims of many crimes, black people are also much more likely to be convicted of crimes and imprisoned as a result than are white people. In 1991, in the USA, the 'incarceration rate' was 396 per 100,000 white adults and 2,563 per 100,000 black adults, a ratio of approximately 1:6.5 (Langan and Farrington, 1998, page 44).

Overall, within a pattern of falling crime rates in recent times, this information suggests that crime in the USA is particularly an urban phenomenon, that for crimes against the person there is a close relationship between poverty and the risk of crime, and that race is also a significant factor in some instances with black people usually more likely to be victims of crime than white people from the same income bands. These elements are, of course, often closely interrelated in many parts of American cities, which is why such areas have often been the subject of place-specific crime-prevention initiatives (Feins *et al.*, 1997).

Within this framework, particular attention has been paid in popular culture to the component of crime in American cities that is to do with violence. US Bureau of Justice statistics show that murder has been a crime more likely to be committed in large cities than elsewhere in the USA, but they also show that homicide rates were falling quite rapidly in the USA during the 1990s. The headline points are as follows:

- Over the period 1976–1998, over half of all homicides occurred in cities with a population of 100,000 or more and nearly one quarter were in cities with a population of 1 million or more.
- But from 1991 the number of homicides in the largest cities was falling, and by 1997 this figure had fallen to a rate below that recorded two decades previously.
- The comparable figures for suburban areas, small cities and rural areas varied relatively little over this same period (source: Bureau of Justice, http://www.ojp.usdoj.gov/bjs/homicide/city.htm).

These trends are confirmed by National Crime Prevention Association data, which show, among other things:

- Serious crime (murder, rape, robbery, serious assault and burglary) was at a twenty-five-year low in 1998 in the USA. Within this, figures for murder showed an 8 per cent drop from 1997 to 1998 and those for robbery dropped by 11 per cent.
- Nonetheless, 8.1 million Americans were estimated to be victims of violent crimes in 1998, and the annual cost of crime per annum was put at $4,500 per household.
- Public concern about these matters was confirmed in a 1998 Gallup Poll, which showed that the American public ranked crime and violence as the most important problems facing the country (source: National Crime Prevention Association, hhtp://www.ncpa.org/studies/s229/s229.html).

Evidence is emerging that some politicians and criminologists in the USA regard all of this as a process which was beginning to bottom out by the late 1990s, with the likelihood of a long-term continuation of the 'good news' represented by these 1990s trends being limited. An Associated Press news report of 22 June 2000 by Brett Martel, for example, in looking at some of these views, makes the point that expert views vary across the country, as indeed do the records of individual cities. So, for example, murder rates in cities such as New Orleans, Los Angeles and New York were reported as being up over the preceding 12 months, although other cities such as Denver and Phoenix had experienced drops.

What does seem clear from this is that as well as broad national patterns, many local factors must also be at work across the USA to account for some of these differences; and many of these are likely to have environmental dimensions to them.

CRIME TRENDS IN BRITAIN[2]

Britain has probably seen itself historically as a country where crime rates are relatively low, and where respect for the forces of law and order is quite widespread; although it is now clear that the first part of that proposition in comparison with the USA is open to challenge (Langan and Farrington, 1998), which will inevitably also undermine the second part.[3] Nevertheless, crime prevention has broadly been seen as a consequence until recent times as being the territory of the police; it was really not until Home Office Circular 8/84 (issued in 1984) placed an emphasis on multi-agency approaches in the wake, amongst other things, of an investigation into a wave of civil disturbances in many of Britain's inner cities in 1981 that this perception could clearly be seen to be changing (Walklate, in McLaughlin and Muncie, 1996, pages 293–331).

This changing perception may well have been related to emerging evidence that putting more resources into policing, the criminal justice system and the prison system did not appear to be stemming what was seen as a growing tide of crime (Fyfe, in Pacione, 1997, pages 255–8). Thus, for example, Smith (in Herbert and Smith, 1989, page 271) reported that recorded crime in England and Wales rose by 63 per cent between the mid 1970s and the mid 1980s, whereas clear-up rates fell from 45 per cent in 1970 to 31 per cent in 1985. It was clear, however, that this trend was not consistent either between or within urban areas of Britain, so people's experiences across the country were likely to be very variable. To illustrate this Table 2.11, based upon work done by Taylor et al. (1996, page 26), compares recorded crimes in Sheffield and Manchester between 1975 and 1990. Taken at face value,[4] Table 2.11 shows that both cities experienced large-scale crime increases over the period in question, with the rate of increase being a little less in Manchester than in Sheffield, but with the overall crime rate apparently being much higher. Indeed, on this basis, nearly one in five of Manchester's population was on the receiving end of a crime in 1990, whereas the figure for Sheffield was a little less than one in ten. More recent evidence seems to suggest that disparities

Table 2.11 Recorded crimes per 100,000 population, Sheffield and Manchester, 1975–1990

Year	Manchester	Rate of increase on 1975 base (1975=100)	Sheffield	Rate of increase on 1975 base (1975=100)
1975	10,368	100	3,565	100
1980	13,180	127	4,893	137
1985	18,732	181	6,207	174
1990	19,724	190	8,602	241

Source: developed from Taylor *et al.* (1996) page 26

Note: Manchester and Sheffield are two northern English cities some 40 miles apart of broadly similar population sizes within their administrative cities, although Manchester is the core city of a much larger conurbation than is Sheffield and has much more wide-ranging regional functions.

between these cities have continued. *The Independent* of 18 July 2000, in reporting recorded crime figures up to March 2000 for particular localities, comments on the perception of Sheffield as a much safer city than Manchester,[5] which it attributes primarily to the nature of the community policing initiatives taken in Sheffield during the 1990s. As an example, the Manchester figures show crimes of violence against the person running at five times the Sheffield per capita rate for 1999/2000, and the Manchester figures for burglary running at nearly twice the Sheffield per capita rate. Without wishing to deny the possibility that particular sets of community policing initiatives can make a difference, we find it difficult to believe that this is a probable primary explanation for these differences, which appear to have existed long before the community policing initiatives in question started. Rather, the figures presented here (assuming that they can be relied upon) would tend to suggest that the phenomena reflected in them are both long-term and deeply rooted in the socio-economic characteristics of these communities, rather than being primarily a function of different local styles of policing embarked upon in recent times.

The chances of being on the receiving end of a crime covered by the data in Table 2.11, high though they may appear to be in many areas, need to be disaggregated, because even by the early 1980s there were major differences between different parts of cities with their very different sets of prevailing economic and social circumstances. Smith (in Herbert and Smith, 1989, page 276), for example, shows that 1983 figures indicate that 12 per cent of households living in the poorest municipal estates in Britain's cities experienced at least one actual or attempted burglary that year, whereas for households living in the more affluent suburbs the equivalent figure was only 3 per cent. It is perhaps scarcely surprising given these large-scale differences between component parts of cities that area-based initiatives have been a significant component of the recent response to this issue in Britain. Indeed, the Urban Policy White Paper (Department of the Environment, Transport and the Regions, 2000b, page 106) summarises comparisons between Britain's cities and the national average carried out as part of the British Crime Survey 2000 as showing that people living in conurbations 'are 19 per cent more likely to experience violent crime, 46 per cent more likely to experience burglary and 35 per cent more likely to experience vehicle related theft'.

The 1998 and the 2000 British Crime Surveys allow us to bring this material nearly up to date. Table 2.12 shows the pattern of crimes recorded in the regular British Crime Surveys carried out for the Home Office between 1981 and 1999, with the four selected categories being responsible for about 50 per cent of the total number of crimes recorded in the British Crime Survey over the period in question.

Overall, the 1981–1995 period saw crime numbers grow by over 70 per cent, before the last two Survey years of the 1990s saw successive reductions from the 1995 peak. Nonetheless, the long-term trend was still upwards, with the overall number of crimes recorded by British Crime Surveys growing by one-third between 1981 and 1999. In rank order terms, the biggest growth rates by types of crimes recorded in Table 2.12 over the period 1981–1995 were for all vehicle thefts, followed respectively by burglary, common assault and vandalism; it is noticeable that both of the 'top two' categories have very specific environmental dimensions to them. This precise rank order is repeated in terms of the scale of the falls recorded between 1995 and 1999, with the figures respectively being −32 per cent for all vehicle thefts, −27 per cent for burglary, −22 per cent for common assault and −17 per cent for vandalism. It is probably too soon on the basis of two Survey years' worth of data to conclude that Britain has permanently reversed its long-term pattern of a significant growth in the crime rate, especially since the absolute level remains well above that for 1981, but clearly the downturn recorded by the 1997 and 1999 results is very welcome to all parties (except perhaps the criminal fraternity) after well over a decade of seemingly inexorable growth.

Table 2.13, then, looks at crime rates, either per 1,000 adults or per 1,000 households, with a particular concentration on the changes recorded in the most recent British Crime Surveys in the 1990s. Crime rates rose (in some cases by large amounts) between 1981 and 1993, then fell back between 1993 and 1999; although in the case of common assault 1995 saw a further rise from 1993 before falling back. In all cases except that of vandalism, 1999 rates were still well above those recorded for 1981; for vandalism, the figure for 1997 was below that for 1981, and 1999 showed a further fall. It should be noted in interpreting the majority of these figures that average household sizes were falling in Britain over the 1981–1997 period and are predicted to continue to fall; this will have an effect on future crime rates measured per household, not only because the number of

Table 2.12 British Crime Survey – numbers of crime incidents (in thousands), 1981–1999, selected categories and all crimes

Category	1981	1991	1995	1997	1999	Percentage change 1981–1995	Percentage change 1995–1997	Percentage change 1997–1999
Vandalism	2,715	2,745	3,419	2,898	2,853	+26	–15	–2
Burglary	750	1,373	1,755	1,628	1,284	+134	–7	–21
All vehicle thefts[1]	1,752	3,825	4,318	3,461	2,956	+146	–20	–15
Common assault	1,403	1,763	2,820	2,278	2,206	+101	–19	–3
All BCS crime	11,046	15,125	19,161	16,371	14,716	+73	–15	–10

Source: Home Office (2000b) Table A2.1

Note:
1 This category includes both thefts of vehicles and thefts from vehicles.

Table 2.13 Key statistics on crime trends, Britain, 1981–1999

Type of crime	1981	1993	1995	1997	1999	Percentage change 1981–1993	Percentage change 1993–1999
Vandalism[1]	148.1	163.8	161.4	134.5	130.0	+11	−21
Burglary[1]	40.9	85.5	82.9	75.6	58.5	+109	−32
All vehicle thefts[1]	95.5	209.2	203.9	160.7	134.7	+119	−36
Common assault[2]	36.2	62.3	68.5	54.8	52.5	+72	−16

Sources: Home Office (1998) Table A3.1; Home Office (2000b) Table A2.3

Notes:

1 Rates are per 1,000 households.

2 Rates are per 1,000 adults.

N.B.: This table should not be compared directly with the apparently similar Table 2.5 (which shows key crime statistics for the USA over a similar period), because the basis of definitions used in some of the cases is different. A more reliable comparison is made later in this chapter in Table 2.17.

households will be growing but also because the number of houses (and hence the opportunity for property crimes) will also be growing.

The 1998 British Crime Survey also contains some useful information on what it describes as 'unequal risks' (Home Office (1998) pages 27–43); this is continued in the 2000 Survey although it is not presented in the same way. The point has already been made that the risk of being on the receiving end of burglary is much less in British cities for people living in one of the more affluent suburban areas than for those living in one of the poorest inner city municipal estates; this broad pattern is confirmed by the 1998 Survey results. Table 2.14 picks out some key elements in this pattern of unequal risk of being on the receiving end of burglary by looking at pairs of results, which demonstrate vividly the differences in risks in these terms: basically, being young, being unemployed, living in a flat or maisonette, living in the inner city, living in a municipal housing area, and living on a main road are all risk factors; there are others. These factors in turn make a major difference to insurance costs and availability (Wong, 1997). Explaining these differences can be both difficult and controversial, and can get quickly into awkward political waters. For

Table 2.14 Some key components in the geographical distribution of risks of burglary, 1997

Component	Percentage[1]
Age of head of household 16–24	15.2
Age of head of household 65–74	3.5
Head of household in employment	5.4
Head of household unemployed	10.0
Detached house	4.1
Flats/maisonettes	7.2
Inner city location	8.5
Rural location	3.4
Municipal housing area	8.1
Non-municipal housing area	5.1
Main road location	6.6
Cul-de-sac[2]	4.3
Average for all households	5.6

Source: Home Office (1998) Tables 5.1 and 5.2

Notes:
1 Percentages relate to the numbers of households who were victims of burglary at least once during 1997.
2 We refer subsequently (in Chapters 7 and 8) to the debate around the apparent support of a majority of police Architectural Liaison Officers in Britain for the cul-de-sac form of housing layout, on the grounds that it limits the escape opportunities available to criminals. This finding (that in 1997 there was approximately a 50 per cent greater chance of being a victim of burglary on at least one occasion if living on a main road location rather than in a cul-de-sac) may go some considerable way towards explaining this preference.

example, if most burglary is opportunistic rather than carefully preplanned (as the police typically say that it is), and if it is much more likely to take place in the poorest rather than the wealthiest areas, the inference that most burglars are residents of the poorest areas is difficult to resist. This is perhaps saying something fairly obvious about the residential location of burglars, but it also carries the risk of stig-matising large numbers of law-abiding citizens who live in those areas; and it can be argued that this has in the past created some reticence in policy initiatives. There is a suggestion, however, that concern about stigmatisation in this way is becoming a little less significant in shaping British policy, as is perhaps illustrated by the announcement of the Youth Inclusion Programme in July 2000 (see *The Independent*, 26 July 2000, article entitled 'Ministers identify 47 crime hot spots'). This pro-gramme not only identifies forty-seven crime 'hot spots' in England and Wales, but also seeks to target within each the fifty worst offenders aged 13–16. Whatever the merits of an initiative of this kind, it is clear that the obvious risk of stigmatisation that it gives rise to is not seen to have outweighed the value of targeting in this instance.

In this brief overview of what we know about the geography of contemporary crime in Britain, it should also be pointed out that the 1998 British Crime Survey data, not for the first time, show that the risks of being on the receiving end of viol-ence vary hugely by age and by sex. Table 2.15 picks out the key points, which are that the group most at risk (by a huge margin) are young men and that risk falls away very rapidly by age group. One of the favourite media images in Britain in recent years in reporting on violence has been of the elderly woman who has been attacked, because of course it is a shocking thing when it happens; but Table 2.15 shows that this group is in fact very unlikely to be on the receiving end of an attack (see Pain, 2000, pages 374–6, for a review of what recent research has con-cluded about some of these matters). The importance of this, of course, is that such reporting has an impact on public perceptions of crime risk, and since the fear of crime is one of the most significant elements in this field the relationship between media coverage and fact is an important matter.[6]

Table 2.15 Proportions of adults who were victims of violence in 1997, by age and by sex

Age	Men	Women
16–24	20.9%	8.8%
25–44	7.0%	4.6%
45–64	3.0%	2.0%
65–74	0.2%	0.8%
75+	1.0%	0.2%
Overall	6.1%	3.6%

Source: Home Office (1998) Table 5.6

Table 2.16 Proportion of victims of violence victimised more than once in 1997

Women aged 25–44	40.0%
Men aged 16–24	34.7%
Women aged 16–24	30.0%

Source: Home Office (1998) Table 5.8

Table 2.15 could perhaps be interpreted as being dismissive of concerns about gender differences, in that it records men as nearly twice as likely to be on the receiving end of crimes of violence as women (and, it should be said, in the case of young men aged 16–24, much more likely to perpetrate those crimes against other young men). This does not, of course, deal with the question of the fear of violence, nor does it deal with different types of violence and the social situations in which they occur, both of which are very important considerations in seeking to understand issues related to gender as far as crimes of violence are concerned. In particular, it does not distinguish between single acts of violence and repeat victimisation, because it treats one or a number of attacks as simply one person who has been on the receiving end of violence. The statistics on repeat victimisation produce very different results from those of Table 2.15, however, as Table 2.16 shows, with women aged 25–44 being the group at greatest risk.

About four in ten of the following groups who were victims of violence at least once were actually repeat victims during 1997:

- women aged 25–44 (which is attributed to the high risk of repeat incidents of domestic violence);
- single parents (who are largely women);
- social renters;
- those in council estate areas (Home Office (1998) page 41).

It is clear from the above that there are important gender differences here, although as yet it is not so clear to what extent environment is a significant explanatory factor in this (see Walklate in McLaughlin and Muncie, 1996, pages 300–2; also Pain, 2000, pages 374–6). It is also clear from recent work that there are important gender differences in terms of 'worry about crime', with the British Crime Survey 2000 (Home Office (2000b) page 48) showing that women described themselves as 'very worried' about certain types of crime in comparison with men at higher than a ratio of 2:1 in respect of rape (29:7), physical attack (27:9), being insulted or pestered (13:5) and mugging (23:11).

Given the statistics reported above, it is scarcely surprising that crime in Britain is big news, as is politicians' reactions to crime. Indeed, there is probably a symbiotic relationship between crime, the ways that crime is reported, and political reactions. One of the sound-bites most remembered in Britain from the Labour Party's successful 1997 general election campaign, for example, was 'Tough on crime, tough on the causes of crime'. As a generalisation, crime statistics are often regarded as fair game politically, with politicians freely blaming each other when they get worse, massaging them to suit their particular stances and quickly claiming credit when they improve, all of which in turn generates further headlines. A typical example of how this relationship between crime rates and the political debate is sometimes reported even in the responsible press is the following extract from a report in *The Independent* of 11 July 2000 under the headline 'Blair raises stakes with Commons showdown':

> Crime has risen to the top of the agenda, with Labour's private polls showing the Tories have re-established their reputation as the best party on law and order after populist initiatives by Mr Hague.
>
> Government sources admitted last night that official Home Office figures to be published next week show crime in England and Wales has risen by almost 3.5 per cent in the past year, largely due to a sharp increase in violent offences.
>
> Although burglary and car crime fell in the 12 months to April, the increase in violent crime could reach double figures. The Home Office will reveal that police successes in combating burglaries in cities has (sic) led drug addicts to turn to robbery to fund their habit.

In a few short sentences, this illustrates both the perceived importance of crime to the battle between the political parties and the extent to which attempts are being made to dampen down the 'bad news' elements of an apparent rise in crime rates by damage limitation tactics (trying to turn the figures into 'old news' and engaging in deflection in explanations). Whatever else this achieves, however, it shows that crime rates and the action to deal with them remain at the top of the political agenda.

The intensity of reporting crime issues in Britain is well illustrated by looking at the four major stories about crime reported in that same newspaper (*The Independent*) in the three-week period that followed the story including the extract quoted above, which appeared on 11 July 2000:

*   17 July 2000 – 'Planners and police surrender city centres to Britain's mass volume vertical drinkers' – near full-page spread reporting the rise of violent (alcohol-related) behaviour in city centres that have fully embraced policies of promoting 'the night-time economy'.

- 18 July 2000 – 'Robberies rise by more than a quarter in a year' – full-page spread reporting new police crime statistics and some local initiatives to tackle crime.
- 26 July 2000 – 'Ministers identify 47 crime hot spots' – near full-page spread showing ministerial reactions to crime problems by 'cracking down' on 'hot spots'.
- 1 August 2000 – 'Crime figures sham as police fail to report 1.4m offences' – front page main story, reporting a research study on the differences between reported and recorded crime, which concentrates on the explanation that this was about massaging the figures to make the police appear more successful.

Readers will readily understand that if this was the intensity of coverage in the broadsheet press, the tabloids were even more prone to screaming headlines and dramatic stories. We believe that there is likely to be a relationship between this level of press coverage of crime issues on an ongoing basis and fear of crime in society, and thus the material that introduces Chapter 7 of this book (on public perceptions of crime as a quality of life issue in Britain) needs to be seen in this context.

CRIME IN THE USA AND BRITAIN: A COMPARISON

As we have already noted, the problems associated with undertaking reliable international comparisons of crime data are very considerable. In terms of the comparison between the USA and Britain, however, we are much helped by a major 1998 study for the US Department of Justice which sought to look at this issue over the period 1981–1996 (Langan and Farrington, 1998). Table 2.17 picks out key figures based upon survey information.

The broad patterns of crime in each individual country have already been noted, with falls in the USA particularly in the 1990s and with steady rises in Britain, and these patterns are repeated in Table 2.17. What this table also shows is that British crime rates were well behind those in the USA for robbery and for burglary in 1981, but well ahead for both categories by 1995; and that for assault and for motor vehicle theft British crime rates were already ahead of those for the USA by 1981, with this gap substantially widened by 1995. Perhaps the most remarkable reversal here is in the figures for burglary, for which in 1981 the British rate was less than half of that for the USA whereas by 1995 the British rate was approaching double that of the USA. The degree of change over the 1981–1995 period can easily be understood by looking at the ratios between the USA and the England and Wales rates for the beginning and the end of the period, as follows (USA figures first):

Table 2.17 Comparative crime rates, USA and England and Wales

Type of crime	1981		1991		1995	
	USA	England/Wales	USA	England/Wales	USA	England/Wales
Robbery[1]	7.4	4.2	5.9	4.5	5.3	7.6
Assault[1]	12.0	13.1	9.9	15.4	8.8	20.0
Burglary[2]	105.9	40.9	64.6	67.8	47.5	82.9
Motor vehicle theft[2]	10.6	15.6	14.2	25.7	10.8	23.6

Source: Langan and Farrington (1998) page 67

Notes:

1 These figures are rates per 1,000 population.
2 These figures are rates per 1,000 households.

- for robbery, the ratio was 1.75:1 in 1981 and 0.7:1 in 1995;
- for assault, the ratio was 0.9:1 in 1981 and 0.4:1 in 1995;
- for burglary, the ratio was 2.6:1 in 1981 and 0.6:1 in 1995;
- for motor vehicle theft, the ratio was 0.7:1 in 1981 and 0.5:1 in 1995.

In the first three of these cases, the changes in the ratios recorded are a function of both the improving figures in the USA and the worsening figures in England and Wales, whereas for motor vehicle theft the change in the ratio is wholly a function of the deteriorating position in England and Wales.

Police records (used here because survey information does not cover all this ground) show that for crimes of violence the USA apparently remains a comparatively more violent society than Britain, although the gap seems to be closing. This may well be linked to the use of firearms in violent crimes, with police statistics showing that they were used in 68 per cent of murders and 41 per cent of robberies in the USA in 1996 whereas the respective figures for England and Wales were 7 per cent and 5 per cent respectively (Langan and Farrington, 1998, page iii). Table 2.18 picks out the key statistics from police records.

On the basis of the evidence contained in Table 2.18, whilst in the case of each type of violent crime the USA has a higher rate than England and Wales, in each case the gap is narrowing. This can be shown by giving the changing ratios between the USA and the England and Wales rates for the beginning and the end of the period as follows (USA figures first):

- for murder, the ratio was 10:1 in 1981 and 8:1 in 1995;
- for rape, the ratio was 17.5:1 in 1981 and 3.5:1 in 1995;
- for robbery, the ratio was 6.5:1 in 1981 and 1.7:1 in 1995;
- for assault, the ratio was 1.5:1 in 1981 and 1.1:1 in 1995 (and indeed by 1996 the rate in England and Wales was recorded as being about 13 per cent above that for the USA).

In the cases of the figures for robbery and for assault contained in Table 2.18, the explanation for this changing ratio appears to lie in a combination of a falling crime rate in the USA and a rising rate in England and Wales. It should be noted, however, that these figures, based as they are on police records, may well under-represent the position in England and Wales more severely than they do the position in the USA. This is because the survey data for both these categories for 1995 contained in Table 2.17 show the rates per 1,000 people in both these cases to be higher in England and Wales than in the USA. The explanation for this difference may well lie in the *police recording* practices in the two countries, which Table 2.3 shows produce very different outcomes, rather than in *reporting* rates to the police which

Table 2.18 Comparative crime rates, crimes of violence, USA and England and Wales

Type of crime	1981		1991		1995	
	USA	England/Wales	USA	England/Wales	USA	England/Wales
Murder[1]	0.1	0.01	0.1	0.01	0.08	0.01
Rape[2]	0.7	0.04	0.8	0.16	0.7	0.19
Robbery[1]	2.6	0.4	2.7	0.9	2.2	1.3
Assault[1]	2.9	2.0	4.3	3.6	4.2	3.9

Source: Langan and Farrington (1998) page 68

Notes:

1 These figures are police recorded rates per 1,000 population. The figures for robbery and for assault are not directly comparable with the figures in Table 2.17, which are based upon survey data.

2 These figures are police recorded rates per 1,000 female population. They may be particularly unreliable given the phenomenon of low reporting rates for rape cases, caused by women's uncertainty about whether they will even be believed or how they will be treated.

Table 2.1 shows are not very different. For murder, the explanation for the changing ratio appears to lie wholly in the falling rate in the USA between 1991 and 1995, since the figure for England and Wales did not change over the period. For rape, the explanation for the changing ratio appears to lie wholly in the rising rate in England and Wales, since the 1981 and 1995 figures for the USA were the same and indeed the 1991 figure was slightly higher than this.

To provide a broader international comparative base, Table 2.19 sets out for selected countries and in selected categories of criminal activity information on crime rates per 100,000 people based upon police records. It is important that readers should understand in looking at this table that it has been constructed to enable them to make a judgment in broad 'order of magnitude' terms about how crime rates in the USA and in England and Wales (the subject of this chapter to date) stand up against some comparator countries in the developed world, and not to facilitate direct statistical comparisons of equivalent data. Readers who wish to pursue international comparisons based upon comparative sample surveys should look at the periodic results from the International Crime Victim Survey carried out under the auspices of the United Nations, which involves a programme of standardised sample surveys looking at householders' experiences with crime, policing, crime prevention and feelings about safety. At the time of writing, the available data from this source were not as recent as those quoted in Table 2.19, but clearly this will change over time.

Bearing in mind these caveats about how Table 2.19 should be used, it does suggest that crime rates in the USA and in England and Wales are broadly in the

Table 2.19 Crimes per 100,000 people, 1998, from police records for selected 'comparator' countries

Country	Total number of crimes	Homicide	Violent crime	Domestic burglary	Theft of a motor vehicle
England and Wales	8545	1.4	633	902	745
Germany	7682	1.2	222	198	193
France	6085	1.6	330	354	710
USA	4617	6.3	567	862	459
Canada	8094	1.8	974	728	547
Australia	6979	1.8	926	1580	703
Japan	1612	1.1	33	188	559

Source: Developed from Barclay and Tavares (2000) Tables 1, 1.1, 1.3–1.5

Note: The statistical basis for the collection of crime data by the police varies between countries, thus this table does not purport to claim that like is being compared exactly with like. Some of the apparent differences will be explained by these differences in statistical practices. In addition, of course, the general comments about the limitations of police recorded crime data introduced earlier in this chapter apply to this material.

same range as are those in many of the chosen comparator countries. In an absolute sense, England and Wales stands out for the high overall volume of crime it displays (but not in every category), and the USA stands out in terms of its homicide rate. Similarly, Japan stands out for the relatively low overall volume of crime it displays and also for its low numbers in most categories. There are also significant differences between the numbers for the various categories of crime for many countries, which in the broadest of senses are probably culturally specific; see, for example, the figures for Australia.[7] The overall conclusion to be drawn from Table 2.19 is that each country in its own particular way clearly has a significant crime problem, and is likely as a consequence to be interested in methods that carry the probability of success in reducing these figures. There is nowhere that can afford to be complacent about these absolute levels of crime, and inevitably there is bound to be a particular interest, given these sorts of absolute levels and the concerns they cause in their respective societies, in what is happening to annual trends.

As far as the demography and the geography of crime are concerned, direct comparisons are more difficult to make because the available survey information is in each case tailored to the particular situation in its own country. We would suggest, however, that the information presented about this earlier in this chapter suggests that the situations in the USA and in Britain are broadly similar. That is to say, crime tends to be more concentrated in urban areas, and within these within the poorest areas; that for many crimes the poorest people in society also have the highest victimisation rates; and that housing tenure patterns are also significant, with higher property crime rates tending to be experienced by households in rented properties, particularly in inner city-type locations, than by those who own or who are purchasing properties. There are also significant racial differences, both in terms of those who are the victims of crime and those who are incarcerated as a result of crime, and these too appear to be broadly common between the two societies. Table 2.20 picks out the key data in support of this statement in respect of incarceration rates.

Table 2.20 Incarceration rates by race, USA and England and Wales, 1991

Racial grouping	USA		England and Wales	
	Rate per 100,000 adult population	Rate in comparison with rate for white population	Rate per 100,000 adult population	Rate in comparison with rate for white population
White	396	1	102	1
Black	2,563	6.5	667	6.6
Other	643	1.6	233	2.3

Source: Langan and Farrington (1998) page 44

Table 2.20 shows that incarceration is more common overall in the USA than in England and Wales (in the ratio of over 3.5:1), but that the racial distribution of this 'incarcerated population' is actually very similar between the two societies, with in particular the black population being in each case over six times more likely to be incarcerated than the white population.

CONCLUSIONS

In an absolute sense, the figures provided in this chapter show why crime continues to be a matter of major public and political interest in the USA and in Britain. While a great deal of political and media attention is devoted to the trajectories inherent in the latest statistics, the overall levels of crime they portray show something that people as individuals are likely to experience in one form or another during their lives, and are likely to be aware of at a still greater level of frequency in terms of what is happening in their neighbourhood or their workplace. We would suggest that it is this sense of crime as a personal or a proximate experience that is also a major factor in the high 'fear of crime' scores we have discussed in this chapter. Crime is not a remote activity affecting a few people, but a tangible threat reinforced by the experiences of friends and colleagues. This perhaps suggests that the overall levels of crime in society actually matter much more than the latest trends, and will continue to do so while crime remains on the scale we have illustrated in this chapter.

This brief examination of the demography and the geography of crime in the USA and in England and Wales also illustrates clearly why both countries have exhibited considerable interest in area-based initiatives to tackle crime problems and in the idea of 'hot spots' (areas of particular concentration of certain kinds of crime). As we have indicated, these are likely to be inner city areas with a predominance of rented housing, concentrations of poverty, and quite probably also a concentration of people from ethnic minority communities. If these sorts of areas are typical crime 'hot spots', they are also areas where the experience of planners has tended to be that community-based initiatives can be particularly difficult to mount successfully. We give several examples of initiatives of this kind in Chapters 5–8. Overall, however, we believe that this review justifies our claim that in these terms both societies face broadly common *problems*, although they are coming at them with very different *trajectories* in terms of recent overall patterns of crime, with significant reductions in crime rates having taken place in the USA in the 1990s and significant increases having typified the British position until relatively recently. We think that this difference of trajectory may be one element in explaining the apparent searching in Britain for an ever-broader policy framework within which to tackle crime in the latter part of the 1990s, which is not visible in the USA; these matters in particular are developed in more detail in Chapters 5 and 7.

NOTES

1   Long-term comparisons of crime data are bedevilled by the fact that they can conceal quite major shifts in what is regarded as socially acceptable or unacceptable. For example, it has been argued that shifts in thinking about domestic violence as part of the emancipation of women in the twentieth century make a real difference to what is kept within the family as distinct from reported to the police, and thus trends drawn from the crude statistics without considering the changing wider social context are potentially misleading. Similarly, comparisons between areas are very difficult when it is all too often unclear whether apparent differences reflect significant variations or merely differences arising from the differential application of some of the types of problems with police records noted in this chapter. Short-term comparisons within the same area simply have a better chance that these variables might be less significant; and in any event, police records may be all that is available at the local level for the purpose of undertaking this kind of comparison. Even so, as noted, care should be taken in using these data to ensure as far as possible that like is being compared with like.

2   There is both a terminological and a data problem behind this use of the term 'Britain'. We use the term in this chapter to mean England and Wales, simply because that is the territory consistently covered by the Home Office's regular British Crime Surveys, which in turn are used in the major USA/UK comparison (the work of Langan and Farrington) upon which we draw heavily in this chapter. But we are conscious that many people would expect a USA/UK comparison to be about the United Kingdom of Great Britain and Northern Ireland, which of course includes both Scotland and Northern Ireland as well as England and Wales. As far as Northern Ireland is concerned, the period over which the statistics in this chapter extend is also the period of 'the troubles', which have undoubtedly affected crime statistics in that part of the United Kingdom; we have therefore chosen not to include material on Northern Ireland. As far as Scotland is concerned, the situation is somewhat complex because there has not been consistent coverage of Scotland during the period of the regular British Crime Surveys. Scotland participated in the 1982 and 1988 British Crime Surveys, but data collection was restricted to southern and central Scotland. Factoring data up from this limited sample to provide estimates for the whole of Scotland would be difficult, however, because it is known that there are significant differences in terms of victimisation rates between the more urban populations in the areas included in the 1982 and 1988 studies and the more rural areas further north excluded from them. Since 1993, Scotland has had its own Scottish Crime Survey, which broadly parallels the British Crime Survey, and to date three Scottish Crime Surveys have been undertaken and published (1993, 1996 and 2000). This means that directly comparable trend data for Scotland relate to a shorter period than

do data from the British Crime Survey. The key points arising from the 2000 Survey (MVA Ltd, 2000) in respect of crime in Scotland are as follows:

- The overall volume of crime fell by 13% between 1995 and 1999.
- Over 60 per cent of crimes in 1999 were against property, approximately half of which were against vehicles.
- The fall in the overall volume of crime between 1995 and 1999 appears to be mainly attributable to a significant drop in relatively minor crimes (such as 'theft from a motor vehicle' or 'other household theft'), but violent crimes appear to have increased over the period. This latter conclusion is a conditional one, however, because it is affected by a change in the questions used in the two surveys at either end of this period.
- Rates of victimisation appear to be lower in Scotland than they are in England and Wales for all categories of crime. A comparison of victimisation rates for Scotland from the 2000 Scottish Crime Survey and for England and Wales from the 2000 British Crime Survey shows the following summary:

Types of offences	Scotland	England and Wales	Figure for England and Wales if Scotland = 100
Household offences per 1,000 households	237.4	428.7	181
Personal offences per 1,000 adults aged 16 or over	78.8	126.4	160

Source: MVA Ltd (2000) Table 3, page 8

Administrative responsibility at central government level for work in this area has shifted as a result of the creation of the Scottish Parliament in the late 1990s. The 1993 Scottish Crime Survey was commissioned by the Scottish Office, which was a UK Government Department with territorial responsibility for most matters of 'home' policy in Scotland, and thus was the equivalent in these terms of the Home Office covering England and Wales. By the time the 2000 Scottish Crime Survey was published, however, this responsibility had shifted to the Scottish Parliament and to the public service structure in Scotland that it oversees.

3   This perception is well illustrated by a full-page article in the *Sunday Times* of 11 January 1998 by Jon Ungoed-Thomas, entitled 'A Nation of Thieves'. The summary of that article immediately beneath its banner headline puts the matter as follows:

> More than one in three British men has a criminal record by the age of 40. While America has cut its crime rate dramatically Britain remains the crime capital of the west. Where, asks Jon Ungoed-Thomas, have we gone wrong?

4   Bearing in mind what we have said earlier in this chapter about the limitations of police data and the difficulties of comparison over quite long periods of time and between

places, it is pertinent to question the extent to which the differences recorded in Table 2.11 are solely attributable to differences in criminality in the two locations, or whether they also include some other types of differences, such as differences in recording practices between police in Greater Manchester and in South Yorkshire.

5   There is some evidence to suggest that Sheffield can justify the claim made by its local press that it is the 'Safest City in England', at any rate amongst the largest cities, and marketing activities in relation to Sheffield have been quick to pick up on this. The Sheffield Hallam University website (at http://www.shu.ac.uk/index.html), for example, includes amongst its publicity designed to attract students to the University a comparative table based upon Home Office collations of police recorded crime statistics; this shows Sheffield as having lower offences rates per 1,000 population in 2000 than all of Leeds, Nottingham, Birmingham, Liverpool, Manchester and Leicester for personal violence, sexual offences, robbery and theft from a vehicle; lower rates than all of these except Liverpool in respect of burglary; and lower rates than all of these except Leicester in respect of theft of a vehicle. By contrast, Manchester was the worst or second worst performer amongst all of these categories in the table. In spite of this, and against a background of a fall in recorded crime of 20 per cent in Sheffield between 1995/96 and 1999/00, the experiences of different parts of the city are very different, as is typically the case in British cities. So, for example, recorded violent crime per 1,000 population is approximately four times greater in Central Sheffield than it is in other parts of the city. This area also has the highest rate in three of these five years for recorded domestic burglary and in all five years for recorded motor vehicle crime, although in this latter case the trend has been sharply downwards (Sheffield First Partnership (n.d.) pages 58–61). Overall, we would suggest that these figures provide some support for the view that community policing initiatives have made a difference in Sheffield in recent years, but that the patterns of lower recorded crime rates in comparison with Manchester are consistent with the evidence we provide in Table 2.11 going back at least to 1975, and are thus primarily about longer-term phenomena.

6   The concept of 'fear of crime' can be two-edged. In other words, fear can affect people's behaviour, but the absence of fear may make groups of people insufficiently aware of risks. Some of the results of the 2000 British Crime Survey reflect this point clearly, in terms of the relative lack of awareness on the part of young men about the extent to which they are at risk of being on the receiving end of crimes of violence. Table A6.1 (Home Office, 2000b) shows that men aged 16–24 were victims of violence from strangers in 1999 in comparison with the chosen sections of the population as follows:

men aged 16–24	8.3% of the population in this group
women aged 16–24	2.3% of the population in this group
men aged 65–74	0.4% of the population in this group
women aged 65–74	0.2% of the population in this group

However, when respondents were asked about their perception of whether they were very or fairly likely to be a victim of attack by a stranger in the next year, Table A7.4 (ibid) records the following results:

men aged 16–29   11% of the population in this group
women aged 16–29   11% of the population in this group
men aged 60 or older   7% of the population in this group
women aged 60 or older   9% of the population in this group

In very broad terms, this comparison of the actual rate of attacks by strangers, as compared with the perception of the likelihood of such an attack, shows that the very significant differences in the actual rate of such attacks on young men are scarcely reflected in any differential perception of risk.

7   A sociological review of crime in Australia (Edgar *et al.*, 1993, pages 480–95) draws attention to two particular features of the Australian situation that should be remembered when looking at the information in Table 2.19. The first is that overall crime figures in Australia are hugely influenced by figures for property crime, which outnumber offences against the person in the ratio of roughly 25:1 (ibid., page 489). This is reflected in Table 2.19, which shows that Australia has by quite some distance the highest rate of domestic burglaries per 100,000 people of all the selected countries. The second is the extent to which the treatment of Aboriginal people by the police in Australia may distort the statistics, since they comprise just over 1 per cent of the general population but nearly 29 per cent of all persons in police custody (ibid., page 493).

CHAPTER 3

ECHOES FROM THE PAST: caves, castles, citadels, walls and trenches

INTRODUCTION

In this chapter we provide an overview of the evolution of defensive design and construction from prehistoric times to the modern era. Although the primary focus of this book is on modern applications of place-based crime prevention strategies, there is much to be learned from the durability of ideas, especially in a field whose applications stretch back into the distant past. Thus, while the use of present-day crime prevention strategies such as urban and building designs and devices aimed at impeding access or facilitating surveillance and territorial control may seem obvious and intuitive, they are nevertheless rooted in experience that spans centuries as well as cultures. Indeed, one could go so far as to say that the history of defensive design parallels the history of humankind. That being said, we make no pretence to exhaust the totality of defensive design experience, as it would be presumptuous to think we – or anyone – could do so in one modest chapter. Rather, we touch upon pertinent examples of defensive designs as a starting place to understand how we got to where we are today and where we may be going in the evolution of place-based crime prevention. We are especially interested in the adaptability of predators – whether invading armies of the past or criminals within our midst today – to the range of successive defensive and protective design strategies and devices that we employ to perplex and impede them.

Because they are so central to the history of defensive design, we focus primarily on the planning, design and construction of walls at the boundaries of cities, citadels, castles and empires. We consider their real and symbolic roles in providing protective edges, their impacts on city form, their vulnerabilities to changing technology and to the adaptive strategies used by predators, their relationship to isolationism, and their linkage to perceptions of security.

Within these contexts, we make connections to modern-day place-based crime prevention issues and principles, such as territoriality, surveillance, access control, activity support and maintenance. In so doing, we suggest that similar defensive design needs and strategies are identifiable throughout history and that they are much more important in determining the form and evolution of urban places and human behaviours than they have been credited.

PREHISTORIC DEFENSIVE DESIGN AND STRATEGIES

Although the archaeological evidence is fragmentary, it seems clear that our species has been shaped by our environment while we shape it in return. Fossil records in Africa now suggest, for instance, that early hominoid ancestors likely became bipedal in response to venturing out from their forest habitat into unfamiliar and dangerous open plains in search of food. They sought the highly concentrated proteins contained in meats to fuel developing brains, which consume a disproportionate amount of the body's energy (Leakey, 1995). Some scientists now believe that early man was much less a hunter, than a scavenger of protein, stealing meat from much stronger predators who had downed it first. Moreover, evolutionary psychologists suggest that the ecological challenges presented by changing habitats and the need to outsmart competitors required the organisation of group efforts, which also contributed to the growth of the human brain (Gore, 1997, 2000). If this is so – and the evidence points in that direction – it was the first step in a long human tradition of organised theft and subsequent attempts to prevent it.

Recent archaeological discoveries point to the migration of *homo erectus* to parts of Asia as far back as 1.8 million years ago and to Europe as early as 900,000 years ago (Gore, 1997). Once out of the tropical womb of Africa and confronted by waves of dramatic climatic changes culminating in three ice ages, our European ancestors were forced to find alternative ways to shelter themselves, not only from the weather but from human and animal predators. Some discovered the natural caves that are found throughout parts of southern Europe, particularly in Spain and France. These provided temporary protection and residences – the first 'true homes' (Childe, 1964) – as long as the local food sources held out. We have a growing history of cave life and early human culture in parts of Europe and Australia based upon surviving wall art and other clues. But most humans were still nomadic even as the last great ice age was approaching about 150,000 years ago; they relied on family units or small social bands for protection along with crude portable shelters or, even more likely, those that could be quickly fashioned out of locally available materials. Because of their decomposition, we can only guess at their structure and design.

Whether for cave dweller or nomad, the selection of sites that could be defended in case of attack was undoubtedly a crucial decision. This is an important principle that humans must have learned early and it has remained with us ever since. A carefully chosen site helps one cope with a dangerous environment which, compounded by an unfriendly climate, places an obvious burden on survival. This is reflected in the density of human populations throughout Europe and parts of Asia that are estimated to be extremely low – 0.1–0.2 persons per square mile in parts of France and 0.03 per square mile in Australia – even as late as 15,000 BC

(Morris, 1979). Indeed, without the intervention of extraordinary luck, humans probably would have remained rare animals.

Population increase occurred during the Neolithic era, beginning about 12,000–13,000 years ago when a fortuitous combination of chance in the mutation of wild grasses into cultivable wheat (the raw material of bread) and the retreat of the last ice age provided humans with the unprecedented opportunity to grow and store sources of energy, rather than needing to harvest them on the move (Bronowski, 1973). The dawning of the agricultural revolution brought the possibility of accumulating the first food surpluses; this has had the most extraordinary implications for human development, profoundly influencing everything from technology to the evolution of place-based crime control prevention policy and practice.

Being on the move makes it difficult for people to develop specialisations and to innovate. Moreover, nomadic life consumes a great deal of energy and makes the accumulation of goods and resources troublesome, inasmuch as they must be transported from place to place. The agricultural revolution of the Neolithic era obviated some of these problems but produced others. With more food on hand than could be consumed over a short time, humans became rooted in specific locations for relatively long periods, and organised themselves increasingly into villages. Here they needed ways to protect their priceless protein treasures against the weather, insects and rodents and predatory humans. To do this required the design and construction of granaries and other storage facilities. Further it required their judicious placement – through planning – within specially shielded areas. As such troves accumulated within villages, they presented inviting targets to those who did not store food. A pertinent example of this is the city of Jericho, a city whose founding predates the Bible.

THE WALLS OF JERICHO: BEGINNINGS OF URBAN SCALE DEFENSIVE DESIGN

The structure and symbolism of this ancient city is synonymous with its almost mythical walls and towers (see Figure 3.1). Built around 7000 BC, almost contemporaneous with the final retreat of the last glacier sheets, Jericho was among the first of many Neolithic settlements in the Middle Eastern and Southern Mesopotamian region. It has survived to this day and is important, not only as one of the earliest urban places in recorded history, but also because it was built to defend the bonus of the great agricultural revolution. Bronowski writes of the city:

> Here wheat and water came together and, in that sense, here man began
> civilisation. Here too, the Bedouin came with their dark muffled faces out of the

Figure 3.1 The Tower of Jericho

desert, looking jealously at the new way of life. ... All at once Jericho is
transformed. People come and soon become the envy of their neighbours, so
that they have to fortify Jericho and turn it into a walled city, and build a
stupendous tower, nine thousand years ago (1973, page 69).

By 6000 BC Jericho had become a settlement of some 3,000 people contained
within ten walled acres (Kenyon, 1957). Whether or not Joshua actually brought
down those walls with a trumpet blast, one thing is clear: they and a hundred
others like it built in the same region were early examples of urban target hardening
in an effort to deter predators and war.[1] In this context, Bronowski notes that war,
rather than being part of human instinct is:

a highly planned and co-operative form of theft. And that form of theft began
ten thousand years ago when the harvesters of wheat accumulated a surplus,
and the nomads rose out of the desert to rob them of what they themselves
could not provide. The evidence for that we saw in the walled city of Jericho and
its prehistoric tower (1973, page 88).

Although not always simultaneous activities, wall building has been connected with city building from the time of Jericho to the Middle Ages and through
the Renaissance, when it was elevated to a science and a high art. First developed
to protect the city's goods and inhabitants from harm, the construction of city walls
is also strongly linked to the forms of community organisation, land economics, and
to technological changes that, as we shall see, can rapidly make defence systems
outdated.

WALLS AS EDGES

The wall marked the boundary of the city, its edges, and these are not trivial things.
As Kostof has pointed out, and as every traveller knows, edges are important since
they distinguish relationships, duties and responsibilities between those within the
jurisdiction marked by the edge and those outside it. For example, the role of
boundaries in determining who pays taxes and customs and who is exempt is of
considerable historic and urban importance.

City edges have been held as sacred ground for thousands of years; in Rome
the *pomerium*, or the ploughed strip where the city walls were to be located, was
celebrated in a fertility rite in the late winter (Kostof, 1991). In some Indian cities
and other parts of Asia the form-giving city edge, whether walled or not, was also
venerated as holy. Walls added even greater import to the city edge. They became
the vessel, however temporary, in which the city was contained, giving it form and
substance, real and psychological. During medieval times walls were 'valued as a
symbol as much as the spires of the churches: not a mere military utility. The
medieval mind took comfort in a universe of sharp definitions, solid walls and
limited views: even heaven and hell had their circular boundaries' (Mumford,
quoted in Miller, 1986, page 117).

While many early cities throughout the world, both in the West and East,
have built walls, they are by no means a universal phenomenon. Wall construction
is an extraordinary investment in human effort and resources and many cities could
not afford to wall their edges.[2] In other places, walls were not used because over-
lords could not justify the costs against the value of what they had to protect. Elsewhere – such as in Japan and what was to become the United States – water

provided natural buffers against attack and mitigated against the construction of walled cities. Many English cities were also protected by large water impediments and generally were not provided with defensive walls. In England this tendency was reinforced by a long domestic peace lasting to medieval times that reduced the need for such expensive constructions. There are, of course, important and interesting exceptions to this such as those found at Berwick and Chester along the English borders with Scotland and Wales. Kostof (1991) notes that for the most part the walls surrounding many interior English towns were more a function of allegiance than defence.

In other places, walls were deemed unnecessary when cities were sufficiently protected by larger, overarching political or military entities. This was the case in much of the Roman Empire up until the end of the third century AD and throughout a vast expanse of the Ottoman Empire at the height of its power. Defensive walls were also often torn down by victors, purposely allowed to fall into disrepair or, as the Mongols did in the thirteenth century in conquered China, forbidden to be built in the first place. (This policy changed radically when the Ming Dynasty came to power in the fourteenth century). Plato approved of the Spartans' practice of building towns without walls, as they feared they would make men 'effeminate, slothful and cowardly' (Duffy, 1975, page 19).

URBAN WALL MATERIALS AND EARLY DESIGN

While there are exceptions as noted above, throughout much of the world, the construction of walled cities was the order of the day, especially during the early Middle Ages. It epitomised an act of political and economic will which, although on a different scale, is not completely unlike the determination of neighbourhoods in the present-day United States to close themselves off from outsiders with gates and barricades. We shall consider examples of place-based crime prevention applications which illustrate this point in later chapters.

Probably the first defensive walls around settlements were simply earthen ramparts piled up using the soil removed from a ditch. When the ditch filled with water, the resulting moat provided additional protection. There was, therefore, a close connection between the size of the ditch and the size of the walls. Whether used to protect towns, cities or nations, earthwork construction persists throughout history as a basic human defensive strategy. Probably its most extensive use was during World War I in the vast defensive trenches dug across France and Germany. Local materials − wood, stone, boulders − were often used to bolster defences by solidifying the soils, and in some cases, cut timber stockades or palisades were constructed across the earthworks, as in the *ostrogi* towns of Siberia

Figure 3.2 Triangular wood palisade fort at Jamestown, Virginia

(Kostof, 1992) or in one of the first American colonial towns, Jamestown, Virginia, constructed in 1606.

Efficiency in defensibility and construction effort were crucial elements in early defensive wall design, especially when such structures had to be constructed quickly. For that reason, settlement walls tended to follow the topography and were often circular in the case of defensive hill towns, or even triangular as in the shape of Jamestown (see Figure 3.2). Kostof suggests (1992, page 28) that a circular shape was ideal in the period before cannon fire because it maximised manpower around a defendable territory; a triangle 'represents the least effort required to enclose a protected space' (Reps, 1965, page 90). Throughout the medieval period, many city walls in Europe came to be further solidified by masonry added on top of the rammed earth foundations. The same strengthening process turned timber citadels and castles throughout Europe into hardened enclaves, as we discuss below, and in China, where, as Kostof reports, the earthworks of such cities as Beijing were studded with 'brick, ceramic blocks and ashlar' (1992, page 28).

Most early defensive walls were built in one layer, as a sheet – a curtain – enclosing the communities within (see Figure 3.3). Some of these shielded

Figure 3.3 Single curtain wall surrounding a settlement

unplanned – spontaneous and 'organic' – villages and towns such as Regensburg, Germany and York, England that had sprung up as market centres (albeit over the remains of Roman frontier military camps called *castra*) and subsequently accumulated sufficient wealth to require the protection of a wall. In other cases, city walls were built to protect carefully planned communities such as the *bastide* towns that were hewn out of the countrysides of France, Spain, Wales, and northern England. Built by royal decrees as Europe was moving from the Dark to the Middle Ages, the *bastide*s were generally rectangular in plan with an internal grid-iron street network protected by a single curtain wall.

Such towns were intended to protect emerging national frontiers and trade routes by dominating the surrounding countryside. Reps (1965) claims that *bastide* towns represent a transitional stage between the feudal castle and the developing cities of the Renaissance. Their design was probably influenced by Roman military camp planning and they, in turn, probably influenced the *Law of the Indies,* Spanish planning specifications that guided the design of towns throughout the Americas beginning in the sixteenth century. There is no question that throughout history cities influence and sometimes mimic each other's design styles and associated ideologies, whether for defensive or other purposes. In modern Britain and the United States, the dissemination of 'sustainability' as a design imperative and 'New Urbanist' ideology – which has a crime prevention thread – are clear examples of this tendency, although implementation, as we discuss in Chapter 5, may be inconsistent across the urban landscape.

CITADELS AND CASTLES

It is not entirely clear whether walled cities developed before citadels and castles, or in tandem with them, which is more likely. What is clear is that citadels and castles represent the ultimate prerogatives of power. Beginning in earliest times in the Middle East, citadels were built as the last retreat against attack for the ruler, whether temporal or sacred, since they were the most difficult targets for attackers to reach and the final ones to fall. From territoriality to maintenance issues their design and use are prophetic of almost all modern defensible space and crime prevention theories and strategies.

Many of the earliest citadels – specially fortified areas, usually built on high ground – were centrally located and their walls completely encircled the entire community. As these population nodes grew by attracting new settlers, additional rings of walls were eventually constructed to encompass the new 'suburban' districts, making the citadel a walled enclave within other walls. In yet another scheme, among the multiple patterns of urban development in both the Middle East and Europe, citadels were sited at the settlement edge in a commanding position and later incorporated into the city walls from that location (Kostof, 1992). Defensive nodes thus grew to become defensive districts, and in some cases, defensive edges along the borders of civilisations.

However they evolved, these sites play an important role in the development of urban forms throughout history. While remaining symbols of centralised political, economic and military power, citadels came also to represent the distinction between the *communal* interests embodied in the building of city walls and the essentially *private* interests represented by the presence of a fortress contained within the city (Kenyon, 1990; Duffy, 1975). As such, citadels – and later castles – were often seen to be as much a threat to the local population as to external enemies.[3]

Aside from their ambiguous political significance, the defensive essence of both citadels and castles – the latter defined as the 'fortified residence of the lord' and, as distinct from citadels, strongly associated with feudal times (Kenyon, 1990, page xvi) – is that their design, siting and construction features were suited to their tasks of extending control and dominion over territories that first included their residents' own living quarters and then beyond that, ever outward into adjacent (and sometimes faraway) lands. Thus, while first conceived as an effective means of holding off the attack of far larger forces, citadels and, especially, castles came to have significant offensive functions. Whether offensive or defensive, the psychology of extending ones' domain, control and responsibility over space is inherent in territorial notions of modern defensible space theory, and was facilitated in much earlier times by the use of design interventions that were clearly fashioned to the task.

Probably the first among these interventions was changing the surrounding environment: moulding the land around the lord's dwelling such that it symbolised and actually functioned as a defensive site. In redefining the face of the land the earliest castles in England were born out of simple ring earthworks carved into the landscape. Kenyon (1990) suggests that these sites were relatively cheap and easy to construct, especially in contested frontier areas, as compared to the more complicated motte and bailey construction. In this latter design, the motte (mound) creates an elevated site on which the early castle structures, made usually out of timber, are constructed (see Figure 3.4).

Surrounding or directly adjacent to the motte was the inner bailey (or ward), consisting of open ground often enclosed by a timber palisade. A ditch formed a protective circle around the inner bailey. Beyond this ditch lay the outer bailey, a larger open area which was also protected by an outer ditch and the earth embankment. The baileys provided living space for castle servants, places of assembly and refuge during attack and, importantly, several layers of defensive protection for the motte with its castle and lord (Hogg, 1975). Indeed, the fundamental concept of layered defences has not changed in millennia: precisely the same strategy is suggested by one of the most widely used modern physical security texts (Fennelly, 1997) and by the United States Department of Defense in a recent anti-terrorism guide (Department of Defense, 1993).

These castle sites, found in significant numbers throughout England, provided defenders with clear lines of sight from the motte – surveillance – and ensured that attackers had to struggle uphill to the stronghold, or the keep ('donjon' to the French), which contained the residential apartments. Elevation also gave defenders more time to prepare – delay being a timeless aid to defensibility – and made it more likely that the opposing forces were fatigued by the time they reached the keep.[4] Altogether, the entire site was designed with hierarchical spaces, providing clear definitions between areas so that 'legitimate users' of these

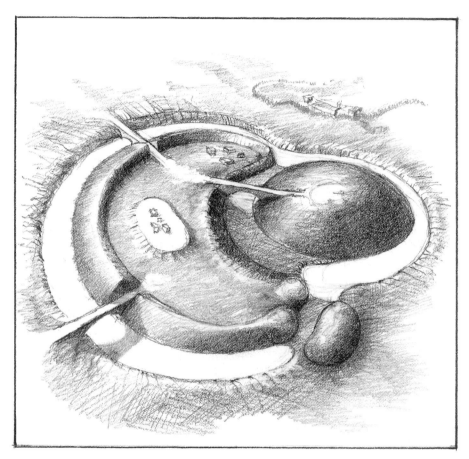

Figure 3.4 Example of motte and bailey construction as a forerunner of castle construction

areas could be clearly distinguished from illegitimate ones. These are spatial strategies suggested by modern day defensible space and CPTED consultants and theorists, and are evident in many of their design suggestions (Newman, 1973; Crowe, 1991, 2000).

Castles were subsequently hardened as the timber structures and earthwork ramparts were replaced or covered by masonry, a development made more likely where the motte was a naturally occurring hilltop that would support the great weight of stone (see Figure 3.5). In England and throughout much of the rest of Europe, the development of stone castles, and their proliferation, was greatly hastened by the advent of feudalism, which lasted from the fifth century to the fourteenth century. During this period power was increasingly vested by monarchs in nobles who consolidated their realms into fiefdoms by exploiting the land and the

Figure 3.5 Section of a masonry castle wall

peasants. With their conscripted labour the nobles built hundreds of masonry castles which, garrisoned by troops, dominated the countryside (Hogg, 1975). In some cases, castles joined the defences of an existing walled town, as in Lincoln. Here, as in the citadels discussed above, the castle was also *protected* from the town by a ditch and drawbridge. In other cases, castles were built outside existing city defences, such as at York, and the walls were subsequently enlarged to include it within the perimeter. As Thompson (1975) suggests, variations on these themes are extensive and generally site specific in nature.

The size and bulk of castles varied too as a function of the relative wealth and status of their owners, and the embroidery of their designs across Europe boggles the imagination, even though many of them share the same origin in the simple motte and bailey concept, which seems to be intuitive. Subsequent technical and design sophistication through the Middle Ages largely aimed at increasing access control and making attack so costly that enemies would be deterred by the effort, which is also a fundamental principle of modern situational crime prevention theory (Clarke, 1997).

Castle gates were strengthened and made more impenetrable by the addition of towers crammed with watchful troops, and an iron, spiked barrier – the portcullis – was set like teeth across the main entrance. Further insulating internal wards was the drawbridge that spanned the ditch (which could be dry or wet) surrounding the castle. Machicolations, or spaced stone buttresses supporting the parapet (the shielding running across the top of the ramparts), permitted defenders to shoot arrows or drop lethal materials (including boiling oil) through holes on attackers who had come too close to the walls. Arrow loops, crenellations and later embrasures were cut into the stone walls, permitting protected bow and artillery fire as well as surveillance. The tall curtain walls were thickened in an (ultimately unsuccessful) attempt to deter breaches from cannon fire, and mural towers (towers incorporated into the curtain walls) were gradually rounded in shape and flared at their bases better to deflect cannon shot.

The sum of this was that by the dawn of the age of truly effective artillery in the fifteenth century, many medieval castles had achieved their objectives: they were impregnable and, assuming a continuing supply of food and water, could and did hold out for years against attackers.

TECHNOLOGY AND URBAN DEFENSIVE DESIGN AND STRATEGY

This era was not to last long, however. Technological change and the adaptations of attackers to the new designs made the tall curtain walls of castles and cities susceptible to attacks from below by mining and from above by bombardment. The first transforming event was the fall (or liberation, for Muslims) of Constantinople in 1453 when the Ottoman Turks were able – assisted by gunpowder invented by the Chinese and cannon devised for them by a Hungarian named Urban – to lob 800-pound cannon balls against the city's walls, breaching them over the course of fifty days. These were the same walls that had withstood the onslaught of Islam for 700 years.

This was closely followed by the second, and in some ways the more important transforming event relative to urban design generally and to the design of fortifications in particular. In 1494, Charles VIII invaded Italy, and successfully used mobile artillery to conquer almost a dozen Italian citadels and cities, including Florence and Naples (Duffy, 1979). For military engineers as well as princes and popes, their fall heralded the advent of a new technology and a new era in city design and military engineering.[5] In so doing these events also helped close the Middle Ages and usher in the Renaissance.

Following the lesson of Constantinople and the conquest of Italy, military engineers such as Vauban, Filarete, Martini, Di Giorgio, and van Noyen, began to design fortified cities for their princes with prickly edges which, while much less graceful than the sweeping curtain walls of the medieval era, were far more effective against the increasingly accurate and destructive cannon that were being deployed against them. City edges in the Renaissance came to feature bulky, low-slung ramparts with massively fortified bastions – multi-faceted masonry projections – that were designed to provide protective fire across a wide circuit of the field of view ahead, covering all flanks (see, for example, Figure 3.6).

Figure 3.6 Example of an arrowhead bastion

As the complexity of built edges grew, they became increasingly expensive to alter or expand. The irony is that, dominant as they were in physical presence, they became outmoded as defensive strategies because of the largely negative spaces – the outworks – designed to make it more difficult for attackers to reach the walls with cannon shot. These often included vast open areas beyond the walls (Kostof calls them 'extramural wasteland' as in the case of Turin, Italy; 1992, page 18), and may have also included an assortment of oddly shaped structural elements such as lunettes, hornworks and ravelins populating the area beyond the glacis, the killing ground at the base of the bastions.[6] Their effect, apart from creating a very defined defensible space beyond the walls, was also to stretch out the distance between the city and the surrounding countryside, further separating urban and rural populations and lifestyles.

Conceived not only for defensive purposes but also as engines of war – 'machine' model cities as described by Lynch (1981) – many of these Renaissance era cities were intended not only to occupy the landscape but utterly to dominate it. Only a few of the most elaborate designs were ever built, such as Palmanova, Italy and Philippeville, Belgium, and these have faded into obscurity except for architectural and urban planning scholars. But many other, less elaborate makeovers were fashioned onto the edges of hundreds of large and small European cities and their surviving outlines are traceable today.

In addition to altering the edges of towns, the new technology of artillery became the catalyst of design for the areas within the walls – its internal districts and street patterns. Interior urban forms, which had been primarily defensive in nature, in some cities took on offensive characteristics as they were modified to facilitate the movement of cumbersome artillery and associated supplies. Thus, as in Philippeville, broad straight avenues were created to supply the bastions with cannon balls and troops more easily and to move the heavy cannon from one point of the city to another. This was further aided by a radial design that focused inward on a central plaza, where the prince or general could, through the use of a raised tower or platform, command a view of the bastions and the entire perimeter.

The radial street pattern, no matter how aesthetically pleasing, was subsequently outmoded by the efficiency of the outworks in defending against attack as compared with bastions, and simpler grid street came to replace or be built over earlier star shaped patterns. The designs of Vitry-le-François, France, and Willemstad, Holland illustrate how the newer internal grid, bastions and outworks function together (Reps, 1965, pages 7 and 11).

THE IMPORTANCE OF DEFENSIVE WALLS IN URBAN DESIGN

Both curtain walls and their successor bastion edges were important elements in early urban life and in later city development across much of Europe. In some cases, as in Constantinople (later Istanbul), single curtain walls were elaborated into double and even triple curtain walls, often containing large open spaces between the walls (see Figure 3.7). Townspeople came to live in these open spaces, which often accounted for a significant proportion of a city's total land area. These inhabitants, in addition to the guards and military personnel who manned the walls, suggest that walls were more than simple inert, mechanical barriers, but were also organic in nature. Together, the walls and people associated with them provided access control and surveillance functions facilitated by a

Figure 3.7 Double curtain walls with open space between the walls

package of defensive design elements previously discussed, such as gates, draw-bridges, portcullis, arrow loops, guard towers, and embrasures.

In many European cities one can trace the growth of the medieval city by the rings of its successive curtain walls, much as one can gauge the age of a tree by its rings. Despite the costs, walls were periodically adjusted to accommodate surging city growth within and suburban 'sprawl' outside the gates. A striking example of this is Paris, with five concentric wall rings built between AD 360 and 1845 (Morris, 1979). Millennia after urban walls have disappeared, their original shapes can still be found in the plan views of cities such as Florence, Italy, Nordlin-gen, Germany and Vienna, Austria and hundreds of other towns where the rem-nants of early defensive walls are traceable in circumferential streets and boulevards that traverse countless neighbourhoods (Mumford, in Miller, 1986; Branch, 1985).

Morris emphasises that the 'role of fortifications as an urban form determinant has been largely neglected by urban historians' (1979, page 129). For example, he attributes the continental tradition of high density urban life and form to the early restrictions imposed on towns by wall building, especially those created following the development of elaborate bastion defences. He says: 'Crammed within their fortified girdles, for ever increasing in population and density, the typical contin-ental European city of the fourteenth to mid-nineteenth centuries could expand only upwards' (page 129). This he contrasts with Britain, where the pacification of the island permitted cities to grow outwards generally without the constraining effects of walls, fostering more expansive attitudes and an anti-urban sentiment, reaching its zenith in the 'garden city' movement at the turn of the last century. Duffy (1979) reaches much the same conclusion, citing the startled and disappointed reaction of English travellers to the dense cities of continental Europe during the eighteenth century.

The same theory could be doubly applied to the United States, a country where only eleven cities had walls of any sort. There are few developed nations with such low density cities, especially in the American South and West, and that harbour such anti-urban sentiment. These are also, interestingly enough, the regions of the USA that lead in the construction of modern gated and walled neighbourhoods and communities according to Blakely and Snyder's landmark study, *Fortress America* (1999).

DEFENSIVE EDGES ACROSS CIVILISATIONS: THE GREAT WALLS

While the walled edges of cities, citadels and castles are central elements in the history of defensive and urban design, so too are edges that stretch across the hinterlands, designed to protect empires and cultures. Examples include the Great Wall of China, Hadrian's Wall, the Wall of Anthemius (or Theodosius) and, in the modern era, the Maginot Line and, of course, the Berlin Wall, which was more a containment vessel than a defensive structure. We focus on the first four examples as they illustrate the changing nature of large-scale defensive strategies, which tend to be cumulative over time by virtue of the massive investment required and which, like city design, are vulnerable to changing technology and to the adaptive strategies of attackers.

THE GREAT WALL OF CHINA

Now a vast historical monument and tourist attraction, the Great Wall of China (also known as the 10,000 Li Wall, the *li* being a unit of measurement equivalent to about one third of a mile) straddles northern China from the Shanhaiguan Pass on the east to the Jiayuguan Pass on the west. The oldest sections of the wall were begun in the Zhou Dynasty in the seventh century BC, when each of several vassal states constructed their own walls for defensive purposes. These subsequently fell into disrepair but were renovated and linked together by the first Chinese Emperor, Qin Shi Huang, who unified the feudal states beginning in 221 BC.

The refurbished walls – a series of connected structures – were intended to protect China's northern frontiers against marauding nomads, particularly the Xiongnu tribes. As in feudal Europe, the walls were built by conscripted peasants, and made of locally collected stone and layers of compacted earth. After Qin's death in 208 BC, the empire dissolved in chaos and the Great Wall began to fall apart from lack of maintenance – a central, but often overlooked, component of defensive design and construction. The Han dynasty, which began to rule in 206 BC restored the Wall and extended it 300 miles westward across the Gobi Desert. In the absence of rock in the desert, they utilised willow reeds and twigs to reinforce a mortar made of water, fine gravel and sand that formed the wall structure.[7]

It was during the Ming Dynasty (1368–1644) that the greatest period of wall building commenced and the present form of the Great Wall took shape. Watchtowers that had been installed at strategic intervals for surveillance were redesigned and modern artillery were added, along with embrasures, peep-holes, and ramparts. Although local inhabitants have through the ages helped themselves to the generous stock of building supplies provided by the wall, one of its best preserved sections is located at Badaling, north-west of Beijing. Here it is 8.5 metres high and 5.7 metres wide, and stretches up and across miles of mountainsides. A central characteristic of the Ming-era wall was its construction of rammed earth faced with mass-produced kiln-fired brick, a technology that surpassed that of the Europeans of the day, who were still using cut stones.

However, like medieval and the even more elaborate Renaissance city walls, the walled edges of the Chinese tended to insulate their populations as much as protect them: in the end, for example, the Ming dynasty turned inward, shunning foreign contact as well as trade with the outside world. One cannot help but wonder whether walls cause such behaviour or are themselves a result of insular behaviour and thinking. The truth is probably a mixture of both. Whatever the answer, it seems clear that wall building and isolationist attitudes stretch across time and cultures.

HADRIAN'S WALL

Another example of an edge across the boundaries of civilisations is Hadrian's Wall. It is a remnant of the Roman occupation of Britain, which began with the invasion of the island by the Emperor Julius Caesar in 55 BC and its conquest and occupation by the Emperor Claudius in AD 43. The wall winds its way across northern England from the River Tyne just east of Newcastle past the city of Carlisle to the Solway Firth on the west. It is approximately 80 miles long and up to 6 metres high, 3 metres wide in places (see Figure 3.8). As such it came to be an unbroken

Figure 3.8 Hadrian's Wall stretching from Housesteads across the English countryside

defensive line protecting Roman Britain from the fierce Pict and Brigantes tribes who lived in the area. Simpson (2000) suggests that its fundamental intent was to 'separate the Romans from the Barbarians' although other historians attribute other intentions, as noted below.

Like the Great Wall of China, Hadrian's Wall did not spring full blown into the world but was rather the product of consolidating a line of existing fortifications established earlier, culminating in the Stangate Line, established under the Roman Governor Agricola in AD 78–85 (Morris, 1979). That defensive line was abandoned and Hadrian's Wall was begun in AD 122, during the Emperor Hadrian's reign (AD 117–138). The most salient existing feature of Hadrian's Wall is Housesteads, one of twelve forts that were built to connect the frontier line of the wall as it marched across the hilly British countryside. A 5-acre site, the ruins of House-steads sit at the peak of the Whin Sill escarpment about halfway between Newcastle upon Tyne and Carlisle. It is an outstanding example of the Roman art and science of military camp construction. Its rectangular (card-shaped) design typifies one of the classic shapes of these *castra*, hundreds of which were estab-lished throughout Europe during the Roman Empire (see Figure 3.9).

Housesteads' grid-iron design with regularly ordered streets, including major and minor roads, and the carefully thought out relationships among land uses, illustrates the attentiveness to planning that characterised Roman camp settle-ments in conquered territories. Many of the early imprints of the *castra* became the

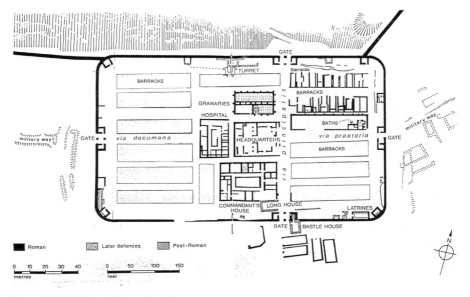

Figure 3.9 Plan view of Housesteads

Source: adapted from *Housesteads Roman Fort*, 1989, London: Crown English Heritage foundations from which villages and later cities grew, although this was not the case in Housesteads. These sites – having both defensive and offensive character- istics – are thus the wellspring of a significant proportion of urbanisation within the vast reach of the Roman Empire which, at its height, radiated from England on the west to North Africa on the south all the way to the Tigris River in Mesopotamia on the east (Morris, 1979). Moreover, as Reps (1965) suggests, it is probable that *castra* design, like later *bastide* examples, influenced the evolution of the 'Law of the Indies' rules promulgated in 1573 by King Philip of Spain to guide develop- ment in the New World, thus helping to shape hundreds of cities there as well.

Like China's Great Wall and the later walls of medieval and Renaissance Europe, Hadrian's Wall was much more than a mere assemblage of stone. In modern place-based defensive design terms, it was a combination of access control features including physical design elements (stones bonded with clay) aug- mented by human guardianship. The latter was organised into formal (military) and informal (civilian settlers) surveillance and activity, all of which served the territorial and cultural interests of the Romans. Simpson notes that 'Hadrian's Wall was an active military zone, a customs barrier, a line of defence and above all "a way of life"' (2000). It was, like so many other grand constructions, a zone of concen- trated human activity which came, by design or simple use, to support its initial defensive intent. A Renaissance poet wrote of the wall:

> Townes stood upon my length, where Garrisons were laid,
> Their limits to defend; and for my greater ayd,
> With Turrets I was built, where Sentinels were plac'd.
> To watch upon the Pict; so me my Makers grac'd,
> With hollow Pipes of Brasse, along me still that went,
> By which they in one Fort still to another sent,
> By speaking in the same, to tell them what to doe,
> And so from Sea to Sea could I be whispered through:
> Upon my thicknesse, three marched eas'ly breast to breast,
> Twelve foot was I in height, such glory I possest.
>
> > (Michael Drayton, 'Poly-Olbion', Song XXIX, 1613, in Hebel 1993,
> > pages 567–8).

While forming a protective barrier, the wall was a corridor in which Roman culture was interposed in an effort to civilise the local 'barbarian' populations. While this proved to be a dismal failure, it was a noble intent, and foreshadowed the hope of modern builders of defensive design that interventions might produce 'spillover' beneficial effects in crime prevention – a 'diffusion of benefits' – that go well beyond their seemingly obvious initial intents or purposes (Clarke, 1997).

THE WALLS OF THEODOSIUS (ANTHEMIUS)

We have already discussed the fall of Constantinople in terms of its significance to the redesign of cities throughout Europe in reaction to the new technology of cannon fire. At the time of its collapse in 1453, the city was the central district constructed within a series of walled edges that extended across the peninsula protecting passage through the Bosphorus between the Black Sea on the north and the Sea of Marmora on the south.

Its location illustrates why it is both one of the best defensive sites among all cities in history, and also one of the most sought-after prizes as the pivot point between eastern and western civilisations. Although scholars differ on the number of walls surrounding the city (Morris outlines four walls, Dunlop depicts five) there is no argument that the most important one was begun under the reign of Theodosius II, in AD 413.

Also called the Wall of Anthemius, who was the regent and prefect of Constantinople at the time, the walls stretched completely across the peninsula – a distance of more than four miles – and shielded the city within from land invasion. Following an earthquake, the wall was reconstructed with an outer curtain and a new moat added in AD 447, and eventually the system contained three walls. These structures complemented a system of seawalls that had been built a decade earlier. While only ruins remain, the original outer walls were 8 metres high, 2 metres thick and included 96 towers. The inner walls were even larger, standing at 12 metres in height and 5 metres thick, also containing 96 towers spaced apart at alternate distances with the outer towers. So formidable were these combined defences, they were able to withstand a succession of attacks by Arab and Bulgarian armies through the centuries.

The breaching of Constantinople's defensive perimeter represented the triumph of one ascending civilisation over another, dying one (the final remnant of the Roman Empire), but also palpable proof of the fragility of stationary access control in a world of changing technology. Successive walls, no matter how formidable and well located, are in the end no match for a determined attacker using tools or strategies specially designed to counter static defences. While there is undoubted truth in Clausewitz's dictum that 'if you entrench yourself behind strong fortifications, you compel the enemy to seek a solution elsewhere,' the question remains whether actual security is not ultimately (if not immediately) outweighed by the imagined sense of security. This difference between perception and reality is a fundamental question of modern defensible space application and certainly applies to our last example of a walled edge between empires, the Maginot Line.

THE MAGINOT LINE: A MODERN DEFENSIVE EDGE

Inspired by French war hero, politician and civil servant André Maginot, the fortified edge that bears his name was built between 1929 and 1940 as a defence against invasion, and specifically German invasion, across France's north-eastern border. At the time it was constructed it contained state-of-the-art weaponry, communications, and armour, all linked together through a vast network of underground tunnels, although concrete blockhouses and pillboxes peeked above ground at intervals. The Maginot Line demonstrated that the fundamental lesson of Constantinople was well learned: that defensive fortifications were safest when sunk low into the earth, leaving a minimum profile for rifle and artillery fire. Trench and underground warfare were natural by-products of this development.

Although the seventeenth-century military engineer, Sebastian Le Prestre de Vauban first masterminded systems of progressively extended trenches to use in attacking fortresses, the art and science of trench warfare reached its zenith in World War I. In that conflict vast trenches were dug across the combat frontiers of France and Germany to shield millions of soldiers on all sides. While they were also used for offensive purposes, such as staging areas to mount attacks, their main purpose was defensive in nature. Using these defensive lines the French and their allies battled the Germans to a draw (albeit at a staggering cost in lives), and this tactic became the inspiration for the Maginot Line. The reasoning was that if underground defensive fortifications could stop the Germans once, they could do so again. Moreover, it was believed that this line of extraordinary fortifications – modelled in part after the fortresses of Verdun that had held out against repeated German assaults – would discourage attack against France or, that if attacked, the line would give the French army additional time to mobilise and deploy its forces (Kaufmann and Kaufmann 1997).

The irony of the Maginot Line is that while it achieved one goal, it nevertheless became the symbol of a much larger failure. The Germans were indeed discouraged from attacking it; rather, they simply flanked the Line by marching into France through Belgium's Ardennes Forest, a tactic that had been considered but rejected as implausible by the French High Command. The result was that, as at Constantinople, a formidable static defence was again defeated by a new approach, but this time with a new twist in that the strategy of high mobility was the essence of the new technologies, as distinct from increased firepower. The lesson that the Germans learned from World War I was that tanks and aircraft defeat trenches and underground bunkers, and that *not* confronting them was the wisest strategy of all. The French, however, assumed what has been termed the 'Maginot Mentality', adopting an unrealistic sense of security based on their belief that building sophisticated static defences was their best protection when, in reality, they were virtually useless against a mobile enemy.

This misdirected faith in a defensive solution that provides, at least initially, a sense of security but later proves impotent, is emblematic of a wide range of modern crime prevention strategies and assumptions. Among these are the notions that we can, almost certainly, prevent crime by addressing defects in offenders' sociological and psychological backgrounds; that increasing street activity and 'eyes on the street' surveillance are infallible crime prevention approaches; and that gating off communities and neighbourhoods, in much the same way that towns, cities and empires and civilisations have walled off their populations throughout history, will protect us against predators who come to steal our grain or our television sets. While each of these modern assumptions and strategies contain valuable kernels of truth, their messages have been overblown by zealots and true believers, often with predictable results.

CONCLUSIONS

While we make no judgements about the inherent nature of man, it is clear from even a cursory review that the history of our species is marked by recurrent predatory behaviour and increasingly intricate efforts to deter or prevent it, which are defeated in turn by ever adaptive predators. We likely began by stealing food from other animals and progressed in Neolithic times to filching agricultural surpluses from our neighbours as large, organised groups. Military fortresses, citadels and walled edges were subsequently used by princes and potentates to dominate the land that produced the food surpluses and the trade routes used to transport them. That each elaborated defence has been defeated is evident in the demise of the curtain walls, castles, bastions and trenches, as we have discussed. But what seems to be elaboration of design is, in the end, only embroidery on simple ideas.

Thus, walls became successively taller, harder, thicker, rounded at the corners, massively extended into the countryside and, ultimately, buried deeper into the ground. They helped change the shape of cities throughout the world; but in the end, they were still defeated. What this suggests is that complex problems – as in war or 'organised theft', in Bronowski's conception – rarely have simple long-term solutions, such as that embodied in the redesign of wall systems, no matter how daring the engineering. Rather, the answers to defensibility are likely to lie in much more complex interplay among social, physical, political and economic forces that we are only starting to recognise and understand in our modern cities and towns.

This is especially so since our new enemies, at least in everyday life in the United States and Britain, are far less likely to be invading armies than criminals who invade our homes and neighbourhoods. They are among us, not outside our borders or hard edges. This means that the responses we offer against them should not be the same, albeit with a few new twists thrown in, as those offered a thousand years ago. To do so, is to take on the 'Maginot Mentality', an expensive self delusion. A fundamental and sobering lesson of this thinking is that we can convince ourselves of almost anything when it comes to our own safety, whether as a society or as individuals, and it becomes easier to believe the truth of the premise, no matter how flawed it may be, as we invest more and more resources in it. We only have to look at the Pruitt Igoe housing projects in St Louis and the Hulme Crescents in Manchester, as discussed in Chapters 5 and 8, to understand the deadly attraction of this thinking.

This is an argument, therefore for critical thinking, for bringing empirical evidence to bear, and for an appreciation of the extraordinary variability of environmental contexts, such that there are few if any defensive solutions that fit all circumstances despite the fact that fundamental principles of defensive design – territoriality, surveillance, access control, and maintenance – have not changed all that much across the centuries. Moreover, it is an argument in support of Ekblom's well reasoned conclusion that designers and planners must change perspectives 'from envisaging use to envisaging misuse' (1997) if they are to keep up with the crafty adaptations of predators in modern society. This is an especially tall order for planners, we suspect, as they are far more accustomed to thinking the other way around.

NOTES

1   The earliest evidence of organised warfare was found at a 14,000-year old site in Jebel Sahaba, Sudan, in the 1960s and the first evidence we have of humans killing one another comes from a 20,000-year old skeleton of a young man whose pelvic bones are riddled by spearpoints found in Wadi Kubbaniya in the Nile valley area of Africa (Gore, 2000).

2   According to Pirenne (1969), more than half of a medieval European city's budget was commonly allocated to the maintenance of the wall and to offensive or defensive weapons. In the sixteenth century the City of Bologna petitioned papal authorities not to force them to refurbish their medieval walls because of the expense and the enormous costs of maintaining them (Kostof, 1992).

3   Duffy (1975) recounts that the use of citadels was the subject of a longstanding debate among political philosophers in the Renaissance since it was 'the only kind of fortification which could be turned equally against foreign enemies and fellow citizens' (page 22). He quotes the French populist Carnot who said: 'A citadel is a monstrosity in a free country, a refuge of tyranny which should be the target of the indignation of every free people and every good citizen.'

4   But elevated locations also have their drawbacks. Duffy (1975) points out that by the seventeenth century, military engineers had begun to resist designing fortresses and citadels on mountains and hilltops. They presented a host of problems as they were difficult to build, supply with potable water and food, garrison, and, in the case of isolated locations, could be blockaded by a small force while the main body of enemy troops bypassed them.

5   Francesco di Giorgio, the Italian military architect and engineer (1439–1502) wrote of the effect of cannon: 'Modern men have recently discovered an instrument of such violence that against it avails neither valour nor arms, neither shield nor the strength of walls, for with that instrument every broad tower must perforce quickly be brought down. By reason of this most powerful machine, called the bombard, all the old devices must certainly be termed obsolete and useless.' (Quoted in Dechert, 1983, page 35.)

6   Excellent glossaries of fortification terminology can be found in Duffy (1975) and Hogg (1975).

7   See (www.discovery.com/stories/history/greatwall/han.html) for an excellent graphic tour of Great Wall sites.

of 'eyes on the street' as a central mechanism to prevent crime, may really not be as effective as supposed. Mayhew cites theory (e.g. Angel, 1968) and empirical evidence suggesting that high levels of street activity may mask certain types of crimes (especially crimes of stealth) and may even encourage other types of crimes, since the offender can easily fade into the crowd. While it is therefore probably inherently desirable for 'somebody to see something' on the street we cannot conclude that this will necessarily result in action relative to the crime because of many intervening variables that affect the process, as well as local socio-cultural issues. The latter often includes fear of retaliation, a common reason attributed by police for the failure of eye-witnesses to report crimes in distressed neighbourhoods.

Mayhew's criticism extends to Newman's theory of surveillance in defensible space design as well as citing problems of costs, safety and privacy issues in modifying existing structures. She further notes that empirical studies of defensible space design implementation show relatively 'small gains' and 'weak effects' in reducing crime rates among projects. Much of the evidence that Mayhew cites is from British 'council' (public) housing studies or research relating to public telephone kiosks (Mawby, 1977; Mayhew et al., 1979) conducted in the 1970s. More recent evidence, however, especially related to the effects of 'mechanical' as distinct from 'natural' surveillance techniques, e.g. closed circuit television (CCTV), suggest contrary yet not undisputed results.

Poyner's (1991) research on parking lot thefts, for example, demonstrated surveillance, operationalised through CCTV, to be an effective tool in helping reduce university parking lot thefts in Britain. Sherman (1997) reports three evaluations of CCTV usage in Newcastle-upon-Tyne, Birmingham, and King's Lynn (Brown, 1995). In the Birmingham case, burglaries, auto thefts, thefts from autos and other types of thefts declined over the forty-one-month test period in which CCTV coverage was employed in the town centre. Reductions in robberies, burglaries, thefts, assaults and thefts from vehicles were also reported (though the data were not made available) in Birmingham and King's Lynn over relatively long periods of time which encompassed periods before, during and after CCTV installation. Because some data were not reported and statistical tests of significance were not performed, Sherman's study does not endorse CCTV as an effective place-based crime prevention tool in open (public) spaces. However, he strongly recommends further, more rigorous, evaluation of its effectiveness, especially given its now ubiquitous placement in Britain and the rapidly growing interest in and use of this surveillance technique in the United States.

CCTV and associated technologically based surveillance approaches have been criticised because of their costs and variable reliability. As structural add-ons (device, cabling and connection), they may be more expensive than designing surveillance facilitation features into construction. There is no doubt that Newman's defensible space approach is far more oriented toward 'natural' design solutions – judicious placement of windows, door, entryway paths – than mechanical or electronic add-ons, even though he did not reject their use. The latter require maintenance and staffing to keep them functioning properly. Moreover, in the case of CCTV there is no guarantee that guardians will be watching in time to actually prevent or intercede in a criminal event. In most cases in urban contexts, helpers are too distant or the criminal event is too rapid for effective intervention. Nevertheless, although the evidence is not conclusive, the increased likelihood of being *apprehended* after the commission of a crime due to CCTV coverage has probable deterrent value for some types of crime, with less value for other, impulse or drug-driven crimes. As detailed in Chapter 7, there are also the suggestions from Britain that the addition of CCTV improves community morale and is a less significant intrusion on city centres than other, more invasive security measures. Further, British studies have found CCTV to be remarkably effective in the *prosecution* of crimes, a virtue which may be of little solace to victims but of great interest to prosecutors and to 'reality' television show producers. It is unfortunate that these latter public spectacles have almost obscured more fundamental issues of the utility and ethics of public electronic surveillance for crime prevention.

Civil libertarians on both sides of the Atlantic have argued against the widespread employment of these tactics, with far more success on the American side. By and large, the British public has supported the growth of CCTV (recent polls put the margin at a 70 per cent favourable level), a trend that does not seem to have been impeded by the sale of embarrassing 'out-takes' of video footage to the public by sleazy entrepreneurs, or by the costs of installing and operating such facilities. The high value that Americans place on privacy, coupled with legal protections not available to the British, have helped slow the widespread implementation of CCTV in America's public places. However, there is evidence that the reluctance to value public order over privacy concerns in the United States is eroding (Nieto, 1997).

An important surveillance 'facilitator' is lighting, since most surveillance techniques are of little use without adequate illumination. Some have argued that lighting is a double-edged sword: it not only permits the offender to be seen, but also allows the offender to see potential victims and other targets. In this view, lighting is a crime facilitator as distinct from being a crime inhibitor. Moreover, most offenders do not inhabit dark and gloomy places, even though that is our picture of their actions in our mind's eye. Rather, offenders, like the targets they pursue, are drawn to reasonably lighted locations associated with known 'criminogenic' (crime generating and attracting) land uses such as bars, liquor stores, pawn shops and adult entertainment districts (Taylor, 1997).

ROUTINE ACTIVITY THEORY

Complementing situational crime prevention further is the work of Cohen and Felson (1979) which focuses on understanding the 'routine activities' of offenders. An approach which is compatible with all place-based theories, in that it concentrates primarily on the criminal event as distinct from the criminal's state of mind or background, routine activity theory also lends itself to the geographic and quantitative analysis of crime patterns and trends. It is associated with theories of behavioural geography and crime patterning (Eck and Weisburd, 1995) in suggesting that offenders, like the rest of us, have day-to-day schedules – trips to and from work, visiting friends, going shopping – and that in the course of such routine travels they search out likely targets. Targets are often associated with offenders' idiosyncrasies, so that paedophiles would likely select schools or playgrounds encountered in the course of routine travel and drug addicted burglars would likely prefer targets adjacent to drug markets. This approach is particularly practical for law enforcement purposes – and especially to the growing field of crime analysis in the USA and Britain – in devising tactical responses to crime grounded in the discovery of order and patterns to raw crime data. Based on empirical studies (Maguire, 1982; Poyner and Webb, 1991), routine activity theory helps one make informed speculations about the search patterns of offenders in certain circumstances and likely venues for crimes based upon adjacent land uses and the socioeconomic characteristics of neighbourhoods. We know, for example, that offenders are likely to prefer home-range areas (part of their 'comfort zones') in which to commit crimes and that targets are often related in time as well as spatially. Clarke emphasises the temporal element as being central to routine activity theory and its stress on 'three minimal elements for direct-contact predatory crime: *a likely offender, a suitable target*, and the *absence of a capable guardian against crime*' (1997, page 11). Taylor (1997) documents recent research by Felson (1995) that further amplifies routine activity theory by suggesting that offenders have a variety of 'handlers' including close associates, relatives and friends who may discourage criminal acts and that settings often have 'place managers' – doormen, security guards, bus drivers – whose scope of responsibility is limited to very small places within the overall urban fabric.

ENVIRONMENTAL CRIMINOLOGY: THE 'FOURTH DIMENSION'

We turn now to environmental criminology, the final major thread in the development of modern place-based crime prevention theory. Environmental criminology incorporates defensible space and CPTED principles, although it focuses much less on design elements of crime in places and much more on the 'geographic' elements of crime, including paths and patterns. These are seen to form 'action' and 'awareness' spaces of offenders which, in turn, contain the 'search areas' in which victims and targets are identified (Brantingham and Brantingham, 1981). Like situational crime prevention, environmental criminology incorporates routine activity theory and rational choice theory. Thus alloyed, the Brantinghams suggest that environmental criminology provides a dynamic 'backcloth': a fluid context to the criminal event, that allows one to grasp both the 'landscape and timescape of crime' (Brantingham et al., 1997, page 7). Influenced by both the small-area zone and sector-based ecological research associated with the famous Chicago School of sociology (Burgess, 1916, 1925; Shaw and McKay, 1931), the Brantinghams nevertheless reject its sociological determinism by asking their most fundamental questions in terms of 'where' instead of 'who'. This is not to say that they discount the value of sociological explanations in describing criminal behaviours, but rather shift these from being the primary (or sole) perspective to one that is supportive of locational data. Patterns are built out of the linkage of geographic and temporal events, and not the social and cultural contexts in which offenders live. An example provided to differentiate the two approaches is that

> a robbery committed by a minority youth one block from his home in the ghetto and a burglary committed by a middle-class white youth one block from home in the suburbs might be treated as unrelated by the sociological imagination, but as identical (one block from home, at noon) by the geographical imagination (Brantingham and Brantingham, 1981, page 21).

The relatively recent development of Geographic Information System (GIS)-based computerised crime mapping by law enforcement agencies in the United States and Britain over the last decade is an outgrowth of historical interest in the spatial identification of crime that harkens back to nineteenth century France (Guerry, 1833) and England (Plint, 1851) and is allied to the development of modern environmental criminology theory. GIS-based crime mapping adds enormous value to the voluminous crime data normally collected by police, by facilitating its rapid transformation into spatial information depicting crime patterns and trends. Crime mapping using GIS technology also has significant utility for comprehensive planning and design issues by providing, among other things, easily understood maps for community presentation. Further, by greatly enhancing crime analysis, it is becoming an important tool in police management by permitting the rapid assessment of problem areas and the deployment of personnel. It is being used to support community oriented policing programmes in a growing number of North American cities and by police forces throughout Britain.

Using computerised crime mapping, police crime analysts can readily distinguish:

- *crime series* (recurrence of similar crimes committed by one offender);
- *crime sprees* (high frequency of criminal activity in a short period of time so that crimes appear to be almost continuous);
- *crime hotspots*[6] (borrowed from geology, this term signifies small areas or specific locations in which an unusual amount of crime activity occurs that may be committed by one or more offenders);
- *crime hot dots* ((Pease and Laycock, 1996) defined as 'an individual associated with an unusual amount of criminal activity, either as an offender or a victim' (Velasco and Boba, 2000));
- *hot products* (types of property that are the repeated target of crime); or
- *hot targets* (defined as particular types of target that are victimised but that are not confined to one geographic location). An example includes a recent Florida case in which a roving band of transvestite burglars victimised dress shops featuring 'plus sizes' across the state.

Routine activity theory and environmental criminology have foreshadowed the advent of computerised crime mapping using Geographic Information Systems (GIS) programs.

New Urbanism

While not explicitly recognised as a place-based crime prevention theory, New Urbanism (also called Neo-Traditional Town Planning, and Traditional Neighbourhood Development) adopts a fundamentally similar premise in suggesting that its physical design prescriptions can profoundly influence behaviour and in so doing, prevent crime and reduce the fear of crime. In many ways, however, the sweep of New Urbanist advocacy is broader and more ideological than place-based crime prevention. First, it is a more comprehensive planning approach with a larger urban design scope than place-based crime prevention. Second, its adherents contend (in the absence of long-term evidence) that the implementation of its design principles can not only reduce crime but can also, among other things, change social relations in cities, increase psychological satisfaction among residents and strengthen their civic commitments – 'stewardship' – as suggested by the recent redesigners of Hulme, Manchester (see Chapter 8). While Newman may have implied those results as an outcome of the implementation of defensible space, especially in connection with his concept of territoriality, the claims are not nearly as explicit or broad as those made by some New Urbanist zealots.

Spurred by revulsion to the automobile dominated, decentralised suburban society that emerged in the United States following World War II, New Urbanists took their ideological cue from Jane Jacobs' (1961) rejection of modern city planning and urban design in favour of a vision of the city composed of small villages centred around vibrant streets, teeming with pedestrians and bustling with activity. Expanding on those visions, the cardinal design principles of New Urbanism have come to focus on the creation of bounded walkable neighbourhoods, the development and use of public transit, and the encouragement of mixed land uses at the neighbourhood level. By far the most significant theme involves the diminution of the role of the automobile as the dominant design focus.

A series of principles (the 'Ahwahnee Principles') and recommendations, summarised by the 'first generation' of New Urbanist theorists and practitioners, Andres Duany, Elizabeth Plater-Zyberg, Peter Calthorpe and Henry Turley, fairly spell out the range of New Urbanist design ideas. Apart from the three overarching ones noted above, these include compacting wasteful community space taken up by large lawns; providing local, pedestrian accessible shopping areas including corner stores; creating bounded edges to communities and having clearly defined and planned internal spaces including a town centre; reducing the influence of the automobile by narrowing streets, using rear access alleys, widening sidewalks, hiding garages, shrinking parking lots and locating them behind buildings; directing night-time illumination to the sidewalk and not to the street; eliminating culs-de-sac in favour of a grid-iron, 'permeable' street network; planting trees along curbs and encouraging the growth of natural vegetation.

They also advocate diversifying housing types, businesses, and the use of sustainable practices to conserve water and energy. To maximise sidewalk activity, 'eyes on the street' and the physical connection to the street, residences are encouraged to have porches, present large front windows, and to have minimal setbacks. Together, with the promulgation of a variety of development codes to implement them, these design principles form the core of New Urbanist doctrine.

Although these ideas have had great press both in the United States and in Britain, and have attracted a growing number of fervent adherents in both nations, only a relatively small number of New Urbanist communities have actually been built. While the promotional material touting a New Urbanist newsletter (New Urban News, 2001) suggests that more than 300 such places are presently being planned or under construction in the United States, that is but a small fraction of the total number of new communities developed annually. Moreover, a recent analysis of advertised New Urbanist communities suggests that developers are often adopting their design principles piecemeal and primarily for marketing pur-

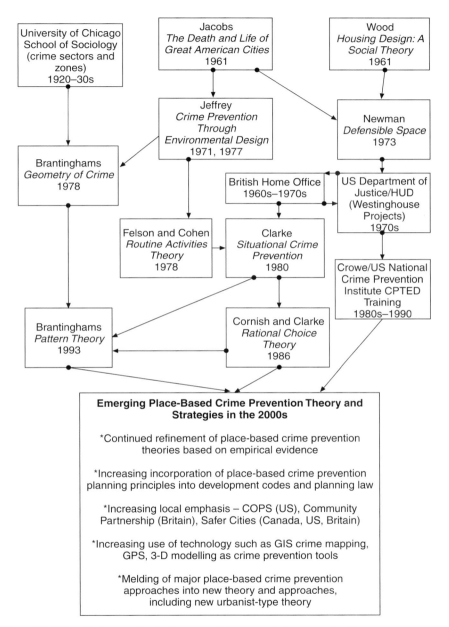

Figure 4.1 Major milestones in the development of place-based crime prevention theory

Source: adapted from Virginia Polytechnic University website, at
http://www.arch.vt.edu/crimepper/pages/home.html

woven together by practice, experience and empirical research. This is as it should be as we move, haltingly to be sure, toward a general theory of place-based crime prevention. Currently, we have a wider theoretical menu from which to choose to test real world crime interventions, which we badly need to do. Woven together, the theories have changed criminology and have had an impact on urban policy in both nations. But they have had a scattered impact on local level planning and urban design practice. One might expect that the principles derived from these theoretical bases would be more influential on planning and design professionals, project owners, builders, developers and local public officials than they have in fact been. But old thinking dies hard, and while police in the United States and Britain have increasingly adopted place-based crime prevention ideas and practice, their influence on the planning and design community has been much less profound.

Part of the reason for this is undoubtedly due to gaps in professional education, and to the fact that this field is in its infancy in many ways; part is also due to the fact that, especially in the United States, there is nothing that has *forced* planners to learn these principles or adopt them into their practices, such as a wellspring of demand from clients or their incorporation into widespread building or development codes. Further, a good deal of the problem lies in the dearth of empirical evidence and reasonably documented case studies that can be used to support relatively general statements about relationships between crime and environmental factors. Thus, a daytime burglary in a specific neighbourhood can be explained within the context of the theories presented here, but daytime *burglaries in neighbourhoods* cannot be generalised (other than to say that they are likely because owners are away at work), no matter how much we would like to do so. It remains difficult to recount empirically grounded general theory when called to do so in public meetings and in court, forums in which planners and designers sometimes find themselves.

Thus, while past empirical research focused on small-scale urban places has increasingly shed light on the connections between criminal behaviour, physical design and the management of some of these places, we are still far from the effective application of place-based crime prevention theories to the vast majority of places. The expectation (the hope) is that increased emphasis on empirical study along with carefully documented case studies will move us forward toward a general theory of placed-based crime prevention planning and, in so doing, a better understanding of the linkage between crime and place at all levels of analysis.

NOTES

1 Jeffrey writes: 'At the time I was writing *Crime Prevention Through Environmental Design*, I had no idea that Newman and his group were working on the same problem. I was also unaware of the police work in Britain until I came into contact with the Institute in Louisville.' (1977, page 45.)

2 In the United States, living in public or government subsidised housing – as a form of welfare – has long been subject to social stigmatisation, inasmuch as tenants are presumed incapable, for whatever reasons, of competing in the mainstream market economy for better housing. Thus, public housing has popularly been seen as generally inferior in quality, construction and location to that available in the private sector (although this is not necessarily true), and associated with lifestyles and behaviours eschewed by the middle-class. Aside from class differences, there is moreover no question that there is a strong racial component associated with the stigmatisation of public housing in the USA by the general population.

3 As advanced by Wilson and Kelling (1982) the 'broken windows theory' suggests, among other things, that community order, disorder and crime are connected in a 'kind of developmental sequence', such that relatively small acts of incivility progressively lead to other, potentially larger ones, including criminal behaviour. An example used is the experiment that compared the treatment of abandoned automobiles left on the streets of the Bronx, New York and Palo Alto, California, where both were plundered and destroyed following initial acts of theft and vandalism. Once the threshold of community civility had been breached, the cars became 'fair game' to other passers-by, even those who would not normally have fitted the 'profile' of vandals. In addressing police patrol assignments, Wilson and Kelling draw from this and related evidence the notion that even small levels of environmental (and behavioural) disorder matter and, if left unattended, send out cues that 'nobody cares', hence encouraging further, possibly more serious disorder and crime. Thus, according to Wilson and Kelling, uncollected trash, broken windows, graffiti, disorderly conduct, and other seemingly minor transgressions not only injure the community generally, but can have a significant cumulative effect. A recent study by Taylor (1999) suggests, however, that relative to long-term neighbourhood stability, revitalisation efforts and the *fear* of crime, neighbourhood status issues (which are historical) and low crime rates are more influential factors than physical disorder. As a result, Taylor advises against 'according grime reduction or zero tolerance a privileged status relative to other community policing efforts' (pages 10 and 11).

4 For example, Poyner (1983, page 11) notes that 'Newman's ideas about territoriality have never been validated by research, even though a number of researchers have tried.' He suggests that the concept has been replaced by accessibility and access control.

5 Although there are no national surveys that assess the spread of CPTED knowledge and use among US police forces, experts such as US Justice Department official Dr Richard Titus believe that it is now widespread, especially within larger agencies. This information is based on personal conversations with him in April 2000.

6   For an excellent discussion of the opportunities and problems associated with the desig-
     nation of crime hot spots, see Taylor's article, 'Crime and small scale places: what we
     know, what we can prevent, and what else we need to know', published as part of the
     Proceedings of the Professional Conference Series of the National Institute of Justice,
     July 1998.
7   Based on field observations and conversations with planners such as David Maltby,
     principal designer for Florida Planning and Design Inc., it is clear that owners seek
     to widen the market appeal of large-scale projects by incorporating into them a range
     of design approaches, from New Urbanist to traditional suburban cul-de-sac neighbour-
     hoods.

PART 2

POLICY AND PRACTICE

CHAPTER 5

AMERICAN POLICY AND PRACTICE

INTRODUCTION

In this chapter we move from the place-based crime prevention postulates offered up by Newman, Jeffrey, Clarke, the Brantinghams and their disciples to constructed projects that either helped generate the theories, or have come to be supportive of them after the fact, and to examples of legislation that are largely grounded in these theories and projects. We look first at the structural context of federalism, since this frames the adoption and implementation of new policies generally in the United States, with implications reaching down to local level jurisdictions, where place-based crime prevention interventions actually take place. Next we concentrate on intervention examples from North America, and primarily from the United States, as a basis for comparison with examples from Britain, which are discussed in Chapters 7 and 8. Our interest is to focus on projects that typify place-based crime prevention in the USA and Britain but that also help distinguish the approaches between the two nations. These projects and legislation suggest a range of fundamental historical, structural and policy contrasts between the USA and Britain that have led both countries to grapple with crime prevention from different perspectives, sometimes with different results. This comparison moves us toward an understanding of where we have come from in each nation relative to place-based crime prevention, as well as where we are likely to go.

Together, the four interrelated place-based crime prevention theories presented in Chapter 4 sought to revolutionise academic criminology, sociology, architecture and urban planning and, by so doing, influence crime prevention interventions in the field. While there is no question that a growing number of academics have come to acknowledge the value of defensible space, CPTED, situational crime prevention and environmental criminology principles as legitimate components of crime prevention theory, the extent to which they are actually put into practice in the everyday planning, design and construction of the built environment is open to question. In the United States new policy and programmes often are far easier to verbalise than operationalise, especially within the context of the highly fragmented federal system in which decision-making plays out.

THE PLACE OF ENVIRONMENTAL DESIGN IN RESPONSES TO CRIME

Place-based crime prevention programmes and planning in the United States remain as the province of local and state governments, even though in recent years the federal government has increased its influence in these fields through a number of grant programmes aimed primarily at housing and local law enforcement. While there are a variety of explanations for the jurisdictional 'place' of environmental crime prevention design within local government in the modern United States, much of the reasoning for its location can be traced to the operation of federalism and to funding approaches, some of which we mention here by example. Moreover, just because local governments have the power to implement many crime prevention strategies, it does not necessarily follow that they will do so, for reasons to be made clear.

It can be argued that the federal presence in place-based crime prevention has antecedents in the series of housing, slum clearance and urban redevelopment acts, beginning with the Housing Act of 1937 and continuing through the Housing Acts of 1949 and 1954 and into the 1970s, when the Housing and Community Development Act of 1974 changed the way federal aid was dispersed to local governments (Gerckens, 1979). It is also evident in HUD's (US Department of Housing and Urban Development) early interest in Oscar Newman's defensible space research in the 1970s. This interest continued, with some interruptions, through the 1990s when place-based crime prevention ideas are seen in public housing redevelopment policies and made explicit in the published viewpoints of former HUD Secretary Henry Cisneros (1995), as we detail later in this chapter.

The federal role in place-based crime prevention can also be seen, albeit sometimes indirectly, in the US Department of Justice (DOJ) administered 1988 Anti-Drug Abuse Act, which provided millions of dollars in both formula and discretionary funding[1] to localities and groups for crime prevention related activities, and in the emphasis on Community Oriented Policing strategies embodied in the Violent Crime Control and Law Enforcement Act of 1994. This latter Act included a provision directing the US Attorney General to establish the Office of Community Oriented Policing Service (COPS), which has distributed several billion dollars in grant funding to communities across the United States. It has been suggested that this emphasis on community policing marks a shift, at least at the federal policy level, from advocating crime *suppression* to crime *prevention* as the chief goal of the police (Greene, 2000). In so doing, Community Oriented Policing is seen as a contextual activity (that is, based in the local environment) which has as a main goal the enhancement of citizens' quality of life.

Police are thus directed toward 'partnership' relationships with local citizens and with other local agencies, much like the thrust of the partnerships envisioned by the British 1998 Crime and Disorder Act, as discussed in Chapters 7 and 8. This is a radical departure from previous local law enforcement styles in the United States, such as 'traditional policing' which has been characterised as reactive, crime focused, inward looking and environmentally insensitive, among other attributes (Greene, 2000). Community Oriented Policing is thus a far more accommodating vehicle for the application of the place-based crime prevention theories discussed in Chapter 4, and this is evident in the linkages between, for example, local CPTED programs and community policing made by the Department of Justice (Fleissner and Heinzelmann, 1996) and the National Crime Prevention Council (NCPC, 2000). Whether Community Oriented Policing is truly effective in reducing crime remains an open question, although there is better evidence that it has a positive impact on relations between community members and the police (Greene, 2000).

Despite these federal efforts in housing and law enforcement, and the fact that 'local crime prevention offices receive more Department of Justice funding than anytime in American history' (Sherman et al., 1997, page 1–12), the goal of a 'comprehensive, and co-ordinated national crime prevention campaign' (NCPI, 1986) remains elusive. Furthermore, the application of place-based crime prevention strategies, such as CPTED, in local communities is extremely variable. There are a number of reasons that this remains so. First, as we have noted in Chapter 1, crime prevention generally, and place-based crime prevention specifically, are relatively new developments; local level bureaucrats, especially in law enforcement, tend to be reluctant to adopt new strategies, particularly when they may dilute their own authority (Greene, 2000). Further reasons include the persistence of the American belief that local government initiatives are preferable to those from the central government, a value reaching back to Jefferson's advocacy of small-town democracy. Allied here is an enduring anti-urban bias that also stretches far back into American history. This is salient in terms of crime since, as we have seen from Chapters 1 and 2, the crimes that people tend to worry about the most and which affect their quality of life are particularly urban phenomena. Additionally, as we have noted previously, planners and urban designers have had little educational background in place-based crime prevention techniques and almost nothing to *compel* them (or their local government) to consider place-based crime prevention planning in development ordinances or policy.

Moreover, an overarching factor affecting the local adoption of crime prevention programmes and planning is the structure of the American federal system itself, which splits power between the central government and the states, and in which cities, regions and special authorities and districts further splinter power, policy-making authority and available funding. The result is an unresolved, dynamic tension relative to policy development, programme application and the governing process itself. In such a system, power is jealously shared among overlapping and competitive governments, creating tension and ambiguity. And in such a system it is possible to have the circumstance where, as in crime prevention funding, it is entirely up to local decision-makers whether or not to apply for, and subsequently adopt, specific crime prevention programmes.

Given the thousands of state and local jurisdictions in the USA – the National League of Cities represents 18,000 municipalities (National League of Cities, 2000) – the potential for variability in the types of programme(s) adopted, as well as the rate of adoption, is extraordinary. This is particularly true relative to building control functions. As the Douglas Commission (1968) pointed out:

> Building code jurisdictions are thousands of little kingdoms, each having its own way: What goes in one town won't go in another and for no good reason (ibid., page XI).

This same variability provides a natural laboratory for innovation: cities and states become 'petri dishes' for experimentation. In this context, jurisdictions have different predilections for innovation: some learn from each other and copy programmes almost verbatim – a 'contagion' effect – whereas others also learn but tailor their programmes depending on local circumstances, politics and environmental issues, and may take years to adopt a programme or policy – a 'stepwise' adoption process (Campbell, 1996). The adoption and diffusion of convenience store crime prevention legislation, presented at the conclusion of this chapter, is a case illustrating both these points.

Finally, while federalism underscores the fracturing of power and policy-making between state and federal governments, it is private economic interests that often shift the balance of power decisively one way or the other, especially where issues devolve to the local level. This is extremely important for crime prevention planning, particularly where it deals with physical interventions to private property in the United States. Why? Because private development is by far the largest financial supporter of local government through local property taxes. We suspect that this tends to heighten conservatism towards policy and development regulatory changes at the local level, such as those suggested by some place-based crime prevention planning strategies. The tendency may be further exacerbated by the sensitivity of builders and developers to the marketability of their products and to their reluctance to experiment with 'risky' innovations. Moreover, local building and development regulatory officials are notoriously conservative relative to changes in codes, and in planning and building regulations (Schneider, 1981), much like local law enforcement administrators, a fact that mediates the spread of innovative ideas. Thus, while local governments are often the ultimate repositories of the power to adopt and implement design and regulatory strategies such as those contemplated by place-based crime prevention theory, they may be unwilling to do so. In the face of these forces, even profound ideas for making communities safer have an uphill battle.

INFLUENCES OF THE ERA

No matter how ostensibly revolutionary, profound ideas nevertheless tend to be products of their times. This is especially true of defensible space and CPTED. The decade in which they emerged in the United States, 1964–1974, encompassed arguably the greatest political and social turmoil ever experienced by the nation, including the civil rights revolution, urban riots and the perceived (and actual) financial failure of large city governments, the Vietnam War, the ascendancy of women's rights, the sexual revolution, the growth of participatory politics, the assassination and resignations of leaders and a fundamental shift in the funding of state and local government though the Nixonian revenue-sharing doctrine. It was an era when paradigms shifted (Kuhn, 1962) as fundamental values were challenged and gave way.

Old elitist 'establishment' ideas in planning, architecture and the social sciences came under attack as it was clear that new answers were needed to address burgeoning social problems, especially those within the nation's largest metropolitan areas, symbolised by the subject matter of the urban graffiti depicted in Figure 5.1.

Crime and social disorder – 'law and order' issues – fuelled political debate across the nation, even as great cities – Los Angeles, Detroit, Washington – ignited in the flames of urban riots. Other cities, such as Chicago, St Louis, Newark and New York, struggled to deal with the problems of social disorganisation in their massive public housing projects, seen by many as emblematic of the breakdown of American civilisation itself.

PUBLIC HOUSING: THE PROJECT SEEDBEDS OF DEFENSIBLE SPACE

While the concepts of defensible space and CPTED sprang from this turbulent era, the predicates of defensible space had been laid down three decades earlier as the nation came to grips with the need to house lower income citizens and to revitalise its largest cities through 'urban renewal'. Tied from the outset to slum

Figure 5.1 'Graffiti and Telephone'
Source: Courtesy of Urban75/Mike Slocumbe

clearance objectives, New York City was the first jurisdiction in the nation to create public housing in 1934. The federal government joined in modestly with the Housing Act of 1937, and then again in 1949 with a much more ambitious attempt that produced a multi-year plan to construct more than 800,000 units across the country. Though a fraction of the British response to the problem, and late in coming when compared to other western industrialised nations, it was a start nevertheless. For a variety of legal and political reasons, most of these units were built in America's inner cities. This is in sharp contrast to the selection of public (council) housing sites in Britain in the same period which, because of the sheer scale of the slum clearance programme embarked upon in the major cities from around the mid 1950s to the mid 1970s, not only re-used the land freed by demolition but also over-spilled to more peripheral locations, including expanded or new settlements away from the conurbations.

Conceived in response to the airless, congested and inherently unhealthy 'dumbbell' urban tenements of the late nineteenth and early twentieth centuries, depicted so graphically by photographer Jacob Riis (1890), that housed generations of immigrants, American public housing development has been classified by Franck and Mostollor (1995) into three general design stages: the courtyard plan stage (1930s–1940s), the high-rise stage (1950s–1970s) and what might be termed the 'neighbourhood connection' stage (1980s–present). A recent development – perhaps too early to be described as a discrete stage – is the incorporation by the US Department of Housing and Urban Development of New Urbanist tenets into several programmes. This trend suggests, as one would expect, that each stage has been markedly influenced by the design doctrines of their times.

In the first stage – the courtyard plan – public housing projects were designed as low-rise, semi-enclosed courtyards, such as those in Newark's 1940 Pennington Court. This design approach was influenced by Garden City advocates in Britain and the United States such as Ebenezer Howard, Raymond Unwin and Clarence Stein, and produced village-like developments on large parcels of urban land which, while different from their surrounding neighbourhoods, were generally compatible with the urban fabric, including connections with the existing street grid. There were, however, few, if any internal streets within these projects. It was theorised that the stark design differences between the new projects and the existing neighbourhoods would 'protect the projects from blight' (Franck and Mostollor, 1995, page 211).

Although the structural outcomes were vastly different, the same fervour of design determinism permeated the second public housing design stage, which saw construction of high-rise behemoths such as Pruitt-Igoe in St Louis, Van Dyke Homes in New York, Rosen Homes in Philadelphia and the thirteen-storey Christopher Columbus Homes built in Newark in 1955. Generally tilted off the street grid of surrounding neighbourhoods, these designs freed up as much land as possible, reducing lot 'coverage', and creating super-blocks of vast self-contained communities, complete with their own identity and project names. Like their predecessors in stage one, it was held as an article of faith by architects, planners and the popular press that the architectural and site distinctiveness of these new high-rises would help them 'break with adjacent "slums"', thereby insulating their occupants from the social and physical disorder of the surrounding blight (Franck and Mostollor, 1995).

Corbusian towers thus poked skyward throughout the middle part of the twentieth century, stacking the poor (after World War II, mostly African-American poor from the South) in ever greater numbers to the sky. Guided by theories of idealised urbanism and implemented through an unholy alliance of design arrogance, political expediency and on-the-cheap construction, these projects established the context for the third stage of public housing planning and design – the neighbourhood connection stage – which sought, among other goals, to reduce the size and impersonality of public housing structures and diminish their isolation from the urban context from which they had been torn.

This third stage, which reaches into the current era, grew largely out of revulsion to the crime and social disorder that came to be inextricably associated with American high-rise public housing. There is no American project which is more directly associated with the demise of high-rise housing for the poor, or the ascendancy of defensible space and CPTED theory, than St Louis' Pruitt Igoe. In Britain it is rivalled by the disaster of Manchester's Hulme 'Crescents' project, which is described in Chapter 8, and met a similar fate in the 1990s.

PRUITT-IGOE

'One cannot discuss crime and environmental design without mention of Pruitt-Igoe' (Jeffrey, 1977, page 193), the quintessential symbol of the failure of both 1950s-style urban renewal and the 'City of Towers' approach to housing the urban poor (Hall, 1988). Pruitt-Igoe was also the structural genesis for the concepts of defensible space. It was from this living laboratory in the early 1960s that Oscar Newman, then a professor at Washington University, enunciated the fundamental principles of defensible space. The term itself was 'born ... in the spring of 1964 when a group involved in the study of ghetto life ... in Pruitt-Igoe, began an inquiry into the possible effects of the architectural setting on the social malaise of the community and on the crime and vandalism rampant there' (Newman, 1971, page 5). Composed of thirty-three identical super-blocks each eleven stories high, the site contained 2,764 apart-ments at a density of fifty dwelling units per acre, as shown in Figure 5.2. It began as an award winning, albeit 'experimental' (for the City of St Louis) design by Minoru Yamasaki. It ended with a project that was so badly constructed that 'locks and door-knobs broke on first use, sometimes before occupancy. Window panes blew out. One lift failed on opening day' (Hall, 1988, page 237).

Beyond construction defects was the overwhelming failure of its design, a testament to what Newman termed its 'compositional commitment and orientation' wherein 'the architect was concerned with each building as a complete separate, and formal entity exclusive of any consideration of the functional use of the grounds or the relationship of a building to the ground area it might share with other buildings' (Newman, 1973, page 58). This sculptural and formalist approach segregated the structures from each other; and the entire project, built off the existing street grid, was also symbolically separated from surrounding neighbour-hoods, although at the same time left vulnerable to them, by a 'permeable' site combined with vast open, unfenced spaces between structures. While this design might have worked for middle or upper income tenants, the fact that the residents were increasingly welfare dependent, single-mother families with children created by the early 1960s an island of utter devastation and despair within St Louis. As Newman recounts:

Figure 5.2 Pruitt-Igoe

Source: US Department of Housing and Urban Development website: http://www.hud.gov/library

The common grounds, which were dissociated from all units were unsafe. They were soon covered with glass and garbage. The mailboxes on the ground floors were vandalised. The corridors, lobbies, elevators, and stairs were dangerous places to walk through and were covered with garbage and human waste. The elevators, laundry, and community rooms were vandalised, and garbage was stacked high around the non-working garbage chutes. Women had to go together in groups to take their children shopping. The project never achieved more than 60 percent occupancy and was torn down some ten years after its construction. It was a precursor of what was to happen everywhere in the country (Newman, 1995, page 150).

In sessions involving police and sociologists Lee Rainwater and Roger Walker, Newman and fellow architect Roger Montgomery began to hammer out the notions of defensible space, or 'those physical features which produced secure residential settings – even in the midst of social disintegration and terror' (Newman, 1971, page 3). To do so, he contrasted Pruitt-Igoe with Carr Square Village, an adjacent neighbourhood that housed tenants with similar socio-economic characteristics but which was designed very differently. He also relied upon the largely untested social and planning theories of Wood (1961, 1967) and Jacobs (1961), repudiating wholeheartedly the 'style metaphysicians' and the followers of the International Congress of Modern Architects (Hall, 1988). In plain language, Newman rejected the design stylists while embracing the 'social' designers. He chose to characterise housing projects as ' "defensible' only when residents choose to adopt this intended role – a choice that is facilitated by the development's design. Defensible space therefore is a 'sociophysical phenomenon' (Newman, 1976). Uncharacteristic of the architects of his day (and many would argue to the present day), Newman sought empirical and evaluative post-occupancy research to bolster design decision-making.

Thus, defensible space was rooted in its outset as a reaction to the urban utopian ideas embodied in Le Corbusier's *Ville Radieuse*, which, while well-intentioned enough, had no empirical bases, and which were especially problematic when applied to low-income families. It is ironic, however, and perhaps speaks to the dualistic nature of defensible space both as an ideology and a theory still in search of a solid empirical foundation, that with some small exceptions Pruitt-Igoe provided little opportunity for rigorous theory testing before it was destroyed in 1972, as shown in Figure 5.3. However, the project's spectacular failure – although demolished with a bang it actually died a long, lingering death – provided the jumping off point for a flurry of empirical and post-occupancy research into the relationship of design to crime prevention.

Figure 5.3 Pruitt-Igoe demolished

Source: US Department of Housing and Urban Development website: http://www.hud.gov/library

and Development (ECOD, 1990), touted in the final report of the national
Commission on Severely Distressed Public Housing (NCSDPH, 1992a),
highlighted in this Commission's compilation of case studies of 'successful
turnarounds' (NCSDPH, 1992b), and heavily funded through the Urban
Revitalization Demonstration grants implemented beginning in 1993 by the US
Department of Housing and Urban Development (Vale, 1995, page 289).

The federal government subsequently came to acknowledge the importance of
Newman's pioneering work in public housing with the publication of an essay by
Secretary of Housing and Urban Development Henry Cisneros in 1995. Cisneros
enumerated the basic principles of defensible space and pointed to Newman's
work at Clason Point Gardens, a public housing complex in New York's South
Bronx, and to Dayton's distressed Five Oaks neighbourhood as examples of
success stories, admitting however that 'it is too early to be sure that Five Oaks
has turned around for good' (Cisneros, 1995, page 20).

IMPACTS ELSEWHERE: PROJECT APPLICATIONS IN THE 1980s AND 1990s

The application of defensible space in federally funded public housing, however, is
not the same as in local-level, neighbourhood-based private residential housing, the
predominant land use in American communities, or in local commercial or industrial
settings. The damage of the Westinghouse and Justice Department studies, along
with the change in political climate, ensured that by the end of the 1980s only a
scattering of jurisdictions around the United States had experimented with a
defensible space or CPTED project application, whether as ordinance, policy or as
an intervention. To be sure, CPTED 'checklists' had found their way into local
development review processes, but these were often counterproductive, since
their 'cookie-cutter' approaches were unsuited to the endless variety of places in
most urban environments. These 'one-size fits all' solutions still haunt serious
place-based crime prevention advocates.

Without federal funding or sustained academic interest some communities
had, by the dawn of the 1990s, done little more than to establish crime prevention
units within their police agencies, perhaps incorporating CPTED or 'security
design' as a public relations 'gesture'. This is so despite the best effort of the
National Crime Prevention Institute (NCPI) CPTED training programmes. Thus,
while Cisneros' ringing endorsement of defensible space in the mid-1990s could
be seen as federal reaffirmation of Newman's work, it was also a reminder that
there were relatively few local-level project applications in communities that could

serve as examples for the nation or as grist for serious research and evaluation.[5] Some of those communities existed to be sure, such as Sarasota, Florida, Ann Arbor, Michigan, Tempe and Tucson, Arizona; they were among the few cities that had initiated innovative CPTED-based planning and development ordinances.

They and others were identified by a 1994 survey of 1,060 cities conducted by the United States Conference of Mayors with support from the US Department of Justice. The survey found that of the 323 responses, 151 cities in the United States reported that they had incorporated CPTED strategies in their development and zoning codes (United States Conference of Mayors, 1998). Unfortunately, the survey instrument was flawed (its first question was badly worded and failed to capture the desired responses) and the sample – a tiny proportion of the total number of US cities – cannot be considered representative of the universe of American cities.[6]

However, the survey results clearly pointed out that while there was a diversity of jurisdictional approaches – a familiar picture in the fragmented American federal system – many responding cities had similar problems with CPTED applications. These included difficulties coordinating internal review teams, problems balancing aesthetics and safety, and, significantly, resistance from neighbourhood groups, property owners, the development community and the general public to CPTED-related design provisions.

For instance, a respondent to the Mayor's survey from the City of Tustin, California noted: 'The builders don't understand the reasons why we don't allow certain types of lighting, locking devices, why we want open carports instead of enclosed, why we frown on screening everything from the roadways.' And University Heights, Ohio's respondent pointed out the 'failure of owners/developers to initiate these concepts into design and/or even to understand the need for them' (1998, page 163). A central problem that the responding cities identified was the difficulty of justifying the increased costs (in time as well as money) of CPTED reviews relative to the benefits (e.g. less crime). This finding is supported by a 1998 survey of a sample of police officers charged with implementing CPTED ordinances in Florida. That survey found that most of these crime prevention specialists had great difficulty explaining the value of CPTED to sceptical builders and few could provide any 'scientific' bases for its principles when challenged (Schneider, 1998). Ultimately the question comes down to being able to 'prove' that CPTED and defensible space interventions are effective in reducing crime.

PROJECT EXAMPLES

Many of the more rigorous empirical studies of defensible space, CPTED or situational crime prevention interventions have been done outside the United States, principally in Britain.[7] However, some documented project interventions in the United States and Canada have, to varying degrees, risen to that level, providing evidence to support CPTED or defensible space applications – whether in legislation, policy or planning or development practice – across national and in some cases, international boundaries. The following are synopses of some project examples which influence crime prevention applications in urban planning and design in the United States and Canada. As we have noted, strategies suggested by the four basic place-based crime prevention theories are interwoven in real world applications. They may be initiated in response to a perceived problem and thus be primarily 'reactive' in nature, or they may have been promulgated as part of a planned or 'proactive' strategy which is likely broader in nature than a purely reactive response.

Moreover, interventions also may be characterised by the relative number of strategies or tactics involved (single or multiple). The matrix in Table 5.1 depicts the possible combinations. This is not to say, of course, that these are always neat and clean classifications since interventions have a life of their own and evolve over time. Thus, a strategy that begins as a single, reactive place-based intervention may generate new approaches that are broader in scope and planned: proactive.

The Miami Shores street closure case illustrates a single tactic, reactive example based primarily upon access control (defensible space and CPTED), whereas the 'rapid-response' graffiti clean-up programmes and ordinances that

Table 5.1 Project classification

Initiation	Tactic	
	Single	Multiple
Reactive	Single reactive Miami Shores, Florida Street Closure	Multiple reactive Gainesville, Florida Convenience Store Ordinance; Sarasota, Florida North Trail Zoning Ordinance
Proactive	Single proactive Graffiti clean-up programmes and ordinances following New York City's Subway Clean Car Program	Multiple proactive Washington DC Metro; Tumbler Ridge Pub Planning; Tempe, Arizona Environmental Design Ordinance

developed in cities across the United States following the apparent success of
New York City's 1984 'Clean Car Program' can be classified as generally proactive efforts that also rely primarily on a single tactic. In this case the tactic reduces
rewards for perpetrators, and flows from situational crime prevention theory.

The Gainesville, Florida convenience store project example demonstrates a
multi-tactic, reactive application with several theoretical roots while the Sarasota,
Florida case is a much broader brush approach than Gainesville's, but is also
largely reactive in nature and draws upon a range of defensible space and CPTED-
based tactics and strategies.

The final examples – the Washington D.C. Metro Subway system design case,
the Tumbler Ridge, British Columbia pub case and the Tempe, Arizona Environmental Design Ordinance – are examples of proactive applications or interventions
which utilise multi-tactic approaches that combine several of the place-based theories. The Tempe example is similar to the New York Subway clean-up programme,
and the Gainesville and Sarasota cases, in that their place-based crime prevention
approaches are largely the results of the efforts of 'champions' who nurtured them
from conception through implementation. Sarasota and Tempe also illustrate some
of the problems inherent in evaluating the results of multi-tactic efforts.

MIAMI SHORES, FLORIDA STREET CLOSURE

The barricading of 78 streets in Miami Shores, Florida between 1988 and 1992
represents a single-tactic, reactive intervention that was intended to stem the
growth in the crime rate of this affluent community of mostly single-family detached
residences north of the City of Miami. With a grid-iron street network bordered by
two major highways and close to low-income neighbourhoods, Miami Shores had
experienced a significant increase in stranger-stranger crimes in the period immediately preceding the closures. Disgusted by the cut-through traffic that also plagued
the community, the inhabitants themselves initiated this intervention, a factor that
has been attributed to its apparent success.

Documented by Atlas and LeBlanc (1994), the project study provides
'promising' evidence (Eck, 1997) that is consistent with place-based crime prevention theory, as well as with other studies (Matthews 1992, 1993; Newman, 1996),
that closing streets (access control) does control certain types of crimes in certain
circumstances, at least over a relatively short period of time. Newman's (1981)
documentation of privately owned and largely closed streets in several St Louis
neighbourhoods anticipated the Atlas and LeBlanc study by more than a decade,
broadly suggesting that closed streets lowered crime rates while increasing perceptions of security and property values. To evaluate the results of the street closures in Miami Shores, the authors compared crime rates for robbery, burglary,
larceny, aggravated assault and auto theft before and after implementation, and

also compared changes in crime rates for these crimes with surrounding municipalities. They found that, while over time, crime rates for all the offences above (with the exception of burglary) had increased in the City of Miami, there were either no changes or, in the case of larceny, an actual decrease in Miami Shores' crime rate. Compared to Coral Gables, another relatively near community, Miami Shores' burglary and larceny rates decreased, while rates for the other crimes remained the same. Attributing these effects to the closures, the study concluded that 'although some crimes appear to be unrelated to environmental road devices, overall crime in the barricaded areas is growing at a slower rate than it is in the surrounding municipalities' (Atlas and LeBlanc, 1994). Other effects, such as the rise in the city's property values and an increase in community cohesion, have also been credited to this single tactic intervention.

The Miami Shores study has been widely cited in the popular press, within real estate and development circles, as well as by some crime prevention consultants to help defend barricading streets and gating neighbourhoods. Its statistics have been embodied in policy and ordinances within untold numbers of communities across the United States as they have sought empirical justification for these actions. As Blakely and Snyder (1999) and Kunstler (1998) among others make clear, this is an enormously controversial area in American planning and development, as it implements not only access control for crime prevention but also facilitates the 'privatisation' of formerly public domains, potentially slicing communities into disconnected pieces. From a historical point of view it is ironic that, while there are differences, street barricading mimics the design and intent of the early public housing site designers who sought to isolate their projects from the contamination – including crime – of surrounding neighbourhoods.

GRAFFITI CLEAN-UP PROGRAMMES AND ORDINANCES BASED ON NEW YORK CITY'S 'CLEAN CAR PROGRAM'

As documented by the US Conference of Mayors (2001), a growing number of cities across the United States including Houston, St Louis, Denver, Little Rock and Cincinnati have followed the lead of New York City's 'Clean Car Program' by adopting policies, implementing programmes or by enacting ordinances aimed at the rapid removal of graffiti from public (and in some cases, private) structures and conveyances. While initially reactive, as in the case of New York City's response to the defacement of its subway system, such programmes and ordinances now have become part and parcel of the daily maintenance agendas of a growing number of local public works agencies. In the process, this has helped move the concept of graffiti-cleaning from one that was once almost entirely thought of as a reactive 'police problem' to one that is now more and more conceived of as a 'maintenance' issue, although the act itself may still be a crime (Kelling, 1996).

The Clean Car Program was born out of the frustration of the former president of the New York City Transit Authority (NYCTA), David Gunn, with the horrific state of the vast subway system when he assumed control of it in 1984. As anyone who used the system at that time can attest, the state of repair of the rail infrastructure was unreliable, the stations were dirty and considered especially dangerous, and the subway cars were almost completely covered, inside and out, with graffiti. Much of this disarray was the result of New York's financial difficulties of the 1970s. Despite these woes, many concerted and unsuccessful efforts were made throughout that decade and early into the 1980s to eradicate graffiti from the subways, an effort given more weight following the publication of a controversial article by Nathan Glazer (1979). Glazer argued that the inability (or unwillingness) of public agencies to stop the graffitists – seemingly 'minor' lawbreakers – sent the message to the general public (and to more serious criminals) that the New York subways were wide open to *any* sort of criminal misbehaviour. Kelling notes that the Glazer article 'galvanized thought about graffiti's potential for disruption in urban settings' (1996, page 116). Embedded in this notion are the seeds of the 'broken windows' theory which Wilson and Kelling (1982) later elaborated in their now famous *Atlantic Monthly* article (see note 3 to Chapter 4).

The ultimate solution to the New York Subway system's graffiti problem lay in understanding the rationale of the act itself, called 'tagging', which basically means to post one's mark, whether it be a name, message or design, in a public place. Gunn removed the *incentive* to tag trains by instituting a policy of thoroughly cleaning subway cars and never allowing them to re-enter service again with any form of graffiti on them at all. Cars were quickly cleaned (within two hours) or, if that was not feasible, they were taken out of service entirely. This approach illustrates a classic situational crime prevention technique in that it destroyed the *reward* inherent in the graffitists' acts: their work would no longer be put on public view.

The Program was successful enough so that five years after being first implemented, the last tagged car in the system was removed from service and cleaned. 'Now', report Sloan-Howitt and Kelling, 'subway trains in New York City are not only graffiti-free, they are among the cleanest subway cars in the world' (1990, page 132). In a subsequent analysis of the Clean Car Program, Smith and Clarke (2000) suggest that it is an exaggeration to say that graffiti has been *completely* removed from the subway trains (something that any present subway rider in New York can attest to), rather it has been 'controlled'. Moreover, they question the linkage between the clean-up programme and purported (or hoped for) reductions in more serious crimes (the essence of the broken windows argument), since they note that New York City Transit Police data for the period following the clean-up show no decreases in crime.

Despite that, few have questioned the efficacy of this strategy in significantly reducing New York's Subway graffiti problem, and this has contributed to its dif-fusion across the nation to other cities. While basically a single tactic strategy, it was supported by a number of related programmes and policies, including improved lighting at maintenance yards, more aggressive policing directed against order maintenance disturbances in the subways (as part of Community Oriented Policing) and better subway cleaning techniques and materials. Moreover, there is no dispute that its success was greatly assisted by new resources pumped into the NYCTA, by a growing political will to act (spurred by the Glazer article and subsequent public debate) and, perhaps most importantly, by the efforts of a champion who was willing to ferret out the causes of the problem and make its resolution a high priority. Some of these elements were certainly learned by other American cities, who were influenced by reports of New York's success in the popular press and in the academic and professional literature. A recent *US Mayor* article on Houston's new 'Operation Renaissance Cleanup Program' notes that:

> Graffiti also contributes to the blight of the neighborhood, so Operation
> Renaissance includes a component focusing on graffiti abatement. Mayor
> Brown presented the keys to a new van dubbed the 'Graffiti Mobile,' ... the van
> [will be used] by the community to identify and cover up graffiti in their
> neighborhoods ... Studies have shown that quick and continual abatement of
> graffiti is effective in preventing future graffiti (DeLong, 2000).

We are not aware of any present empirical studies comparing the results of rapid, concerted graffiti clean-up programmes across the United States or elsewhere. While anecdotal reports suggest that it is indeed effective, it would be interesting to know (among other things) if 'tagging' activity is displaced to other targets and if so, how.

GAINESVILLE, FLORIDA CONVENIENCE STORE ORDINANCE

This case represents a combination of CPTED and management (situational crime prevention) strategies – a multi-tactic approach applied as a reaction to a wave of violent crimes affecting convenience stores in a small college town in north-central Florida. While it stands alone by virtue of its impact on subsequent state-level leg-islation, the case is also part of a long stream of evaluations, beginning in 1975 (Crow and Bull) of the effects of crime prevention interventions on robberies in convenience stores.

Convenience stores have been important enough venues of robberies that they have merited their own subclassification within the FBI's Uniform Crime Report's Part I Crime Index.[8] They are generally small grocery and sundry stores strategically placed within a community, typically in highway strip malls (in the USA) or within easy neighbourhood walking distance (in the UK). They have a much more limited selection of goods and staff than larger grocery stores (such as 'Sainsbury's' in the UK or 'Safeway' in the USA and the UK), but their operating hours are generally longer (often extending into the early hours of the morning) and they cater to clients who typically need only a few items at a time and are interested in transaction speed as distinct from comparison shopping. Shoppers generally pay a premium for these conveniences. Examples of such stores are 'SPAR' in Britain and '7–11' in the United States. The incidence of crimes affecting these establishments has ebbed and flowed through the years, with peaks reported during the early 1980s, shortly before the City of Gainesville, Florida enacted what came to be known as the 'two-clerk' law. The city's police chief championed the ordinance after a particularly brutal 1985 murder that occurred during the course of a convenience store robbery. Police-sponsored research subsequently found that while convenience stores constituted only 5 per cent of all retail businesses, they accounted for 50 per cent of all retail store robberies in Gainesville, and that 96 per cent of all convenience stores in the city had been robbed, compared to 36 per cent of fast food stores, 22 per cent of hotels, 21 per cent of service stations and 16 per cent of liquor stores and lounges (Clifton, 1993). Most robberies had been committed in stores that had only one clerk on duty at the time of the robbery.

The law was modelled on versions that had been adopted in Kent, Ohio and Coral Springs, Florida and provided for CPTED-related elements relating to *surveillance* (e.g. prohibiting signs from covering windows, placing the clerk so as to be visible from the street, providing parking lot illumination standards, security camera requirements), *cash management elements* (limiting the amount of cash available to clerks, requiring a drop safe, signage) and *managerial elements* (required robbery prevention courses for clerks). Far and away, the most controversial element was the requirement that stores operating between the hours of 8 p.m. and 4 a.m. (when most robberies were found to have taken place) have two clerks on duty at that time. While the CPTED provisions were generally accepted by the large corporations that owned many of the city's convenience stores, they strongly challenged the two-clerk provision, a situational crime prevention element. The corporations contested the police research with their own studies (Scott *et al.*, 1984), and ultimately fought the city in federal district court, where they lost decisively in 1987. In the first seven years following its enactment in Gainesville, convenience store robberies declined an average of almost 80 per cent over the previous six-year time period (Clifton, 1993). While there are rival explanations for this decline (the police had locked up some of the most serious offenders) and some research that shows contrary findings, the local crime statistics are still compelling.

The irony is that the city's apparent success was its undoing. Gainesville was not the only city in Florida to be plagued by convenience store robberies and the ordinance soon became a model for state law. But what the convenience store corporate lawyers could not do in federal court, their political lobbyists could accomplish in the state legislature. The state law, ultimately passed in 1990, so diluted the original city provisions that many became meaningless. It narrowed considerably the definition of convenience stores, excluding 'mom and pop' stores – often the most vulnerable to robberies – and required stores to implement the two-clerk rule (or provide a bullet-proof glass enclosure for after-hours shifts) only after a serious crime such as a murder, robbery, sexual battery, or aggravated assault had been committed there. Since state law pre-empts local ordinances in the United States, the Gainesville legislation was voided and was ultimately repealed in 1998. Recent research has shown that convenience store robberies in Gainesville have once again crept upward, so that 113 were recorded for 71 stores between 1995 and 1998, a figure that approaches the 124 robberies mark for the three-year period preceding the original ordinance's enactment (Leistner, 1999).

Despite these local-level drawbacks – unintentional consequences of success – the Gainesville convenience store ordinance has become a model for other states (Virginia, Oklahoma, California, and Texas), for the federal government (the Occupational Safety and Health Administration's voluntary guidelines to protect convenience store employees) and for other nations. We will know whether the specific crime prevention design and management strategies embodied in the ordinance are effective across cultural boundaries depending upon the results of future evaluative, empirical research.

SARASOTA, FLORIDA'S NORTH TRAIL ZONING DISTRICT

The creation of Sarasota, Florida's North Trail Zoning District was a reactive, multi-tactic intervention that is far broader in scope than Gainesville's Convenience Store Ordinance but narrower than Tempe's broad brush Environmental Design Ordinance (below). Like most crime prevention approaches, this legislation was a reaction to a local circumstance, although in the case of Sarasota the problem was more diffuse than that which caused Gainesville's or Miami Shores' reactions.

A tourist-oriented community of about 55,000 people, Sarasota was in the late 1980s facing a problem that troubles many cities in the United States, the deterioration of a once prospering neighbourhood. In Sarasota, this was the North Trail District, an area surrounding the city's main entrance corridor, US 41, also called the Tamiami Trail. The Tamiami Trail links Sarasota and Miami, and during the 1940s and 1950s, was a booming commercial and tourist strip. By the advent of the 1990s it was a deteriorated relic of a past era. Many of the small businesses that flourished there, especially older tourist hotels that could not compete with

more modern ones, closed down and were not replaced.[9] Compounding the
problem were the widening of the Tamiami trail, which sliced off front yards, and
the adoption of new, more restrictive land development regulations that altered
density requirements and changed setbacks, parking, landscaping and storm water
retention rules (Carter, 1997). An unintentional consequence of the new regulations was a further degradation of the area through the creation of a district where
many of the pre-existing structures, sites and land uses did not conform to the new
regulations, hence generating 'non-conforming' uses, buildings and lots. As the
area decayed further over time, it attracted prostitution, drug dealing and related
crimes. Carter notes that 'by 1990 many considered it the worst area in town'
(1997, page 1).

Public reaction from area residents finally prompted the city to act and a
'CPTED Task' team was created, initially consisting of police, planners and building
officials under the direction of the city manager. While the team's broader goal was
to use CPTED tactics throughout the entire city, it chose the North Trail corridor as
a prototype. The team subsequently coordinated input from the local university
(student architectural projects), city planners (a new zoning district to deal with
constraints to viable redevelopment), the public (consensus building), city police
(new law enforcement strategies) and local designers (plan visualisations and
public education) in the development of the North Trail District's new land development regulations.

These regulations incorporate CPTED principles within substantive areas and
review processes. For example, the new regulations sanction natural surveillance –
'eyes on the street' – by encouraging open air facilities, by promoting safe pedestrian access to streets and stores from parking lots, by requiring windows on all
street frontages, by providing shade trees and enhanced landscaping and by providing illumination standards for businesses. Setback requirements are adjusted to
facilitate increased use of front yards and the structural height requirements are
changed to encourage increased residential redevelopment within the entire district, but especially along the Tamiami Trail corridor. Sherry Carter, an original
member of the CPTED task team, notes that other CPTED principles, such as
natural access control, territorial reinforcement and maintenance, were also
embodied in the new development regulations for the North Trail District (1997).

Like Tempe, Arizona (below) Sarasota's review of construction plans is performed by a multi-agency team consisting of law enforcement, planning and building officials. And like Tempe, this is a mandatory review process (albeit only for the
North Trail District zone). However, while the review is required, plan changes
made by the city officials are recommendations – suggestions – which may or may
not be implemented by the designers or owners. Unlike Tempe, the CPTED review
team does not have the power to stop construction, although in both cities the

parties tend to negotiate design and construction outcomes rather than rely on hard and fast rules.

Carter (1997) reports evaluative results of the Sarasota North Trail District CPTED intervention through a comparison of North Trail Sector,[10] North Trail Corridor and city-wide police calls for service data and FBI Part I crime data for 1990 and 1996. The data show that while calls for service to the police grew for both the North Trail Sector and the Corridor in 1996 compared to 1990, they increased at a much lower rate (5.93 per cent and 0.11 per cent) than did calls for service city-wide, which grew at a 13.26 per cent rate for the same years. Further, Part I crime rates for the North Trail Sector and the Corridor are reported to have declined at a much higher rate (dropping 40.72 per cent and 29.56 per cent respectively) than did city-wide rates for these types of crime, which fell by 8.69 per cent. She also reports a growing regeneration of the area through increased building permits, new development, and growth in property values (Carter, pages 10–11), and the diffusion of CPTED applications into other city programmes and areas, particularly Sarasota's downtown.

Like the Tumbler Ridge and the Tempe examples presented below, the Sarasota project evaluation is weak on a number of methodological grounds. For example, the comparison of changes in calls for service and crime rates for the North Trail Sector and the Corridor with the city's rates overall is statistically questionable, inasmuch as the 'comparison groups are ... too unlike the target group given the program' (Sherman et al., 1997, pages 2–16). Moreover, we are not entirely sure whether the programme simply attracted people who were less prone to commit crimes and, if that were the case, can we say that the programme's design and code strategies actually were the cause of the reduced crime? Probably not. In that context, there are no real alternative explanations for the declining rates offered and, in the end, we are not entirely sure of the cause and effect relationship between the programme and reduced crime, no matter how much we want to believe it to be the cause. Nevertheless, like the other examples, it presents a well-documented community-level project in which to assess further the credibility of the place-based crime prevention theories presented here.

THE WASHINGTON, D.C. METRO SUBWAY DESIGN

Although criticised for not having a strong research design, this case by Nancy La Vigne (1997) nevertheless provides the 'best available evidence' (Eck, 1997, pages 7–24) that the *design* of subway systems has an influence on crime. While the system designers were not driven by CPTED or other crime prevention theories, La Vigne notes that the concepts were nevertheless incorporated into the system's architecture, policing and management from the outset in the 1970s. Her study carefully documented the design of the systems' *platforms* (open and

Figure 5.4 Washington, D.C. Metro system

uncrowded by structural elements facilitating good sight lines) (see Figure 5.4), *entrances, exits and pathways* (shortened passageways to reduce loitering, winding and curved pathways avoided), *lighting and maintenance* (uniform minimum lighting standards, reflective durable and easily maintainable wall surfaces, rapid graffiti and damage repair policies generally similar to those used in the New York Subway System, as described above), *security devices* (widespread use of CCTV and station guardians), *signage* (criticised as being weak), *money handling policies* (limited commercial activities and use of farecards and automated systems that reduce fare evasion) and *transit police and personnel* (quality of life violations enforced, vigilant attendants).

LaVigne notes that the Metro system's construction and design operationalised many CPTED and situational crime prevention prescriptions and she compared its crime rates with those of generally similar systems in Boston (MBTA), Atlanta (MARTA), and Chicago (CTA) that did not incorporate similar defensible space or CPTED applications. Her findings were that the Metro's mean crime rate was significantly lower than the other three systems. She also compared the Metro's robbery, aggravated assault, and total Part I crime rates to crime rates at aboveground locations throughout the Washington, D.C. area, reasoning that 'if Metro's environment is structured in such a way to reduce criminal opportunities, one would expect to find little variation from station to station, compared to that occurring above ground' (La Vigne, 1997, page 293). Though her findings were mixed (robbery and Part 1 crimes were significantly lower in Metro stations but assault rates were not significantly different), they were also generally supportive of the hypothesis that Metro's environment thwarted crime opportunities and incentives.

LaVigne's carefully crafted study provides scientific support for the inclusion of CPTED and situational crime prevention measures in subway design across the United States. Clarke (1997) notes that the lesson learned by Metro's experiences also have been instructive to designers of other new systems throughout the world.

THE TUMBLER RIDGE, BRITISH COLUMBIA PUB

An example of proactive, multi-tactic crime prevention design is the case of the Tumbler Ridge pub reported by Brantingham, *et al.* (1997). A new town, Tumbler Ridge, was laid out by planners with a special concern for crime prevention. Of particular interest to planners was the location, site layout, parking and access design of the pub since 'heavy drinking and associated assaults and accidents are major problems in resource towns in northern British Columbia' (ibid., page 6). As a result, the pub was situated in the town plan so that walking to and from it was facilitated, while the connecting street pattern and overall road network were designed to reduce drunk driving incidents as well as increase the ability of police to keep an eye on drivers who were entering or leaving. The pub's entryway and parking lot were separated from the entry area of an adjacent hotel in order to min- imise potentials for assault and vandalism. These proactive design considerations were part of a much larger town plan in which 'housing types, parks, pathways were specially considered' (ibid., 1997, page 6). Such large-scale conceptual design, which builds in crime prevention applications from smaller pieces to a grand scale, is similar to that undertaken in some new towns, such as Celebration, Florida, the multi-million dollar Disney-sponsored development in central Florida.

While follow-up research in Tumbler Ridge is necessary in order more directly to connect crime rates to design intervention and to eliminate (or at least explain) rival hypotheses, the Brantinghams report:

> since its inception the town has maintained one of the lowest crime rates amongst all British Columbia policing jurisdictions. In 1995, its criminal code offence rate of 76 crimes per 1000 population was about half the provincial average across all 192 policing jurisdictions and only about a third of similar nearby resource towns such as Dawson Creek, Fort St. John or Mackenzie (ibid., 1997, page 6).

TEMPE, ARIZONA'S ENVIRONMENTAL DESIGN ORDINANCE

The City of Tempe, Arizona's environmental design code, incorporating defensible space, CPTED, and situational crime prevention principles, is among the most sweeping laws of its type in the United States. It is an example of a multi-tactic, proactive strategy that, like the case of Sarasota, Florida above, requires the sustained cooperation of planners and police in the review of the development of the city's built environment. Because of their breadth and the presence of numerous intervening variables, the impacts of Tempe's environmental design provisions, also like Sarasota's, are difficult to assess empirically. However, they serve as a model by virtue of that comprehensiveness and because of their implementation strategies.

First broached publicly in 1989 by a police officer who had become a CPTED 'convert' and champion,[11] the Tempe CPTED code provisions were negotiated among city agencies and with the local development community over a 6-year period, and ultimately implemented in 1996. Their genesis was therefore not a reaction to a specific crime wave or a horrific act. Following complaints from the city council that elements of the first draft of the ordinance were too restrictive and that they sacrificed some public amenities and aesthetics, such as landscaping, for security (a problem also voiced by other cities responding to the 1994 US Conference of Mayors CPTED survey cited previously), the sections were redrawn to be more flexible, and subsequently enacted at the end of 1997 within the city's larger design review process.

The CPTED provisions amended Tempe's Chapter 11, Design Review Ordinance, adding four general 'Environmental Design articles' (Tempe Police Department, 1997). These are intended to synchronise with part of the city's zoning ordinance that regulates land uses identified as particularly crime-prone, such as bars, adult-oriented businesses, pool halls, hotels, motels and convenience stores, among others. For these, the police department is empowered to review and approve special security plans. But the ordinance extends far beyond these areas of focused concern to include *all* new construction in the city, additions, alterations and use enlargements (exceeding 50 per cent of value), and existing multi-family dwelling units converted to private unit ownership. Most single and two family dwelling units are excluded from the ordinance (Tempe Police Department, 1997).

Within this broad spectrum, ordinance sections regulate interior spaces, lighting, landscaping, wall and access control gates, identification signs and addresses, directories, vision panels and parking structures. The rationales driving these regulations are defensible space, CPTED and situational crime prevention principles, all of which are recited in the ordinance under the familiar rubrics of territoriality, surveillance, access control, activity support, and maintenance, basically unchanged from Newman, Jeffrey and Clarke's original formulations.[12]

In its enforcement, the Tempe ordinance incorporates a strong multidisciplinary, multi-agency approach, although it is a fundamentally police-based function. Thus, the city has established a CPTED section comprised of police officers within its development services department who work directly with city planners, fire officials, park department, transportation and other agency representatives to review site and development plans. In many ways, this approach is similar to the Architectural Liaison Officers (ALOs) model used in Britain (see Chapter 7), although the British officers generally remain housed with their own police agencies. To the best of our knowledge, the Tempe example is unique in the United States in one crucial aspect: CPTED section officers can stop, or 'red tag', construction that does not conform to the ordinance. This is a formidable power, usually reserved for building inspectors and fire marshals in US jurisdictions.

As previously noted, empirical evaluations of the ordinance's impacts are difficult, if not impossible.[13] Lacking clear evidence of effectiveness, some prominent members of the development community have strongly opposed the new ordinance, with one former mayor–developer going so far to say that 'it's a cumbersome process. It's almost impossible to get final (building) approval here' (Kuykendall, 1999, page 40). Other problems relate to internal administration since development review staff turnover means that new personnel, most of whom have no prior knowledge of CPTED, have continually to be trained. The police, who admittedly have a large stake in its outcome, rate the ordinance as a success. However, as Henry Cisneros noted relative to Newman's Five Oaks Neighborhood in Dayton, it may be much too early to tell.

Certainly, one of the strongest arguments to the private development community that CPTED or other place-based crime prevention applications actually 'work' is that it is in their financial interests to implement them. Unfortunately, to the best of our knowledge, there are no empirical studies that detail cost savings or advantages of either specific or general interventions to owners. What we do have, however, is indirect evidence based on the costs of *not* utilising place-based crime prevention approaches. This comes from the rapidly growing field of premises liability law, where property owners – from individuals to large corporations – are being successfully sued in American civil courts for failing to have exercised reasonable care in property design, maintenance and use. In noting that CPTED now equips property owners and managers with proactive crime prevention tools, Gordon and Brill (1996) point to the trend in American courts, beginning in the 1970s, to expand concepts of 'special relationships' between business inviters (typically business owners/managers) and invitees (typically customers), and widen the scope of 'foresee ability' to include the 'totality of circumstances' in determining whether or not a crime was indeed foreseeable. This now broadened view includes a variety of elements, such as 'the nature of the business, its surrounding locale, the lack of customary security precautions as an invitation to crime' (ibid., page 4), as well as whether previous similar incidents have occurred on the property. The authors note that courts in the United States are increasingly amenable to allowing juries to 'hear theories about the relationship between how properties are managed and designed and criminal behaviour' (ibid., page 10). A study of trends in 186 security-related lawsuits conducted by Sherman and Klein (1984) between 1958 and 1982 clearly demonstrated that the number and the size of the awards in such cases rose dramatically during that time. Kennedy (1993) has documented the growing legal and financial importance of security design to architects, engineers, and property owners, although he notes that 'criminogenic aspects of the physical environment have not been routinely selected for analysis by design teams' (page 110). There is, therefore, a body of indirect evidence that place-based crime prevention is cost effective to the far-seeing owner and property manager insofar as the implementation of appropriate strategies will help them defend against costly lawsuits. In the absence of federal or state mandates, this may, in the long term, be the most effective way to insinuate place-based crime prevention strategies into the design and development of many types of private land uses.

CONCLUSIONS

It is clear that the implementation of place-based crime prevention theories – defensible space, CPTED, situational crime prevention, and environmental criminology – in the United States has been uneven over the past four decades. This is due to many interrelated factors that include the relative newness of the ideas, the discovery (and for some the rediscovery) of the importance of city street life in America, the social, political and economic upheaval of the 1960s and the search for responses to crime set loose by 'law and order' demands, the disenchantment of some academics and professionals with old ideas and solutions based on offender-based models in criminology and the rejection of purely 'sculptural' approaches to architecture. Further, the evolving sophistication of housing and human-environment research and the erratic interest in place-based crime prevention planning at the federal government level, have also played major roles in the evolution of place-based crime prevention theory and applications in the USA. Perhaps the latter point has been the most important, yet most understated, of these factors inasmuch as public policy in America's fragmented federal system plays out much differently than it does in Britain's more centralised system.

The structure of the American federal system splinters jurisdictions and policymaking among many, sometimes competing levels of governance. In this polyglot system, place-based crime prevention theory and applications have become largely the province of public housing and law enforcement organisations to the relative exclusion of most other local agencies. Indeed, while CPTED may be widely used by police in the USA (although we suspect this applies primarily to larger agencies), we do not believe the same to be true of local planning, development and building code enforcement agencies, or their city and county commissions, who have the power to make design and construction details binding. The alliances that we have illustrated in this chapter between the police, planners and designers in the Tempe and Sarasota cases are, we believe, rare phenomena in the United States.

This is so even though in recent years some engineers, planners, architects, real estate developers, office managers and professors have 'discovered' place-based crime prevention planning, and despite the fact that the Department of Housing and Urban Development, the Department of Justice and some state agencies (such as Florida's Office of Attorney General) have provided training assistance and funding to public housing agencies and police in these areas. By and large, in the absence of federal or state law, executive orders, federal or state court decrees, or significant demand from client groups, local government agencies, professional groups and societies (as well as individuals) tend to be attentive to central government policy (whether at the state or federal level) and innovation programmes primarily through grants and related discretionary funding inducements. Moreover, as a whole, it is arguable that American planning and zoning (which substitutes for planning in many communities) is far more sensitive to market demands than is the case in Britain, insofar as local government in the USA is supported primarily from property taxes, which are generated by private development decisions. And, although significant increases in the numbers of premises liability cases have made place-based crime prevention planning more of an issue to property owners, developers and insurance companies (Gordon and Brill, 1996), we believe it to be still relatively low on their 'radar screens'.

Thus, there is little compelling incentive to focus the attention of local agencies (other than the police or public housing officers) on many aspects of place-based crime prevention theory and applications or to galvanise professional or academic interest. The United States Department of Justice does not by dint of policy announcement have the same authority or influence over the thousands of police agencies or the local, regional or state planning and development agencies in the United States that the equivalent British Government Departments have (as exemplified by DoE Circular 5/94; see Chapter 7). Thus, when federal interest and funding in defensible space and CPTED dried up during the 1980s, local adoption, implementation and experimentation with these approaches also flagged. And academic interest, which had also been piqued, foundered as well, although it revived during the 1990s. Despite that, it is nevertheless clear that federal leadership in introducing defensible space and CPTED concepts into public housing has been important to the gradual diffusion of these concepts to this arena, and this has influenced design and construction policies and professional practice even through periods of relative inattention. Such leadership in the United States has been generally lacking, however, in other land use categories, as we shall discuss further in the next chapter, such as in private (non-distressed) residential, industrial and commercial land use development, where direct federal intervention has been historically weaker. Thus, we would hypothesise that the role of central government is pivotal in the introduction and dissemination of new design and building concepts, especially when these include funding over time, as a way to overcome the natural diluting tendencies of the federal system.

The way forward in the United States is thus through a much more fractured and truncated structural system than in Britain, and the result of this shows in the history of the differential implementation of these approaches between the two nations. We look more formally at this comparison in Chapter 9. There are, of course, other factors at play here, including different cultural and value systems (which, for example, show up in discussions about privacy concerns and CCTV), different levels of urbanisation (Britain is a more dense and more urbanised society than the United States), different types of development review and planning processes (British planning tends to provide more discretionary power to local planning authorities than is granted to American planners), and differences in the resort to legal action to redress civil wrongs (Britain is far less litigious than the United States).

However, the essence of these differences – which on the whole argue for more rather than less adoption of crime prevention planning applications in Britain than the USA – may be obviated ultimately by the potential for innovation that the federal structure leaves open. Thus, if this structure is a hindrance to the adoption of central policy, it may also be a boon to experimentation at the local level, assuming there are some inducements to do so. Whether those inducements are forthcoming is arguable, and will likely depend on the establishment of strong empirical bases for these place-based crime prevention theories and applications. But this leaves us with a 'chicken and egg' dilemma portending an evolutionary answer far different from the seemingly revolutionary spirit that heralded the beginnings of this field.

NOTES

1   Federal funding to localities is provided in a variety of ways depending upon how the resources are allocated by Congress. *Formula* funds (sometimes called block grants) are generally provided to certain classes of grantees (say cities over 100,000 population) on the condition that they satisfy specific application requirements. *Discretionary* funds may

be open to any qualified applicant but may be limited by Congress by specific eligibility criteria, such as the provision of matching funding or the passage of state or local legislation that addresses a nationally designated purpose. *Earmarked discretionary* grants are directions from Congress – whether written into the legislation itself (a 'hard' earmark) or as directed by congressional hearings and conference reports ('soft' earmarks) – as to how to spend portions of the funds allocated within the overall funding, usually for a designated specific purpose or group. An example of an earmark within the Office of Justice Program (OJP) Byrne Discretionary Grant Program is the funding ($3 million in FY1996) allocated to the National Crime Prevention Council. Finally, *competitive* grants, which are generally the smallest amount of funding available, are awarded based upon meritorious application (Sherman *et al.*, 1997, pages 1.13–1.20).

2   While giving credit to Newman's contributions, C. Ray Jeffrey, originator of the term CPTED, suggests that his later work was much too simplistic in that it moved away from design and deeper into hardware and target-hardening solutions, a 'not very imaginative approach to environment-behaviour interaction' (Jeffrey, 1977, page 224).

3   Gardiner, an advocate of comprehensive environmental security, criticises defensible space's focus on public housing projects as being limited and 'as applied to date, (it) isolates the resident of the public housing project from his surrounding neighborhood and forfeits the neighborhood streets to possible offenders' (1978, page 15).

4   This perceived inadequacy gave increased credence to the notion of place-based, situational crime prevention strategies, insofar as those are intended to extend beyond both defensible space and CPTED's foci on physical space to include design, use and management. In fairness to Newman and Jeffrey, it should be pointed out that, while both placed a high value on the role of physical environment in preventing crime, they also advocated multi-faceted strategic approaches that included social (community) and managerial (institutional) interventions as well.

5   This is in contrast with the diffusion of defensible space, CPTED and situational crime prevention applications to communities across Britain, where the more centralised structure of government and greater sustained research, police and political interest in these theories helped disseminate place-based intervention strategies.

6   Moreover, it does not account for CPTED or defensible space policy or ordinances included in county, state or special authority codes, nor does it include the independent CPTED interventions by private designers or developers.

7   See Eck, 'Preventing Crime at Places' in *Preventing Crime: What Works, What Doesn't, What's Promising*, US Department of Justice, 1997.

8   These are available at http://ww.fbi.gov/ucr/ucr.htm. Part I crimes refer to the first eight offences listed in the Federal Bureau of Investigation's Uniform Crime Reports (UCR). These are the so called 'index crimes' that identify the most serious violent and property crimes in order of their presumed seriousness. They consist of murder and non-negligent manslaughter, forcible rape, robbery, and aggravated assault, burglary, larceny-theft, motor-vehicle theft, and arson. The UCR consists of crimes reported to the police, and then reported to the Program Support Section of the FBI. Index crimes are used to compare crime rates nationally and across jurisdictions. Part II crimes consist of

arrest reports for such crimes as curfew and loitering violations, disorderly conduct, drug abuse, and a host of other, non-traffic violations. Chapter 2 discusses some of the problems of dealing with reported crime rates of several sorts. An excellent recent article dealing with the subject of crime data in the United States is 'Bridging gaps in police crime data' by Michael D. Maltz (1999).

9   In the words of a university assessment of the area in 1990, 'Today, it is a random string of small commercial and retail facilities, a decreasing number of "host" facilities such as hotels and motels, restaurants, a small number of residential options and an increasing number of vacant properties' (University of South Florida Urban Design Group 1990, page 2).

10   'Sector' is used as the geographic bounds of the data here since, presumably, police reporting areas for calls for service and crime rates rarely correspond with zoning districts.

11   Officer Dick Steely played the major role in developing and implementing the ordinance.

12   The ordinance also recites and defines the 'three-D's' – designation, definition, and design (Crowe, 1991 and 2000).

13   This is true, as Clarke has noted (1997), even in relatively small scale applications, since urban environments are extraordinarily dynamic places unlike the laboratories of physical scientists who can control intervening forces.

CHAPTER 6

CASE STUDIES IN NORTH AMERICA

INTRODUCTION

In this chapter we focus on several examples of existing applications and case studies that relate to general land use classifications found in most American planning and zoning codes and that illustrate specific CPTED, defensible space, situational crime prevention or environmental crime prevention principles. We employ cases whose focus is very narrow in scope (micro) as well as those which are broad (macro). These cases are documented in the literature or based upon our own field observations.

DIVERSITY OF THE AMERICAN EXPERIENCE

As noted previously, the US federal system encourages the splintering of public policy as it moves through various layers and levels of government throughout the nation. This is an important reason why there is little consistency in approach or application of place-based crime prevention measures from one community to the next. Some applications involve the adoption of ordinances that implement CPTED techniques, whereas others are grounded not in law but in practice as carried out by owners or designers on their own initiative. Tempe, Arizona and Sarasota, Florida have chosen broad brush applications, incorporating defensible space principles and CPTED into fundamental planning and zoning ordinances and site review procedures, whereas other communities selectively embed CPTED in narrowly focused law, such as Gainesville, Florida's convenience store ordinance. In still other places, CPTED, defensible space and situational crime prevention techniques have often been 'unconsciously' inserted – much as Newman's defensible space principles have found their way into public housing design – in a range of planning, zoning and land development ordinances and professional practice. For instance, surveillance and access control concepts derived from defensible space are woven into countless Automatic Teller Machines ('ATMs' in the US and 'cash points' in Britain) siting ordinances in jurisdictions across the nation, whereas many of these communities have no other CPTED provisions in their codes. As the 1998 US Conference of Mayors' survey attests, place-based crime prevention approaches tend to be recent additions sprinkled throughout land development and life safety codes. These codes, as Zahm (1998) argues, have not historically been developed to consider safety from crime as a fundamental objective.

The upshot is that, while CPTED applications are numerous across North American communities, they are likely to be idiosyncratic and are often unrelated to broad-scale comprehensive planning initiatives. Moreover, to reiterate a point made in Chapter 5, relatively few of them have been documented and fewer still have been carefully evaluated for their effectiveness in preventing crime.[1] Rarer still are rigorous longitudinal case studies: a comprehensive, illustrated catalogue of case examples (which is sorely needed) is at present non-existent.

TOWARDS A CATALOGUE OF CASE STUDIES

Place-based crime prevention case examples may be organised and illustrated:

- based on classical defensible space and CPTED principles (e.g. 'territorial reinforcement, surveillance, access control, activity placement and genera-tion, maintenance'),
- by using Wekerle and Whitzman's (1995) three-fold urban safety typology ('awareness of the environment, visibility by others, finding help'),
- by employing Clarke and Homel's matrix (1997; Clarke 1997) depicting sixteen situational crime prevention techniques from 'target hardening' to 'facilitating compliance' (see Chapter 4),
- by using Fisher and Nasars' (1992) trilogy of physical features that relate to victim-offender dynamics ('prospect, refuge, escape'), or
- through the Brantinghams' (1993) environmental criminology scheme ('nodes, paths, edges') that owes a debt to Kevin Lynch's approach to understanding urban environments and images (1960).

To be sure, this is not an exhaustive list of conceptual classifications. But whatever crime prevention typologies are used, they must all somehow connect with the physical environment they describe and with the crimes they seek to prevent.

For planners and probably for most citizens, that environment is most readily conceived in terms of general land use categories: residential, commercial, indus-trial, recreational and parks, educational, healthcare, and transportation uses, each with its own series of subcategories. While a comprehensive catalogue of cases based upon all land use categories and subcategories arrayed against all place-based crime prevention principles is beyond the scope of the present work, we provide four representative samples that fall within the residential, commercial, industrial and transportation land use categories. As noted in previous chapters, some of these examples demonstrate proactive strategies while some are reactive; some are single-tactic strategies while others employ many, sometimes very different, strategies and are therefore multi-tactic. Within these contexts, we also present examples of situations where no place-based crime prevention interventions are employed, as a means to discuss and demonstrate their potential application(s), especially at micro-scale levels.

RESIDENTIAL LAND USES

In the United States residential land uses constitute the largest proportion of all urban land uses. They are also the most likely venues for crime. As we have noted previously, 'distressed' neighbourhoods and public housing projects stand out among all residential areas as places where crimes are clustered, specifically homicide, sexual assault, robbery, aggravated assault, burglary and drug law violations. These are the crimes that citizens tend to fear the most, and to which they adjust their behaviours accordingly.

In comparison to Britain, American residential areas tend to be much less densely populated in terms of both people and structures. This is especially true in suburban areas, where land allotments are more generous in the United States and single-family, detached housing tends to be the norm. Although there are similar suburbs in Britain, by and large housing there tends to be attached, with common walls and adjoining entryways bordered by small, carefully tended garden areas allocated to each home. British residential CPTED approaches are often focused on micro-level access controls, such as fencing back and side yards which may lead to common back lots or shared spaces, and target hardening by securing doors, windows and other building entrances. While these approaches are common in the United States as well, the wider separation between structures and land uses fosters more macro-level approaches, epitomised by the gating of entire suburban communities accompanied by changes in community traffic circulation patterns. The result is the tendency to create broader swathes of 'privatised' space in the United States than in Britain. We shall discuss the implications of these differences in more detail in Chapter 9.

RECENT INTERVENTIONS IN NEIGHBOURHOODS AND IN
PUBLIC HOUSING

CPTED and related interventions and experiments in residential neighbourhoods can be found throughout the United States and Canada. Examples include Bridgeport, Connecticut ('Phoenix Project'), Fort Lauderdale, Florida ('Riverside Park'), Los Angeles, California ('Design Out Crime'), Toronto, Canada ('Safe Cities'),

Vancouver, Canada ('Safer City Task Force'), Phoenix ('Safe Communities Programs'), Knoxville (integrated into its Community Policing programme), Houston ('Neighborhoods to Standard') and in Dayton, Ohio ('Five Oaks'). Of these, one of the best documented cases comes from the Five Oaks neighbourhood where Oscar Newman-designed interventions (traffic pattern changes, addition of gates and fences, target hardening, capital improvements) combined with community policing were reportedly responsible for a 15 per cent decrease in crime between 1989 and 1993 and a 26 per cent decline between 1992 and 1993 (Feins *et al.*, 1997). Other widely reported CPTED applications are found in a variety of public housing projects across the nation, such as in Cincinnati (Cincinnati Metropolitan Housing Authority), Chester, Pennsylvania (Ruth Bennett Homes), Philadelphia, Pennsylvania (Richard Allen Homes), Louisville, Kentucky (Cotter Homes), Lexington, Kentucky (Bluegrass-Aspendale Housing Project), Macon, Georgia (Macon Housing Authority), Portland, Oregon (Iris Court), Los Angeles (Mar Vista Gardens), New York (Clinton Hill Block Association), and San Francisco (Robert B. Pitts Plaza) among others.

Among the best documented residential cases, including public housing and neighbourhood studies, are found in the National Institute of Justice publication, *Solving Crime in Residential Neighborhoods: Comprehensive Changes in Design, Management and Use* (Feins *et al.*, 1997) which provides extensive research and evaluations of four residential areas where place-based crime prevention measures have been instituted. These include Castle Square Apartments (Boston, Massachusetts), Lockwood Gardens (East Oakland, California), Genesis Park (Charlotte, North Carolina), and Oak Park, Illinois. This NIJ study is careful to note that these cases are 'suggestive' that place-based crime prevention tactics – tailored to specific locales and that coalesce multiple stakeholders – do indeed reduce crime, although they are not 'proof' that this is the result. In practice, it would be as difficult as untangling a spider web to evaluate the effectiveness of specific place-based crime prevention measures applied to these residential areas. Despite the fact that the crime data support the contention that place-based applications work, the physical, management and community organisational interventions in these cases are woven together in complex ways that defy individual analysis.

One study that does provide strong empirical evidence for a place-based, situational crime prevention application in residences is Eck and Wartell's research into the use of nuisance abatement programmes in San Diego (1996). In a randomised and controlled experiment, the researchers found that letters threatening landlords with property seizures for illegal drug dealing were effective in significantly reducing such activity over a six-month period. Although other nuisance abatement programmes tended to corroborate their results, this evaluation was the only place-based residential research to rate a '5' – the highest score for the most rigorous research methods – in the US Office of Justice Program's landmark report, *Preventing Crime: What Works, What Doesn't, What's Promising* (Sherman *et al.*, 1997).

A NEIGHBOURHOOD EXAMPLE: HARBORDALE, FLORIDA

A previously largely unreported case that resembles the NIJ cases noted above is that of Harbordale, a neighbourhood within St Petersburg, Florida. Like Sarasota's North Trail District example presented in Chapter 5, Harbordale is an example of a distressed neighbourhood within an otherwise prospering resort and retirement community. It provides the opportunity to discuss place-based crime prevention strategies at macro and micro-scale levels.[2]

Consisting of approximately 2,300 residents occupying 1,437 single and multiple-family dwelling units as depicted in the base map in Figure 6.1, this predominantly African-American community was in serious decline by the mid-1990s. Its structures and infrastructures were far below city-wide standards. It contained a high proportion of vacant, abandoned and dilapidated buildings, poor property and

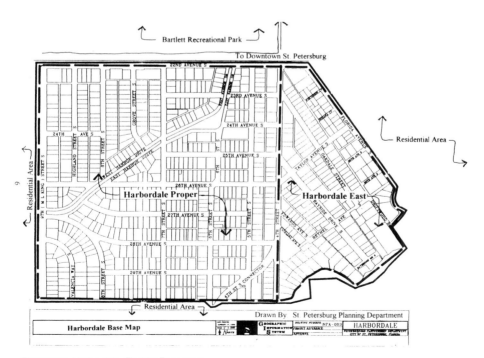

Figure 6.1 Harbordale, Florida: Base map

Source: Ajoc, 1996

landscape maintenance, missing or inadequate sidewalks, bike paths and lighting, and low property values compared to the city generally.

Approximately 38 per cent of the residents had incomes below the federal poverty rate and most lived in rental housing. Between 1992 and 1995 the neighbourhood's crime rate was significantly higher than the city's crime rate, with drug activity, assaults, robbery, burglaries and prostitution accounting for the most serious and pervasive criminal activity. In late 1996, following the fatal shooting of a black citizen by the police, rioting broke out throughout St Petersburg's minority neighbourhoods, including Harbordale. A number of buildings were burned and vehicles destroyed in Harbordale and adjacent neighbourhoods. Implementation of the neighbourhood plan – containing the CPTED-related interventions noted below – was delayed by these 'disturbances', as they euphemistically came to be known locally.

The neighbourhood is emblematic of many similar venues in the United States, not only as a crime vector but also as an example of a distressed community containing badly needed affordable housing located within the urban core. Figure 6.2 is a map of crimes, including prostitution, strong arm robberies, drug trafficking and assaults, showing their relative distribution in 1993–1994.

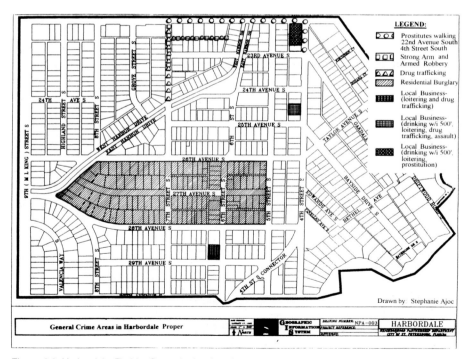

Figure 6.2 Harbordale, Florida: General crime locations

Source: Ajoc, 1996

Response to Harbordale's deteriorating situation was framed within the City of St Petersburg's 'Neighborhood Planning Program' established in 1989 as an effort to shore up the city's neighbourhoods by defining their goals and addressing expressed needs. Executed in tandem with a state programme (the 'Urban Partnership Initiative'), the programme employed city planning staff to work directly with neighbourhood groups in solving their problems. It also involved other city agencies, such as the police, that have a role in the process. Development of neighbourhood plans based on issues raised at 'brainstorming' sessions was a key aim of this effort. At sessions in 1995 Harbordale neighbours and planning staff identified seven issue areas to be included in the neighbourhood plan submitted to the City Council. These were: crime and public safety, housing and building codes, mangroves, infrastructure, parks and recreation, landscaping and neighbourhood identity, and transportation. Within these areas, specific place-based crime prevention elements included concerns over insufficient street and alley lighting, the incidence of burglaries, drug-dealing, prostitution and vandalism, the extent and condition of ill-maintained properties, the overgrown mangrove swamp area ('Salt Creek'), and vehicle speeding and cut-through traffic on neighbourhood streets (City of St Petersburg, 1999).

Of particular interest is the 'mangroves' issue. It had been identified by the neighbours as their primary concern in that it was symptomatic of their inability to resolve crime and neighbourhood appearance issues. Figure 6.3 shows the central location of the mangrove swamp area in Harbordale. Mangroves consist of dense woody plants that are found in tropical climates throughout the world. They provide habitat for many types of animals and their distinctive root system acts as a natural filter, which can improve water quality and reduce pollution. In Florida, State law protects them. Untended, their foliage can grow to heights of 20–30 feet, which is what happened in Harbordale. The wild mangroves bisected the neighbourhood, forming a complete visual barrier from one side to the other and, due to inadequate street lighting, they provided a convenient place to dump trash and stolen goods, consummate drug and prostitution deals. Many residents were fearful of this area and avoided it, especially at night. Initial attempts to secure approval to trim the mangroves had been unsuccessful; the uncontrolled growth along the spine of their community became a symbol to the neighbours of their ineffectual voice and the lack of the government's concern about the neighbour and the neighbourhood.

Accordingly, the mangrove issue became the first implementation priority under the new neighbourhood plan. Following significant effort, state agencies ultimately granted permission to trim the mangroves in 1996, and they are currently maintained to a low level on a regular basis. The residents credit the trimming with reductions in illegal dumping and criminal activity and improvements made to private properties along the creek. Moreover, the effort galvanised local planning

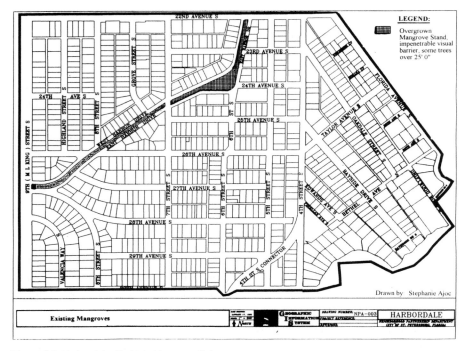

Figure 6.3 Harbordale, Florida's Mangrove Spine

Source: Ajoc, 1996

efforts and provided neighbours with the sense that they could, if organised, effect positive changes. Though delayed by the riots in late 1996, other plan implementations in the neighbourhood included the addition of infrastructure improvements (speed plateaus (speed ramps), road striping and sidewalks), housing demolitions and acquisitions, street beautification and signage (including neighbourhood entrance signs), and the planning and development of a linear walking park – a viable common space – along the Salt Creek mangrove spine of Harbordale.

Coupled with community policing and a new sense of neighbourhood efficacy, St Petersburg planners credit these improvements with increasing property values (4.55 per cent rise in 1996–1997 and a 5.5 per cent increase in 1997–1998) for the neighbourhood, and a significant decline in its crime rate. This has been reflected in a steady drop in the area's UCR (Uniform Crime Rate) index.[3] It slid from 390 in 1995 to 298 in 1996, and from 292 in 1997 to 222 in 1998. Police calls for service in Harbordale have also declined, dropping nearly 12 per cent from 1997 to 1998 alone (City of St Petersburg, 1999). Residents and the community police officer assigned to the neighbourhood point specifically to reductions in prostitution, robberies, and drug-related crimes in the triangle formed by NW 22nd Avenue, West Harbor Drive, and 7th Street south, once Harbordale's chief crime generator. Place-based crime prevention changes are given much of the credit for this decline. As with the NIJ neighbourhood studies noted above, it is impossible to say what changes actually deserve what credit since physical, management and community organisation changes were implemented together in Harbordale. Moreover, other intervening variables, including the expansion of the American economy and age cohort factors related to the reduction in crime generally, probably also account for the positive changes seen here. However, there is no doubt that residents *perceive* crime to be lower and the quality of life to be improved by virtue of the City's place-based crime prevention interventions in Harbordale.

RELATED PROBLEMS AND APPLICATIONS

Harbordale's concerns with surveillance and lighting (the mangroves and alleys), cut-through and drug related traffic on local streets, and neighbourhood appearance and upkeep as problems related to crime generation and facilitation, are not unique. They are problems that are often unexpressed and consequently not addressed in many American – especially minority – residential areas. A recent examination of several such neighbourhoods revealed the following examples.

As the experience with Harbordale's mangroves demonstrates, landscape maintenance is a relatively inexpensive yet effective means to improve sight-lines, facilitate 'eyes on the street' surveillance and improve neighbourhood morale. However, it is often overlooked, as the photographs in Figure 6.4 illustrate. Both were taken at the same public housing complex in north central Florida. They show residences located in distressed neighbourhoods in high crime areas. Untended growth inhibits surveillance from the structures to the street and vice versa and contributes to the general impression to residents and visitors that nobody is concerned with upkeep. Unlike Harbordale's mangroves, no state permits are needed to cut this foliage.

Surveillance also can be impeded by man-made structures, built with the best of intentions. The results of such constructions are often counter-intuitive, as was the case with the screening walls shown in Figure 6.5, also in a high crime neighbourhood. Here, and throughout this complex, both garbage and side entrances are completely obscured from view. The intent was to provide residents some additional privacy and to shield sight-lines to trash receptacles from the street and apartments. In fact, residents claim that these barriers have created 'entrapment' zones, where drug deals take place and violent crimes occur. The landlord has not responded to the neighbours' complaints.

Street design and traffic circulation patterns are particularly important for neighbourhoods with crime problems related to cut through traffic and vehicular

Figure 6.4 Maintenance disasters

Figure 6.5 Counter-intuitive design examples

Figure 6.6 Long straight street in a distressed neighbourhood

drug sales. Neighbourhood layouts that are extremely 'permeable', with many entrances and exits and with long straight roadways ('straightshot streets', as shown in Figure 6.6, a photograph of part of a street in a public housing complex) tend to promote escape and excessive speed, according to police. Many of Harbordale's streets follow this pattern and, until the addition of 'street plateaus', could be considered crime facilitators (Clarke 1997).

Some communities adopt the most extreme options by gating or barricading entire neighbourhoods, as in Five Oaks, Ohio or Miami Shores, Florida, whereas others utilise street calming techniques that slow traffic and make quick getaways problematic, yet do not seal off neighbourhoods from the outside world. The photographs in Figure 6.7 illustrate street calming techniques used in Orlando, Florida neighbourhoods. In one, a planted median is used to slow traffic; and another depicts a closed traffic lane, creating a one-way street with the other lane now used for pedestrian and bike travel on that block.

There are dozens of street calming interventions that are considerate of all forms of transportation and that can also accommodate emergency vehicles, often the biggest sticking point in their implementation in residential neighbourhoods. American cities have been glacial in their adoption of such devices, unlike the British and other Europeans whose use of roundabouts, woonerfs (a Dutch

Figure 6.7 Three street calming approaches – *continued on page 168*

Figure 6.7 *Continued*

innovation designed to incorporate compatibly between cars, houses, pedestrians and playing areas in neighbourhoods), pinch points and speed humps is commonplace. Rather, an American response has been to shut down whole streets in certain neighbourhoods, a solution that Kunstler notes:

> is a drastic remedy for an uncivil society and must not be thought of as normal. It is one thing to tame traffic, it is another to create paranoidal fortifications. The best way to bring security to streets is to make them delightful places that honorable and decent citizens will want to walk in. They become, in effect, self-policing. The disadvantages of an interrupted street network in all other respects far outweigh any supposed gain in security (1998, page 130).

Finally, we consider the use of common space in residential areas, an issue that was addressed in Harbordale through the trimming of the mangroves and the creation of a linear walking park. This amounted to the reclaiming of enemy territory and has proved to be a rallying point in bolstering neighbourhood morale. Newman was among the first to point out the problem with the creation of large tracts of undefined lands within distressed neighbourhoods, noting in connection with the Bruekelen project in New York City that 'residents view these interior areas as the most dangerous in the project' (1973, page 53). This is especially true for spaces that are permeable to surrounding neighbourhoods such that it is difficult to know who 'belongs' in areas and who does not. Gilbert Rosenthal, an architect in charge of remodelling Philadelphia's Richard Allen Homes, reported a conversation with residents where they were presented with various configuration options for common space and courtyards. They rejected them all saying, 'You don't get it, do you? We don't want any common space: it's all too dangerous' (Rosenthal, 1995, page 6).

A tenet of defensible space and CPTED theory subsequently developed around the conception of spatial hierarchy, advocating clear distinctions among public and private space (with gradients between them), and the assessment of spaces using Crowe's 'Three-D' approach of designation, definition and design (1991, 2000), as noted in Chapter 4. While one result has been more careful attention to the delineation of open common space through the use of real (i.e. fences and gates) and symbolic (i.e. pavestones) barriers, especially within American public housing projects and high-crime neighbourhoods, there are many exceptions, as illustrated by the photographs in Figure 6.8 of open spaces in a Florida public housing project.

Poor maintenance and undefined common space are characteristics of the central section of the public housing project depicted above, surrounded by a low-income neighbourhood. As a consequence, few residents actually use this area and it is vulnerable to pedestrian and vehicular drug activity, especially at night. Easy access for outsiders is available through the large parking lots, which provide unimpeded entry to apartment rear entrances and to the common open spaces, as shown by the tyre tracks between the trees in the following photograph (Figure 6.9).

In contrast, a number of residents living on the site's perimeter have personalised adjacent open spaces using territorial markers such as gardens, lawn furniture and low hedges. The fence line shown on the far right of the photograph at Figure 6.10 provides a boundary to the common space, insulating this part of the property from outsiders and allowing residents to develop a sense of territorial control over otherwise common lands. The only gardens that exist in this project follow the fence line. We leave open for now the question of whether Kunstler's rejection of street closings is as applicable in the context of the commons and if not, why not.

Figure 6.8 Undefined open spaces in a public housing project

Figure 6.9 Open access to the commons (note the tyre tracks)

Figure 6.10 Gardens along the fence

COMMERCIAL LAND USES

Case studies of place-based crime prevention applications in commercial land uses are rare, with most being confined to the convenience store studies cited previously, ATM design (NCPC, 1997), pay phone toll fraud (Bichler and Clarke, 1996), shopping bag theft in central markets (Poyner, 1983; Poyner and Webb, 1992), banks (Clarke et al., 1991), and shoplifting (DiLonardo and Clarke, 1996). This is unfortunate since, although commercial land uses in the United States generally comprise no more than 5 per cent of developed urban areas (Goodman and Freund, 1968), they account for a disproportionate amount of criminal activity. They are obvious targets for crime.

Depending upon the individual community, these areas may contain central business districts, neighbourhood-shopping areas, regional shopping centres, as well as wholesale and retail establishments of varying size and complexity. In the past, communities in the United States tended to overzone lands for commercial purposes to provide for business expansion along transportation routes. At the urging of business leaders, city and county commissions zoned an overabundance of commercial lands, reasoning that such lands would ultimately be more valuable than residential properties to owners and to the jurisdictions. Insufficient demand for this excess property caused owners to be reluctant to improve it, especially where residential uses fell into commercial zones.

A consequence was the creation of large amounts of urban 'waste' lands that deteriorated into slums, often adjacent to existing business districts within downtown areas. These districts contain multiple crime targets and are often within the routine paths of would-be perpetrators within urban settings.

A 1985 study of the security needs of three commercial centres undertaken by New York City's Crime Commission and the Regional Plan Association suggested that fear of crime was hindering economic development in these centres, but that behaviour was more important in that respect than physical signs of disorder (see the 'broken windows' theory; endnote 3, Chapter 4). Following surveys and interviews in a total of twenty-three cities across the nation, the authors concluded that a combination of physical and situational crime prevention strategies should be employed to decrease crime and the fear of crime in commercial areas. These included more dense development with increased housing and mixed-use projects, the hosting of downtown special events to draw people and activity and the increased use of police foot patrols (Citizens Crime Commission of New York City, 1985). There is no evaluation as to the impact of these recommendations – some adapted directly from Jacobs and Newman – on any commercial areas. Indeed, as we have stated, such evaluations are rare in the United States. There is, however, a growing body of research from Britain on mixed-use neighbourhoods and crime (Poyner and Webb, 1991; Pettersson, 1997); most show that a complex series of micro-factors such as neighbourhood design, the specific mix of land uses, and local policing style can have an impact on the fear of crime and actual crime rates in such districts. Some of the findings are inconsistent with the ideology of the 'New Urbanists' and 'eyes on the street' adherents, noting that mixed uses may in fact promote more crime insofar as 'the greater level of activity; more people (especially tourists unfamiliar with the area) increases the potential for street crime', even though those living in some mixed-use neighbourhoods tend to feel safer than those living in other urban districts (Pettersson, 1997, page 195).

One of the few American evaluations of place-based crime prevention interventions in a commercial area was a re-evaluation of the impact of a CPTED programme in a declining commercial neighbourhood in Portland, Oregon. This 1981 study, sponsored by the National Institute of Justice, assessed the use of increased access control, surveillance, and security advisors for local businesses; it found that commercial burglaries were reduced following CPTED interventions and that there was a 'stabilisation' in the neighbourhoods' quality of life, physical appearance and social cohesion among the business community. Of all the CPTED strategies – increased street lighting, security surveys and the use of security advisors – the report credits the use of security advisors and the subsequent mobilisation of the business owners and managers as the most effective interventions. It concluded that:

(1)   a realistic timetable should be established for CPTED projects;
(2)   changes in the social environment are more difficult to accomplish than physical changes;
(3)   changes involving a smaller number of agencies and special interests are more likely to be implemented than large-scale changes, and
(4)   a successful CPTED program generally depends on augmenting existing resources (Kushmuk and Whittemore, 1981).

Perceived and real crime problems associated with downtown commercial areas combined with burgeoning road development to the hinterlands, insufficient parking, and the high costs of urban land and construction, have helped push commercial activities from the urban core to the urban fringe, and ultimately to the strip commercial development and to large scale suburban shopping centres which are spread over the American landscape.[4] The not unexpected irony is that crime has followed these commercial developments to the suburbs.

From modest beginnings in the Southdale Shopping Mall outside of Minneapolis in 1955, enclosed shopping centres (which account for about 65 per cent of all malls) have grown to become multi-million square foot behemoths featuring almost every form of modern service and entertainment imaginable. It was not until 1993, when the National Shopping Center Security Survey was conducted, that anyone had an inkling of the dimensions of the crime problem in shopping centres and malls in the United States (Hollinger and Dabney, 1998). Until that time, there was no extant database that compiled information about shopping centre crimes or their associated security services. The Survey, sponsored by an industry magazine, sought to provide crime information to centre managers, owners and store tenants. The 350 shopping centre respondents revealed that shoplifting was by far the most prevalent crime they had to deal with, followed by disorderly conduct and then by a combined category of trespassing, vagrancy, and begging. Part I crimes such as rape and homicides were far down the list. Unfortunately, the Survey did not provide much information about crime prevention approaches.

Despite their growing dominance of the American commercial scene, there are no independent, reasonably comprehensive case studies in the literature of before and after place-based crime prevention applications in shopping malls. There are, rather, studies of theft of cars from shopping centre parking lots (Hollinger and Dabney, 1999), theoretical examinations of environmental criminology and shopping centres (Brantingham et al., 1990), and shopping malls as predictors in the ecological distribution of crime (LaGrange, 1999). This paucity of evidence is due, no doubt, to the complexity of the subject matter, to the intimidating array of intervening variables presented by the environment and most of all, we suspect, to the proprietary and hence generally secretive nature of the shopping centre industry relative to the release of crime data and security responses.

We do have one small-scale case study of a CPTED intervention in a strip shopping mall, the Council Ring Plaza, a neighbourhood commercial centre located in Ontario, Canada. Documented by Peel Regional Police Officer Tom McKay (1997), this study considers the effects of physical changes made to a problematic waste-space adjacent to the shopping mall and the resultant impact on crime. Strip malls are inherently problematical: longitudinal design makes them more vulnerable to crime than other types of shopping areas since their orientation to the street makes casual surveillance relatively difficult. It is even more problematic when they are located along higher speed roadways, as many are. Moreover, they are designed for easy vehicular access and egress, factors which facilitate escape.

According to McKay, during 1991–1992, the Council Ring mall had experienced ten burglaries and one sexual assault, with many more unreported incidents. The police performed a CPTED survey of the area that identified the southern portion of the property – leftover space – as a significant problem. While adjacent to the mall, it was isolated and visually disconnected from it and from the street, and had become a favourite place for vagrants. The police response was to recommend that the area be opened up visually (a wall and slats were removed from a privacy fence) to the street and to passers-by. In addition, the waste space was made physically uncomfortable for vagrants through the removal of landscaping and the substitution of a concrete deck that further threw open the area to passing surveillance.

The results, according to police, were a reduction in loitering and vandalism and, during the 5 years since the changes, a 92 per cent reduction in break-ins and declines in assaults, sexual assaults, robberies, thefts and other crimes as well. As with so many other crime prevention case studies, this is not a scientific evaluation but rather an impressionistic one, and the total number of crimes is so small (eleven) that the percentage reduction, while dramatic, is statistically questionable. Further, there is no discussion of alternative explanations for the crime decrease, there are no adjacent area crime rates compared and there are no control groups. Nevertheless, the results are in line with other empirically based reports in the literature that support increased surveillance and the removal of 'facilitators' as means of preventing crime (Clarke, 1997). It is clear that further research needs to be devoted to commercial land uses, insofar as they are significant targets of criminals and often present opportunities that, while difficult for them to pass up, may be thwarted by rather rudimentary assessment and design changes.

INDUSTRIAL LAND USES

In the United States, industrial land use districts are generally divided into two types: light manufacturing and heavy manufacturing, which are distinguished by the relative amount of noxious emissions, noise, vibration, odours and dust emitted from each. Other sub-classifications may also be established for special purpose districts, based on community needs and ordinances. According to Leary (1968), industrial zones were once considered 'catch-all' districts, such that other land uses that could not otherwise be zoned were dumped into that category. Over time, communities have come to recognise the value of industrial zones and they have become increasingly popular as venues for industrial parks, which aggregate generally similar types of manufacturing firms under centralised management.

In describing the use of CPTED and situational crime prevention measures in two California industrial parks, Peiser and Chang (1998) note that research on crimes in industrial parks is scarce. Despite that, they are significant crime targets since, like many downtown urban commercial centres in the United States, they contain valuable assets but are likely to be deserted at night and on weekends. Moreover, industrial parks are commonly located adjacent to low-income residential areas with high crime rates and are inviting foci for criminal activity, especially perpetrated by juveniles.

Such was the case with a 20-acre site, the Cerritos Business Park, located between Los Angeles and Long Beach, California. According to Peiser and Chang, the Park was plagued by automobile thefts and break-ins, break-ins of warehouses and buildings, and thefts from buildings, vandalism and graffiti. Crime prevention responses centred around access control and reducing escape routes (perimeter fencing and fencing between building), improved signage ('for lease' signs that advertised that buildings were vacant were removed), target hardening (installation of retractable window bars), improved lighting, CCTV surveillance, and night-time security patrols. To reduce the problem of teenage loitering, the managers turned on lawn sprinkling systems periodically throughout the day.[5]

After the changes were implemented, Peiser and Chang report that break-ins were drastically reduced (from every weekend to one every 2 months), as were reports of vandalism and graffiti. Moreover, the Park's occupancy rate jumped from a low in 1995 of 75 per cent to 98 per cent in 1996. According to Park management, costs of the improved security measures were far outweighed by income from increased rents, higher occupancy rates, and shorter vacancy periods for individual buildings, all credited to the security improvements (Peiser and Chang, 1998).

Peiser and Chang also discuss the Paramount Industrial Complex, an industrial park located in the City of Paramount, California. Located adjacent to a high-crime community, the park experienced a high incidence of auto theft and a series of burglaries accompanied by vehicles' 'ram-raiding' roll-shutter doors in loading areas. This latter 'smash and grab' technique appears to be more common in Britain than in the United States, although there is no comparative data to support that impression.

Situational and CPTED crime prevention measures for the Park included increasing guardianship (random night and day patrols instituted), target hardening (removable bollards installed in front of loading docks), surveillance facilitation (improved and better maintained exterior lighting) and improved access control (fencing between buildings). Peiser and Chang report that these interventions 'have been effective' but unfortunately give no further details as to crime statistics or related impacts.

The Cerritos and Paramount cases share design similarities. Prior to interventions, they were both highly permeable, car-oriented suburban sites containing a myriad of isolated interior spaces, such as loading docks, that were prime crime attractions. Both are located in generally suburban areas, adjacent to relatively low-income residential neighbourhoods, a problem inasmuch as these contributed motivated offenders as distinct from 'eyes on the street' surveillance.

While we do not have enough information from the case reports to know, we can speculate that these parks are likely similar to many others in the United States and Canada in that they have limited public transportation options and that previous to the application of the place-based crime prevention measures, little thought was given to the security of shift workers, who come and go at odd hours of the day and night. These issues have been addressed by a number of prescriptive studies (as distinct from cases), including Wekerle and Whitzman's *Safe Cities* (1995), one of the most comprehensive public-service texts published to date. While they speak to many of the same remedies for industrial zones suggested by the case analyses above – lighting, surveillance, and access controls – they focus much more on protecting the workers and clients (as distinct from the property) and look to the nature of changing land uses within industrial zones, especially in urban industrial areas. Wekerle and Whitzman address the problem of 'gentrifying' industrial areas where residential and commercial conversions have turned shop and storage spaces into 'boutiques or restaurants, or into loft living spaces' (1995, page 107). The book's grasp of the fluid nature of urban zones and neighbourhoods, and its focus on the needs of residents (especially women), are important contributions to the discussion of planning for crime prevention.

Like commercial land uses, it is clear that there are insufficient empirical studies of place-based applications to make sweeping statements about industrial land uses or about specialised subcategories within them, such as industrial parks. Rather, what is more productive and logical, at this stage in the development of the science and art of place-based crime prevention, is the tailoring of interventions to each case which, while unique, nevertheless tends to present problems found elsewhere in terms of surveillance, access control, maintenance and activity support/generation.

TRANSPORTATION LAND USES: BUS STOPS

Our final illustration is less an example of a crime prevention intervention than a carefully drawn empirical study of a transportation land use subcategory that has largely been overlooked in the literature: urban bus stops. The 'transportation' category, with a focus on terminals (e.g. the BART system in San Francisco) was considered for inclusion in the original Westinghouse Studies of the 1970s but was dropped because the study designers believed that defensible space principles such as 'territoriality' would not be much applicable to such 'transient places'. However, a recent study of Los Angeles bus stops using updated models of place-based crime prevention strategies puts that notion to rest – although it focuses less on territoriality and more on 'aggregate' environmental features – and seeks to demonstrate the potential applicability of place-based crime prevention principles in urban 'micro-environments' (Loukaitou-Sideris, 1999). As such, the study sets out a host of 'environmental responses' – suggestions rooted in empirically based research – to guide transportation and land use planners in their decisions on where to locate urban bus stops.

After a careful review of the extant literature on place-based crime prevention planning, Loukaitou-Sideris concludes that there are sufficient theoretical and empirical bases to analyse bus stop crime patterns using environmental planning variables as independent variables, and employs a 'qualitative and ethnographic' approach as distinct from one that is 'quantitative and cross sectional' (ibid., page 398). To carry that forward, she analysed the environmental attributes of ten high-crime bus stops in Los Angeles and compared these to four low-crime bus stops that are located reasonably nearby. Bus stops were chosen for study since in Los Angeles they account for a disproportionate amount of bus system crime (67 per cent compared to 33 per cent of crimes reported while riding buses), are important places for many low-income citizens who have limited transportation options, and are the focus of a significant level of perceived crime and fear for bus riders, particularly in the Los Angeles inner city.

Moreover, as nodes within the urban transportation system that forms the skeleton against which all urban elements, including buildings and landscape, are framed, bus stops are important gathering and dispersal places – pulse points – for large numbers of urban citizens. They are numerous in large cities (Los Angeles has almost 20,000), and their locations are highly correlated with the growth and shifting of populations. In that context, they obviously are far easier and less expensive to move and to alter than to move or redesign train stops or train and aeroplane terminals. Indeed, in some jurisdictions, notably smaller urban areas, bus stops are left to the discretion of the driver, ensuring that the system will be tailored to rider needs.

In Los Angeles, bus stop locations generally are fixed and the author concentrated her research on those stops in the inner city area that accounted for a high proportion of the total number of bus stop crimes (18 per cent) over a two-year period, 1994–1995. She analysed the immediate surroundings (the micro-environment) of each bus stop using structured observations, systematic mapping techniques, interviews and systematic random surveys of passengers. The environments of four adjacent low-crime rate bus stops were also carefully examined and compared as paired sets with four of the high-crime sample.

Although this research could be criticised for the small sample size, the findings are nevertheless pointed: Loukaitou-Sideris notes significant environmental differences, characterised in five categories of features, between the high and low-crime rate bus stops that account for the differences in crime. The feature categories are 'bad neighbours' (which includes 'negative land uses that can be considered crime generators', such as bars, liquor stores, single room occupancy hotels, vacant buildings and surface parking lots), 'desolation and lack of surveillance', 'crowding', 'broken windows', and 'easy escapes' (ibid., pages 401–4). These factors are by and large familiar to students of place-based crime prevention theory. One, crowding, usually receives more attention now in this literature as it is related to pick-pocketing and to spaces between shoppers and thefts from bags (Poyner and Webb, 1992) than it has relative to crime generation. Early in the history of CPTED and defensible space theory, Angel's research (1968) predicted that certain levels of street activity and population density were linked to the likelihood of crime occurrence. In this concept, a critical crime zone was one that could support a relatively low number of people but of sufficient density to contain both targets and perpetrators. Loukaitou-Sideris adds to Angel's theory by postulating a second level of population density, one large enough to mask less serious crimes such as pick-pocketing within crowds.[6]

Her research concludes that environmental variables play a significant role in crime at bus stops in Los Angeles, in that deteriorated surrounding structures and uses or ones that attract or facilitate crime ('bad neighbours') characterise the most dangerous bus stops. Further, those stops which are isolated or do not lend themselves easily to nearby surveillance, and especially those that have easily accessible escape routes, are more prone to crime than nearby stops that do not have those environmental features. Stops that have high density usage – and hence become crowded to the point where relatively minor crime such as purse snatching can be concealed in the confusion – are more likely to be venues for this type of crime than stops with less usage. And, finally, the high-crime stops were far more likely to have 'broken windows' attributes than low-crime bus stops.

Loukaitou-Sideris' research leads her to a series of suggestions that could be the basis of a 'best bus stop practices' siting manual. In line with what is preached by most crime prevention advocates, she emphasises that crime control cannot be left entirely to the police but that it requires a coordinated approach among agencies and citizenry. According to her research, safer bus stop siting must take into account surrounding land uses, avoiding where possible areas containing crime generators and crime attractions such as bars, liquor stores, pawn shops and adult theatres. Further, siting should be attentive to the signs of public incivility that distinguish areas that are cared for as distinct from those that are not. And in line with other evidence about the importance of convenience store locations (Leistner, 1999), she suggests that bus stop sites should not isolate riders by placing them amongst 'dead spaces' where surveillance opportunities from nearby businesses or activities are minimal, since serious crimes were found to take place at bus stops in desolate areas. In the opposite situation, crowded bus stops can facilitate less serious offences, and Loukaitou-Sideris endorses sidewalk design alterations ('nubs' that broaden sidewalks) to lessen crowding at high-use stops and the use of barriers to shield bus patrons from pedestrians in these circumstances. Adequate lighting, reducing visual obstructions from man-made and natural features and the removal of sidewalk space impediments ('newspapers stands, signs, poles') are also proposed as design and maintenance considerations of good bus stop siting. However, one would have to question whether it is truly in the interest of bus patrons to do away with newspaper stands and signs in all but the most congested situations.

Finally, Loukaitou-Sideris reports tangential evidence that increased levels of criminal activity are associated with grid street design (as distinct from culs-de-sac) insofar as these provide a myriad of escape routes to fleeing offenders. Noting that the higher-crime bus stops in her study tended to be located near intersections and areas with alleys, she suggested that where feasible, escape routes near bus stops be fenced or barricaded so as to diminish opportunities of offenders to vanish into the urban fabric.

This study of bus stop design and siting is valuable inasmuch as it focuses on micro environments spread throughout the urban landscape, in contrast with the relatively large-scale sites (neighbourhoods, shopping centres and strip malls, industrial parks) that we have presented heretofore. As such, it clearly demonstrates that place-based crime prevention interventions and research can be applied across a spectrum of urban sites and scales and within a range of land uses.

CONCLUSIONS

This latter point is crucial, for if place-based crime prevention theory is to be meaningful to the urban planner, police official, building and zoning officer, architect, developer and property owner and, not least, to the person on the street, it must translate into clearly effective applications within the land uses and experiences each come into contact with in the course of daily living and work. But, as we have seen, while there is a growing body of knowledge based on residential – primarily public housing – applications, there is relatively little case or project evidence to support the diffusion of applications based on these approaches within other land use categories. For example, much of what we know about the application of place-based crime prevention in commercial areas as noted in the Ring Plaza study, in office parks as demonstrated by the Cerritos and Paramount cases or at Los Angeles bus stops is imported from empirical studies in other areas. While this may be adequate for many purposes, there is no doubt that each land use type presents unique problems and possibilities, as does each individual site within land uses. There is the need for a systematically constructed casebook of place-based crime prevention studies within and for specific urban land use categories, something which may be far in the future. This is all the more relevant, we believe, in a society like the United States whose fragmented governmental structure makes it difficult to discern the emergence of clear-cut policy and trends.

This being the case, there are nevertheless some fundamental themes that are becoming evident within particular land use categories. One, demonstrated by the Harbordale study and supported by reports from throughout the literature, such as Wekerle and Whitzman's 'Safer Cities' work in Canada, is that outsiders cannot assume what is important to residents in making place-based crime prevention design changes. For instance, to Harbordale residents, the untamed mangrove swamp common space running through the heart of the neighbourhood presented a physical, psychological and political barrier that was underestimated or unrecognised for years by local and state government agencies. On the other hand, *too much* value has been ascribed by outsiders to the provision of common open spaces in many public housing complexes, much to the chagrin of residents who often fear and avoid such spaces. The lesson is that truly safer communities and improved qualities of life must be designed for specific places with the vision of residents clearly in focus, otherwise even the best laid plans will, as they say, go astray. Our expectation is that such conclusions can be applied to other land uses and activity generators within the urban fabric.

However, it is wise and prudent to resist the temptation to dictate to others what we think is preferable and to stretch the implications of the available studies beyond the boundaries of the available evidence – which is often difficult for consultants, professors and local officials to resist. But to do so is to raise expectations among citizens that may be dashed and that ultimately discredit place-based crime prevention theory as well as those who would preach and apply it to urban settings.

NOTES

1   Sherman *et al.* (1997, page 3) note that 'many evaluations funded by the Federal Government – perhaps the majority – are "process" evaluations describing what was done rather than "impact" evaluations assessing what effect the program had on crime . . . Evaluations containing both process and impact measures provide the most information but they are rarely funded or reported.'

2   We are indebted to Susan and Stephanie Ajoc, planners for the City of St Petersburg, who provided information on Harbordale and access to neighbours and local police for interviews.

3   As described in endnote 8, Chapter 5, the UCR (Uniform Crime Reports) consists of so-called 'index crimes' that identify the most serious violent and property crimes in order of their presumed seriousness. They consist of murder and non-negligent manslaughter, forcible rape, robbery, and aggravated assault, burglary, larceny-theft, motor-vehicle theft, and arson. The UCR is derived from crimes reported to the police, and then reported to the Program Support Section of the FBI. Index crimes are used to compare crime rates nationally and across jurisdictions.

4   Citing Jacobs (1961), both new urbanist ideologues and CPTED advocates argue that the development of commercial districts separated from residential zones has contributed to the decline of the American city as a vibrant and exciting place and to the growth of crime as such districts are deserted for many hours of the day. Although they are compelling arguments, the empirical evidence to support both theses is mixed at best.

5   Some convenience store managers have addressed this problem by playing 'MUSAK' in their parking lots.

6   It should be clear that 'crowding' is a psychological and cultural notion distinct from population density, which is strictly a physical phenomenon. Crowding has also been the subject of numerous comparisons between aggressive and pathological behaviour in animal and human populations, many of which are discredited (de Waal et al., 2000).

CHAPTER 7

BRITISH POLICY AND PRACTICE

INTRODUCTION

This chapter looks at how policy and practice in relation to crime and the design of the built environment have evolved in recent years. Britain is distinguished from the USA in these terms (the subject of Chapter 5) by several factors, but one of the most significant is the existence in Britain, particularly during the 1990s, of a strong central government policy thrust in this area, framing and hopefully complementing initiatives at the local level. This chapter therefore has this component running through it as a consistent thread, while Chapter 8 has a more local focus as it looks in much more detail at three case studies of particular types of initiatives.

One potential consequence of the stance adopted for the purposes of this chapter is that it can create the impression that the British experience is characterised primarily by uniformity.[1] In comparison with the American experience which has been described in Chapters 5 and 6, it is undoubtedly true that a primary distinguishing feature of the British approach in recent years has been both a strong central government policy thrust and the creation through legislation of a common framework within which most of the local work in this field is expected to take place; thus in a book of this nature it is both appropriate and necessary for a chapter with the title 'British Policy and Practice' to concentrate largely on this superstructure. However, this should not be taken as implying that the British system is lacking in diversity or in the willingness to experiment at the local level. The differences that exist in British society, not only between its urban and rural areas and its economically well favoured and less favoured regions but also in terms of the very segmented nature of many of its urban areas, in which neighbourhoods characterised by relative poverty frequently sit alongside those marked by relative affluence, inevitably mean that there is both a need and an opportunity to respond in different ways to crime prevention issues. It would grossly misrepresent the efforts of large numbers of people in these localities to imply that all they do is sit and wait for Government directives before taking action in this field. There is, therefore, a very considerable variety of initiatives to be found both throughout Britain as we have defined it for these purposes (and indeed throughout the length and breadth of the United Kingdom), to which it would be impossible to do full justice without the kind of detailed survey information that is not at present to hand.

Nevertheless, the existence of a strong Central Government policy thrust in recent years is the primary distinguishing characteristic of the British system, which is why it is the focus of this chapter. This in turn also affects the three case studies chosen as the focus of Chapter 8, since they all derive from component elements of this Central drive: the police Secured By Design initiative, the arrangements set in train as a result of the Crime and Disorder Act, 1998, and an example of how crime prevention initiatives relate to urban regeneration issues.

The chapter commences with an overview of the public perceptions of crime and the fear of crime as a pair of closely related quality-of-life issues. It then examines the place of environmental design alongside other policy responses to crime, and looks in more detail at how the police service organises itself to contribute in this area. The specific emergence of national policy via DoE Circular 5/94 leads into a wide-ranging discussion of the sustainability, urban regeneration/revitalisation and social inclusion contexts within which this issue is increasingly viewed in Britain, including the partnership approach underlined in the Crime and Disorder Act, 1998. The chapter concludes with some reflections on the current state of British policy and practice.

PUBLIC PERCEPTIONS OF CRIME AS A 'QUALITY-OF-LIFE' ISSUE

The recognition that crime rates in Britain are a major political issue that we noted in Chapter 2, with the success or otherwise of a Government being at least partially reflected in whether crime rates have gone up or down, is not merely a function of sensationalist media reporting. Such concerns about crime rates and the fear of crime are often also reflected in the results of the studies that have been undertaken which ask people about their perceptions of the factors that affect the quality of life in the areas where they live. Indeed, these two phenomena (the sense that this matters to the national political tussle, and the recognition that it does matter locally) may well be mutually reinforcing.

A major study of this issue was undertaken in the early 1990s by Robson *et al.* (1994), as part of an appraisal of the effectiveness of initiatives undertaken to date under the broad heading of 'urban policy'. This study asked 1,299 residents in fifteen different areas of Greater Manchester, Merseyside and Tyne and Wear to rank twenty variables they were given in terms of their importance to the quality of life in the area. The results are summarised in Table 7.1. This shows that, by quite some distance, violent crime was the issue of most concern to local residents, and that non-violent crime, ranked fourth highest in the list, was ahead of issues such as the quality of housing, the quality of the local environment and unemployment.

Table 7.1 Public perceptions of factors affecting the quality of life in major urban areas

Variable	Percentage of sample ranking variable as 'very important'	Rank order
Violent crime	79.3	1
Quality of healthcare	73.7	2
Cost of living	71.9	3
Non-violent crime	67.2	4
Quality of housing	64.2	5
Quality of welfare services	61.7	6
What the area looks like	61.3	7
Employment prospects	59.2	8
Pollution	58.2	9
Unemployment levels	58.0	10

Source: Robson *et al.* (1994) page 340

Table 7.2 Public perceptions of safety in major urban areas

Category	Do you think your area has become safer over the last three years?	Do you expect your area to become safer over the next three years?
Safer	14%	28%
The same	37%	37%
Less safe	49%	35%

Source: Robson *et al.* (1994) page 342

The same sample was also asked about perceptions of safety in their residential areas, both over the last three years and in terms of their expectations over the next three years, and the results are summarised in Table 7.2. This shows that about half of that sample felt that their area had become less safe during the previous three years, and only just over one-quarter expected to see any improvement over the next three years. This latter result could be seen as the triumph of hope over experience, since twice as many people thought their area would become safer over the next three years than thought it had become safer over the past three years.

Similar pictures have emerged from more local studies. For example, a document which tells in promotional terms the story of the Nottingham City Challenge programme over the period 1992–1997 describes the issues as follows, under the banner headline of 'Winning the Fight against Crime':

> In the past, St. Ann's in particular has hit the national press headlines as one of the most crime ridden areas in the country, with the perception that it is literally crawling with drug dealers and those perpetrating motor crime. Yes, it is a tough

area and it was realised that the network of alleys and cul-de-sacs [sic] provided havens for the small minority intent on car stealing, domestic theft and violent crime.

Crime, and the fear of crime continued to be the number one priority of local residents throughout the programme – and has indeed, continued to do so. A reduction of 7.5% in crime overall has been achieved through partnership with the police, city council, residents and business; this reduction is a significant achievement and compares very favourably with the city and national crime figures.

A survey of residents' views of crime in the City Challenge area carried out in 1995 back[s] up the statistics, revealing that people perceived that there was less crime in the area than they did in 1993 when they were originally asked.

Challenge implemented a radical programme of security improvements to the St. Ann's Estate; closing off unwanted footpaths, creating parking spaces next to homes, providing safe walking routes for residents with good lighting and eradicating hidden areas, installing thousands of new toughened doors, fitting locks and bolts to windows and doors and spending over £3m on improvements to these (Nottingham City Council, undated, page 5).

Similarly, the final review of the Dearne Valley City Challenge programme in South Yorkshire over the 1992–1997 period (the same Government Programme over the same period as the Nottingham example quoted above), written in rather less promotional terms than was the Nottingham example, says the following:

Following the 'Priority Search' survey carried out at the beginning of City Challenge and subsequently used as a working document, year 5 saw a MORI poll return to the concerns of the local residents. 'Better crime prevention and Safety on the Streets' was now seen as the highest priority. City Challenge funding has continued to reinforce the security and safety message via the security grant scheme. Open to application from community groups and small businesses in the area, it has been able to directly target this issue.

Assistance to small retail outlets to provide CCTV, support to Neighbourhood Watch Schemes which promote crime prevention and reduce the fear of crime and securing the premises of local groups are some of the initiatives supported by the community programme. The victims of crime have not been forgotten. Our support of the Dearne Valley Victim Support scheme has been instrumental in ensuring its long term future and it continues to be a help and benefit to people in the area when they most need it (Dearne Valley Partnership, 1996, Strategic Objective 4).

The important point about both of these City Challenge examples, which were con-centrated five-year programmes tackling some of the worst problems of urban deprivation in the country, is that in both cases when asked the local residents indi-cated that crime and safety were their number one concerns. This example, which is wholly consistent with the results of the Robson study quoted above, could be repeated several times over in terms of recent studies in British urban areas,[2] and it is clear (as was the case in the Nottingham and Dearne Valley instances) that find-ings of this nature have influenced the contents of major public intervention pro-grammes undertaken in those areas. It is also clear from the quoted descriptions of what was done in these two cases that the actions taken included a considerable amount of 'target-hardening',[3] in large measure in response to public concerns. If the planning process is to be seen to be successful in tackling the problems that are extant in these sorts of urban areas, it is clear from this evidence that it will need to address this type of agenda; it is part of our thesis that to date it has done this too little and too ineffectively.

The 2000 British Crime Survey returned to the broad issue of public attitudes towards crime and the fear of crime under the heading 'Concern about crime' (Home Office, 2000b, pages 41–54). The headline findings from this work were as follows:

- 33% of respondents felt that crime had increased nationally 'a lot more' over the previous two years and a further 34% felt that it had increased 'a little more', although in fact on British Crime Survey counts crime levels had been reducing over that period.
- Perceptions of crime rates in people's own localities were a little more posit-ive, with the figures for 'a lot more' being 20% and for 'a little more' being 30%.
- When asked about whether they thought they were likely to be on the receiv-ing end of crimes over the next year, car-related crimes were well ahead of other types of crime, with 33% of car owners saying they were 'very' or 'fairly' likely to experience theft from their car and with the equivalent figure for theft of their car itself being 29%. Responses generally tended to be well-ahead of 'actual' rates, with (for example) 21% of households saying they were 'very' or 'fairly' likely to be on the receiving end of a burglary as compared with an actual burglary rate of 4.3% of households in 1999.
- When asked the more general question about whether people were 'worried' about crime (as distinct from whether they expected as individuals to be on its receiving end), the top six areas of concern when adding together 'very worried' and 'fairly worried' responses were:

  1 = burglary   57%
  1 = theft of cars (owners)   57%

3. theft from cars (owners)   53%
4. credit/bank card fraud   50%
5. mugging/robbery   44%
6. physical attack   43%

This provides very clear evidence from a recent national study that the major public concerns about crime recorded in the more locally based surveys undertaken earlier in the 1990s and reported above are continuing.

THE PLACE OF ENVIRONMENTAL DESIGN IN RESPONSES TO CRIME

It is important, of course, to keep this matter in perspective: in no sense is it being suggested here, nor could it be said to be a feature of the policies being promoted by successive British Governments, that by itself environmental design can solve the problem of crime in localities. Essentially, environmental initiatives need to be seen as one of a suite of measures addressing this problem in a comprehensive way. Walklate (in McLaughlin and Muncie, 1996, pages 293–331), in summarising current British thinking in the early/mid 1990s, describes four inter-related themes as being visible in crime prevention policy:

- offender-centred strategies, which tend to be about enforcement and punishment and which would be regarded as the traditional major concerns of the system;
- victim-centred strategies, which tend to be about how to avoid the major problems in the field of crime, but are also about improving victim support once crime has taken place;
- environment-centred strategies, also described by Clarke and Mayhew (1980) as 'situational crime prevention'. This component is, of course, the primary focus of this present book. It spans a broad spectrum of activities, including both 'target-hardening' approaches, which both make individual potential crime scenes more difficult for criminals to access and to escape from and which increase surveillance of them (see for example Bottoms, 1990), and the approaches of 'New Urbanism' which seek to reduce crime by promoting environmental design approaches; these stimulate human activity on streets, in buildings and in and overlooking public spaces and thereby increase natural surveillance (see, for example, Rudlin and Falk, 1999).

- community-centred strategies, which raise many definitional and social policy issues but which are essentially about involving local communities directly or indirectly in various ways in crime prevention activities. This sort of broad 'community safety' approach is argued for (see, for example, Osborn and Bright, 1989) on the grounds that it focuses on the role of other public authorities and organisations as well as the police; that it addresses the particular needs of groups that are most vulnerable to crime; that it considers the relationship between levels of crime and the facilities, services and opportunities of particular neighbourhoods; and that it tries to divert young people from offending in the first place and young offenders from further offending. The approach found expression in the Home Office's Safer Cities Programme launched in 1988, with sixteen cities initially being chosen to participate and with a wide range of strategies being visible (see Walklate in McLaughlin and Muncie, 1996, pages 317–20 for a useful general summary).

Tilley (1992, page 29) argues that the initiatives taken here can be seen not only in physical and in social terms, but also in terms of three levels of intervention: the conduct of new dedicated initiatives, incorporation into new and potentially relevant initiatives, and the re-examination of existing patterns of practice. The wide-ranging nature of the social interventions at this third level of intervention was seen by Tilley as providing the greatest scope for the police to begin to threaten the strategies of other agencies rather than to concentrate primarily on their own responsibilities. While this can be seen to be widening the agenda without always sharpening the focus, it can also be seen as a precursor to some of the more holistic approaches embarked upon later in the 1990s which we discuss later in this chapter. It should be noted, incidentally, that although this sort of approach has been seen as having potential by many writers, it has also been criticised for its lack of clarity and for the fact that its advocates are promoting its virtues before much firm evidence from carefully researched cases has become available (Hughes, in Jewson and MacGregor, 1997, pages 153–65). More recently, Gilling (1999) has added to this a concern about whose values are actually driving community safety debates, and has expressed doubts about whether much of what is being done in Britain is helping to tackle the problems of social exclusion as distinct from, in effect, reinforcing them.

This apparent broadening of the range of types of crime-prevention initiatives in response to the problem of rising crime levels does not mean that traditional attitudes to the roles of the police and of the criminal justice system have necessarily been supplanted. Locke (1990, pages 245 and 246) described this development in thinking in the late 1980s as follows:

Strategic thinking seems to have moved away from being satisfied only with controlling crime, towards an albeit tentative confidence that crime can in fact be reduced. The machinery of criminal justice policy is still dominated largely by lawyers, with their traditionally myopic visions of how to respond to crime. This domination has been increasingly challenged by magistrates, probation officers, voluntary organisations, police officers and by those in local government. The view that the criminal justice system alone cannot effectively respond to crime has by no means been displaced. ... What has been added to current thinking is a clearer idea of what needs to complement the workings of the criminal justice system – crime prevention, diversions and community based measures.

Critics of police operations have undoubtedly added to this debate by arguing that in some localities police approaches can contribute more to the problem than they do to the solution. Lea and Young (1993, but first published in 1984), for example, argue that police practice in the large cities has often tacitly divided those cities into 'respectable' and 'non-respectable' parts, resulting in two different styles of policing: 'one in the inner city based on force and coercion, the other in the suburbs and the smart part of town based upon consensus' (ibid., page 65). They argue that it is little surprise that the former style, which they describe as 'military policing', is reacted to in very negative ways by many of the residents of inner city areas whereas the latter style, which they describe as 'consensus policing', generates a much more positive response.

This ferment of ideas appears to include an acceptance of the broad notion that environmental initiatives have a part to play in crime prevention, but it is clearly only a part (and a contested one at that, in terms of what works where) in a broad field containing many contested elements. The broad position in Britain by the late 1990s, as it prepared itself for a new round of partnership initiatives required by the Crime and Disorder Act, 1998 (see below), can be summarised by reference to the contents of the manual prepared to support this initiative (Crime Concern, undated). This argued that approaches needed to be tailored to the local situation, but that in particular the problems of the approximately 2,000 residential neighbourhoods in the United Kingdom exhibiting the following characteristics required special attention:

- crime rates three to four times higher than surrounding areas;
- high levels of repeat victimisation;
- above-average rates of disorder and anti-social behaviour by young people;
- high incidence of neighbourhood disputes and anti-social behaviour by adults;
- widespread drug dealing and prostitution. (ibid., page 3)

In such areas, crime was seen as being likely to be one of many problems albeit, as we have already seen, one that local residents are likely to put very high up their lists of problems needing to be tackled. The other common features were seen as:

- high levels of poverty and deprivation, with up to 60 per cent of families dependent on state benefits;
- high unemployment rates, often spanning generations and including up to 35 per cent of young men;
- a shifting population, with annual turnover at 20 per cent or more;
- above average proportions of lone-parent households (20 per cent or more) and of children under 16 (30 per cent or more);
- run down, defective and unattractive housing stock, some of which goes unfilled for long periods;
- physical dereliction such as graffiti, abandoned cars and boarded-up shops;
- a struggling local economy;
- few play and leisure facilities;
- physical isolation (ibid.).

Within an holistic approach to tackling this range of problems (because the manual accepts that attempting to tackle crime in areas such as this as if it were a free-standing issue would not be likely to succeed), the recommended approach is that:

... successful crime reduction depends on:

- *effective local partnerships* involving the police, local authorities, the community and other key agencies;
- *consulting, motivating and involving* residents and young people as an integral part of their work;
- *a problem-solving approach* based on sound information, analysing the problems clinically and listening to the experience of local people;
- *tailor-made packages of measures*: single steps are rarely enough to reduce crime, criminality and fear of crime. At most they are 'fire-fighting' exercises to contain the problem. What is needed is an across-the-board approach which may include not only security, policing and surveillance initiatives but also improved housing management, family support programmes and good youth facilities (ibid., page 5).

THE ROLE OF THE POLICE SERVICE IN ENVIRONMENTAL DESIGN

Part of the changing nature of the responses described above has been an acceptance on the part of the police service that since environmental design is one of the elements that impacts upon crime and crime prevention, and has very practical implications for police operations, it would be helpful from a police perspective to try to influence decisions about the layout and organisation of physical space. This has resulted in the establishment in virtually all of Britain's police forces of Architectural Liaison Officers (or equivalent title). Some of these posts are civilian posts, and sometimes they are serving police officer posts carrying a rank; no doubt within the police service itself there are arguments about the strengths and weaknesses of each approach at a time when 'civilianisation' has been an important issue in policy developments in police forces. Whichever way this is handled in individual forces, their duties in practice tend to fall into three broad groups:

a   'spreading the gospel' to all interested or affected parties;
b   liaising with development interests over the design of proposals, helped by the conferment of a 'Secured By Design' award to projects which meet the principles expressed. (The award, among other things, has been used as a marketing tool by private housing developers.) The 'Secured By Design' approach is the subject of a more detailed case study in Chapter 8 of this book; it should be noted that, as well as being a significant award in its own right, the guidelines laid down in order to secure it illustrate also the kind of advice that Police Architectural Liaison Officers are likely to give on free-standing cases;
c   responding to consultations from local planning authorities at the stage when planning applications have been received.

Table 7.3 presents a more detailed description of this role in terms of the way in which it is conceived by the Nottinghamshire Police.

The first of these roles, the task of 'spreading the gospel', is well illustrated by the appearance at the 1996 Town and Country Planning Summer School for Councillors (which is typically attended by about 300 elected members who are on the Planning Committees of local planning authorities) of two serving police officers from two different forces to talk about their work and philosophies (Pearson, 1996; Stokes, 1996). The more senior of these officers summed up the value of the approach as follows:

> Police experience has demonstrated that where the local authorities, the community and the police operate together, good housekeeping methods can go a long way towards helping us achieve the desired effect of reducing not only crime but also the fear of crime (Pearson, 1996, page 81).

Table 7.3 The Architectural Liaison Officer role in the Nottinghamshire Police

The Crime Prevention Officer and Architectural Liaison Officer roles are combined in this description of the 'core duties' of the three officers who fill these posts in the 'C' Division of the Nottinghamshire Police:

- identifying potential solutions for crime 'hotspots', highlighted by the monitoring and analysis of local crime and incident statistics, produced by Local Intelligence Officers and intelligence inputs;
- assisting in promoting all aspects of crime prevention to both the Police Service and the public, while maintaining contact with other agencies and community groups who promote these issues;
- liaison with local authority departments, architects and other agencies, with the view to 'Designing out Crime' by evaluating and reporting upon new developments and planning applications from a security aspect;
- providing information to members of the local community regarding relevant prevention advice, in the way of talks, seminars and presentations;
- working with under-represented minority groups in order to encourage and instil confidence, so that crime is reported and underlying causes of crime are identified;
- surveying domestic and business premises, where there are special or difficult security features which need to be considered;
- keeping up to date on crime prevention techniques as produced by the Home Office Crime Prevention Agency and relevant external organisations, regarding best practice;
- design, delivery and evaluation of training in the crime prevention arena both internally and externally;
- carrying out all duties with full regard to the Police policies and procedures.

Source: Nottinghamshire Police website at http://www.nottspolice.org.uk (accessed July 2000)

The third of these functions, responding to consultations by local planning authorities on planning applications, is of particular relevance to the subject matter of this book. It may be helpful, therefore, to try to put a scale against this sort of activity. Before doing so, however, it is important to understand that such consultations are not of themselves mandatory. Local planning authorities have been urged to do this in paragraph 9 of DoE Circular 5/94 (Department of the Environment, 1994) by the Secretary of State for the Environment as good practice, and since most local planning authorities are likely to take the general view that such consultations lead to better informed decision-making there would not usually be any inhibition in doing this. Nonetheless, this is a matter for the exercise of local discretion; there is no compulsion behind such consultations.

At the time of the 1993 White Paper on the then Government's proposals for the reform of the police service (Home Office, 1993), there were forty-three separate police forces in England and Wales covering an area with a population of approximately 50 million people. Thus a police force on average covered just over 1 million people. The White Paper, incidentally, claimed that this was too large a number of police forces, although it was unable to advance any very rational criteria for reducing the number! Within each of these forces, the Architectural Liaison Unit typically might consist of a couple of officers plus some administrative support, and in some forces it is even smaller than this. There is inevitably a limit in this situation to what such a unit can do, and particularly to how many cases it can pursue effectively at any one time.

In contrast, there are well over 400 local planning authorities in England and Wales, or approximately ten times the number of police forces. This ratio, for example, is repeated exactly in Greater Manchester, where there are ten Metropolitan District Councils covering an area with a population of approximately 2.5 million people policed by the Greater Manchester Police Force. In any one year, these ten local planning authorities together will typically deal with around 20,000 planning applications. Clearly, the Architectural Liaison Unit of the Greater Manchester Police, given that it is of the typical size described above, would be swamped by consultation on this scale. Practicalities dictate that consultation needs to be on a selective basis. In any event, of course, many applications are small-scale and do not raise significant or non-standard issues. Thus, the fact that individual planning case officers exercise their discretion over when to consult the force Architectural Liaison Unit is not of itself a problem, provided that the cases are sensibly chosen; and informal liaison usually produces some agreed guidelines about this. Indeed, this process can be seen as another example of the discretionary nature of the British planning system (Booth, 1996). Perhaps the more important question is what local planning authorities do with police comments of this kind once they have received them. There is very little research on this, but Kitchen (1997a) suggested two broad probabilities based upon his own professional practice experience. The first is that, where local planning authorities adopt a consultative style of development control decision-making, adverse police comments would be likely to be referred back to the developer and/or the developer's agent for further consideration, and most such people would be likely to take police advice about these matters seriously. The second is that, if this process resulted in no amendments to the application having been made that would now make it acceptable, both planning officers in making a recommendation and elected members in taking a decision would be likely to attach weight to the views of the police. This would not be the case universally, however, and Kitchen has recorded instances of high-profile cases where police views seen as coming from the 'target-hardening' stable were ignored in favour of a rather different philosophical stance (Kitchen, 1997b, pages 156 and 157).

Overall, it is probably correct to say that police consultation has by now become an established part of development control practice in many local planning authorities, and that while police views on major developments do not always carry the day (because other considerations may be regarded as dominant) they are often on the table when such decisions are taken. This represents a very radical change from the situation of a decade ago, when the policy guidance, the police staff capability and the planner awareness simply did not exist. That is not to say, of course, that there may not be substantial scope for improvement to this process on both sides, and scope also for more meeting of minds on substantive issues based upon research findings about what appears to work on the ground and in what circumstances. An example of the kind of issue that this kind of research-driven approach could help with is the development of policy towards roller-shutter blinds and doors on commercial premises, which were often installed on police advice for security reasons but are often criticised by planners because at night they can make commercial areas look dark and intimidating (see the photographs at Figure 7.1). Manchester City Council's development guide (Manchester City Council, 1997, page 7) puts the matter as follows:

> There is ample evidence that the sensitive combination of good management, good design and community involvement is an effective way of creating more secure environments and of reducing vandalism and the threat of crime and violence. We want to see high-quality crime prevention measures being adopted across the whole City. Alongside this we believe that increased and properly-controlled public use of buildings and commercial facilities will enhance community ownership of the city's buildings and spaces. Manchester can be made a more secure city without resorting to the obtrusive and offensive spectre of universal barbed wire, bollards, shutters and other crime prevention devices. The creation of fortified territories is a confession of defeat. We see the application of many such architectural approaches to public security as negative and an inhibition to the City's creativity.

It may well be that the partnership framework introduced by the Crime and Disorder Act, 1998 will help to bring together some of the views about issues of this nature by providing a more effective framework within which this can take place.

The advice that Police Architectural Liaison Officers (ALOs) give, as reflected in the Secured By Design scheme, is sometimes presented as coming out of the 'target-hardening' school, thereby reflecting a fortress mentality (see, for example, Rudlin and Falk, 1995, page 56). Whilst there is undoubtedly some truth in this, it is also an over-simplification of a complex reality. This is partly because such a perception sees Secured By Design as essentially a static concept coming from a

Figure 7.1 The impact of roller-shutter blinds and doors

These two photographs (taken of the same local shopping parade from more or less the same position at two different times) are typical of the situation to be found in thousands of similar locations throughout Britain. The negative effect on the street scene of shops being closed and roller-shutters being down is obvious from comparing the two photographs. At night, the problem is even worse, because while windows reflect street lights roller-shutters do not.

particular and limited perspective, whereas both in theory and in practice (because there are mechanisms in place for updating the available guidance) this need not be axiomatic. It also overlooks the fact that Architectural Liaison Officers, while starting from a common base, have to deal with a wide range of situations and of people. In giving advice, therefore, they are engaged in processes of social inter-action as well as in debates about building and space layouts. Police ALOs are also individual human beings in their own right; and how they deal with situations and with people will thus vary from person to person. In spite of this, it is certainly possible to summarise what is in essence the common basis for what police advice is aiming to achieve. In relation to domestic burglaries, Pascoe (1993b) identifies two immediate aims of police advice and a longer-term objective. The two imme-diate aims are:

- to reduce the opportunities for crime; and
- to increase the chance of catching an offender.

The longer-term objective is 'to design housing layouts that will encourage resid-ents to bond as a community unit. The community should then take action to defend its territory against criminals, resulting in less crime and an improvement in the quality of life for the residents' (ibid.). Thus, the approach seeks to combine target-hardening at the level of the individual property with more generalised approaches to estate design around the creation of defensible space, well lit and well defined circulation routes, and the concept of natural surveillance. Pascoe reports, however, that the majority of Police ALOs appear to emphasise the target-hardening elements of this rather than the estate layout elements, and to favour one particular form of estate layout (based around culs-de-sac linked by main feeder roads) despite the flexibility offered by the Secured By Design model (ibid.). This finding is perhaps not wholly surprising, since, as a typical police response, it reflects the classic stance of 'situational crime prevention': if a crime target is made as difficult as possible from the criminal's perspective that individual will act ration-ally and not commit the crime (Clarke, 1980; Barr and Pease, 1992). In itself, this is a contentious approach, since it is very doubtful whether it offers a model which can be assumed to apply either to all types of crime or to the complex range of criminal motivation (Pascoe, 1993a; for a more general review of some of the liter-ature in this field, see Pascoe and Topping, 1997). In any event, this approach inevitably raises the issue of the extent to which measures of this nature stop crime or merely deflect it to less secure locations, which is how one might expect the rational criminal to behave (Barr and Pease, 1992). It is perhaps not too surprising, therefore, that an approach as rigid as this will from time to time come into conflict with other views about these matters. The Secured By Design scheme is one of the three case studies presented in Chapter 8, which looks at these debates in more detail.

One particular type of initiative in Britain which has been particularly associated with police advice, and which has been widely introduced in the 1990s, is closed circuit television (CCTV). The reliance on CCTV in towns and city centres to provide security has grown considerably, with strong Government backing including financial support, which continues at the time of writing; for example, under the headline 'Thousands of new cameras filming streets', *The Independent* of 18 January 2000 reports further government funding for CCTV of £170 million over a three-year period. Fyfe (in Pacione, 1997, page 257) records the growth of such schemes in town and city centres from two in 1987, to thirty-nine in 1993, to approximately ninety in 1995. Growth has continued apace since then, and CCTV schemes increasingly are now to be found not just in town and city centres, but in many other types of areas as well. The available research seems to suggest that these schemes are broadly successful in their own terms, in that they both deter some crime and help achieve subsequent arrests once crimes have taken place (Brown, 1995), and also that their reception from the general public has been 'broadly positive' (Honess and Charman, 1992). Superintendent Pearson of the Strathclyde Police, when talking to the Town and Country Planning Summer School for Councillors in 1996 about his experiences with the introduction of a CCTV scheme in Airdrie town centre, described the matter thus:

> Probably (most important) was the effect on community morale. The public felt that at last something constructive was happening within their community. The convergence of interests on behalf of the various authorities was seen as constructive, and the creation of safeguards to ensure the proper management of the system further enhanced the public view of the system. Even criminals appeared to show their support for closed circuit television – at any rate they were heard to observe that because of the presence of cameras, police officers no longer stopped them to ascertain if they had been involved in crime – as the cameras detected the real offenders, ensured they were properly identified, and led to their arrest (Pearson, 1996, page 82).

One of the early decisions taken in relation to the redevelopment of that part of the city centre of Manchester which had been devastated by the IRA bomb of June 1996 was that the response would include a significant extension in the use of CCTV cameras (Kitchen, 2001). The photographs at Figure 7.2 give an impression of the visual appearance of these cameras. This was based upon a view that CCTV cameras were preferable to much 'harder' forms of security that would run the risk of making the City Centre a less attractive place to visit, and also upon the belief

Photograph 1

Photograph 2

Figure 7.2 CCTV Cameras in Manchester city centre after the IRA bomb

Photographs 1 and 2 show externally-mounted CCTV cameras looking respectively down a street and at the entrance to a major facility. One of the issues raised by wall-mounting of this nature is the relationship between the camera and the architectural form of the building.

Photograph 3

Figure 7.2 *continued*

Photograph 3 shows a CCTV camera in an internal pedestrian space (in this case, near the entrance to a retail arcade), where there is much less architectural form to hide its intrusive appearance.

Photograph 4

Figure 7.2 *continued*

Photograph 4, taken at the entrance to another retail arcade, shows that telling people that CCTV is in operation is seen as having a deterrent value in itself.

that there would be a very high level of public acceptance of CCTV in this situation, particularly in the wake of the IRA bomb. To date, both of these propositions
would appear to be correct; or, to put it more accurately as a double-negative,
there is little available evidence to show that they are incorrect.

   Schemes of this nature inevitably give rise to concerns both about the possible displacement of crime to adjacent areas not covered by the scheme
(Dawson, 1994) and more generally about the civil liberties implications of this kind
of surveillance (see, for example, Graham and Marvin, 1996, pages 225–7). Oc
and Tiesdell (1997, pages 130–42), in an overview of the role of CCTV in helping
to create safer city centres, agree that these matters need to be kept under constant review, but conclude that overall the effect of CCTV has been a positive and
well-received one and that it is 'here to stay' as an element of public policy.[4]

DoE Circular 5/94 and other planning guidance

DoE Circular 5/94 (Department of the Environment, 1994) is rather optimistically
entitled 'Planning Out Crime', although in practice it is less a document that tells
planners and others how to do this and rather more a list of issues to think about,
sources of information, and processes that need to be gone through. This is not said
to belittle the value of this advice in its own right, but simply to record the point that
despite its title it is not a recipe for the elimination of crime via the planning process.

   Indeed, paragraph 2 of the Circular puts the contribution of planning in realistic terms, as follows:

> Successful crime prevention often depends upon a wide range of measures.
> Crime prevention initiatives on housing estates, for example, are known to
> require a package of measures which address a range of issues – not just
> crime itself – and involve several agencies. The planning system is one, but only
> one, important factor in a successful crime prevention strategy. Good planning
> alone cannot solve the problem of crime, but when co-ordinated with other
> measures, its contribution can be significant.

The primary significance of the Circular, which represents advice from the Secretary of State to local planning authorities rather than anything which has a more
formal legal status, can probably be summarised in five points:

*   It represented a formal acknowledgement of the relationship between crime
    prevention activities and the planning system which had not previously
    existed in such explicit terms.

- It provided a much more formal status for the work of Police Architectural Liaison Officers in terms of the planning system.
- It urged local planning authorities to reflect crime prevention concerns in their development plans through the incorporation of principles for the design, layout and landscaping of new residential or commercial development, which should aim 'to reassure the public by making crime more difficult to commit, increase the risk of detection and provide people with a safer, more secure environment'. (ibid., paragraph 13)
- It argued for strategic and collaborative approaches to areas, seeing planning and crime prevention as complementary and mutually reinforcing activities.
- It argued for some key concepts, such as mixed uses, that are about the promotion of activity via planning policies and environmental design rather than security measures in relation to buildings, and as such started to open up some of the debates promoted by 'New Urbanists', particularly in relation to town centres (ibid., paragraph 14), as well as covering more familiar ground such as the promotion of CCTV.

This basic approach has continued to be developed in subsequent guidance, alongside the development of the policy ideas which form the next section of this chapter. Many towns and cities, for example, have picked up on ideas such as mixed uses, promoting the night-time economy and 'the 24-hour city' as a means of revitalising the economies of their city centres, implicitly or explicitly accepting in this process the view that the promotion of activity is the best way to deter crime. Some of these, it is now being suggested, are becoming the victims of the success of these policies, in the sense that so much night-time activity has been promoted that the police cannot cope with the sheer volume of lawlessness that is now happening in such areas, often fuelled by over-indulgence in alcohol. *The Independent* of 17 July 2000, under the banner headline 'Planners and police surrender city centres to Britain's mass volume vertical[5] drinkers', reports research showing this as a common phenomenon in parts of Nottingham, Manchester, Liverpool, Newcastle, Leeds, Hull and Birmingham. Manchester City Centre, for example, is reported as receiving an influx of 75,000 people every Friday and Saturday night (as compared with 30,000 in the early 1990s), with the Gay Village being both a major destination and also 'the key hotspot for assaults'. The Greater Manchester Police are reported as having forty officers on street duty in the city centre at such periods plus another fifteen in vehicles, as compared with 3,200 registered door staff in 1999 (although presumably not all of these will be on duty at the same time); as a consequence, effective control of the problems of violence and disorder that have accompanied this growth is said to have passed from the police to the private security system.[6] It might be argued that the headline blaming planners (as well as the police) for this problem is somewhat unreasonable, since planners, while promoting the policy in these areas, were not responsible for decisions about policing them or about the resources this would require; but this example perhaps serves to underline the point which has already been made elsewhere in this book about the often emotive nature of reporting in this field.

Mixed uses, as distinct from the segregation of land uses that often characterised previous generations of planning activities (Coupland, 1997), has been carried forward as an idea into advice about areas other than town centres. The 1999 public consultation draft of the revision of PPG3 (the Planning Policy Guidance note about housing), for example, sees mixed-use development and mixed communities as not only being desirable concepts in their own right but also as an essential component of successful housing areas in the future (Department of the Environment, Transport and the Regions, 1999a, paragraphs 9–12). Some of this is about seeking to increase the density of housing areas, both because of considerations of urban sustainability and in order to generate more activity in such areas with, among other things, benefits in terms of crime prevention because of the natural surveillance this would generate. The final version of PPG3 (Department of the Environment, Transport and the Regions, 2000a) sets a target of achieving residential densities of between thirty and fifty dwellings per hectare net, as compared with the current average of twenty-five dwellings per hectare and an achievement of under twenty dwellings per hectare by more than half of all new housing (ibid., paragraphs 57 and 58). The principles that should guide the design of these housing areas are stated (ibid., paragraph 56) as being:

- create places and spaces with the needs of people in mind, which are attractive, have their own distinct identity but respect and enhance local character;
- promote designs and layouts which are safe and take account of public health, crime prevention and community safety considerations;
- focus on the quality of places and living environments being created and give priority to the needs of pedestrians rather than the movement and parking of vehicles;
- avoid inflexible planning standards and reduce road widths, traffic speeds and promote safer environments for pedestrians; and
- promote the energy efficiency of new housing where possible.

This advice reflects a concern about the continuing spread of urbanisation, which is described in more detail below. But it must also to a degree represent a challenge to the sorts of developments that to date have been taken through the Secured By Design scheme (see above, and also Chapter 8), which have tended to be relatively low density, and also to extant guidance on highways layouts in residential areas where that pre-existing advice has undoubtedly contributed to the achievement of low densities by virtue of the land-take it involves (see below). As PPG3 puts it (ibid., paragraph 57), 'local planning authorities should therefore examine critically the standards they apply to new development, particularly with regard to roads, layout and car parking, to avoid the profligate use of land.'

The argument about urban sustainability in recent years in Britain has been intimately connected with debates about the need in a highly urbanised country for new housing and related developments to meet the changing needs of the population without further large-scale suburban expansion intruding on the countryside on a massive scale. The numbers in the calculations that have been made have changed as this debate has ebbed and flowed, but in essence the argument is unchanged. This is that new housing units need to be made available on a large scale to cope with major shifts in the nature of the family in Britain, producing far more one- and two-person households than has been seen in the past and hence for a given population size a larger number of housing units. Of the order of 4 million new housing units on this basis are said to be needed over a 20/25 year period, and the Government's policy is that at least 60 per cent of these should be constructed on previously used urban land (Department of the Environment, Transport and the Regions, 1998a). This is seen in some quarters as a major opportunity to promote urban living based upon the application of 'New Urbanist' principles because of the densities of development it will require (Rudlin and Falk, 1999, pages 125–46); others, however, have been more cautious in arguing that the extant problems of education, crime and social welfare to be found in Britain's cities will need to be tackled more effectively than they have been to date and that the merits of urban living will need to be promoted to a largely sceptical public if such a policy is to succeed (Breheny and Ross, 1998). Nevertheless, there is a strongly urban push to British policy about meeting housing needs in sustainable ways at present, and this inevitably raises issues about how urban crime is tackled. Indeed, this linkage between urban crime and sustainability may become a key to the need, for which we have been arguing, for planning and planners to take the relationship between crime and the design and organisation of the built environment more seriously, since if planners see tackling the problem of urban crime as an integral part of working towards sustainability (which is now a central theme of British planning practice) they may find it much easier to conceive of work of this nature as a mainstream activity.

This link is taken further in the reworking of the companion volume to PPG3 offering design guidance in relation to residential roads and footpaths (Department of the Environment, Transport and the Regions, 1998b), as follows:

The design of housing layouts can make a major contribution to both the prevention of crime and alienating the fear of crime. Most crime is opportunistic, and common sense measures can make an area secure for both people and property. The main points to be borne in mind are:

- Crime depends upon concealment. Well used or overlooked streets and spaces make the criminal feel uncomfortable and exposed.
- Anonymous and uncared for spaces can cause long-term problems. The design of layouts should provide a clear definition of ownership and responsibility for every part of a development.
- Clear and direct routes through an area for all forms of movement are desirable, but should not undermine the 'defensible space' of particular neighbourhoods.

. . . In terms of detailed design, the principal means of crime prevention are:

- Natural surveillance: neighbours should be able to see each other's houses, and where cars are parked outside (at front or back), owners should be able to see them.
- Routes that are overlooked and busy. If separate footpaths or cycle tracks form part of a layout they should be on routes which generate high levels of movement and should be as short as possible. Long, indirect pedestrian and cycle links may feel threatening for users and may provide escape routes for criminals.
- Play areas or communal space located where they are well-related to surrounding areas and are overlooked. They should not be regarded as just a use for parcels of land left over after the rest of the layout has been drawn up.

The development of a good community spirit is the most obvious way of deterring crime, but that cannot be relied on as a solution on its own. Mutual support works best when the design of an area has taken account of security issues at the outset (ibid., page 46).

As noted above, however, some of this advice does represent quite a challenge to hitherto conventional traffic engineering views about such issues as road widths and visibility splays at junctions, which have a major impact on many residential layouts, and indeed as questioning the relative significance of the cul-de-sac which, as we have already seen, has been a favoured form of layout for many Police Architectural Liaison Officers. As yet, however, the advice cannot be said to have fully resolved these issues, since it both begins to shape these challenges and at the same time persists with highway layout advice of the type it is questioning, although it has begun the process of re-examining the extent to which highway layout standards need to be amended if its other objectives are to be achieved (ibid., pages 50–75).

The Urban Task Force chaired by Lord Rogers of Riverside (Urban Task Force, 1999) urges the Government to take this further, by arguing that crime reduction strategies under the Crime and Disorder Act, 1998 ought to include six principles:

- policies and guidance for 'designing out crime'. The key elements here are seen as being 'the creation of lively areas with public spaces that are well overlooked, interconnected streets and a fine grained mix of uses with plenty of windows and doors that face onto streets';
- joint action on a multi-agency basis;
- engaging residents and businesses in the fight against crime;
- making ways of using statutory orders for tackling particular kinds of crimes as easy as possible;
- bringing local services together to focus on crime and vandalism 'hotspots';
- improving public confidence in the police (ibid., page 127).

What is clear from all of this is that ideas about how urban areas, and particularly residential areas, should be laid out – ideas that have had the status of 'conventional wisdom' for some time – are now being challenged in contemporary Britain. Considerations of crime prevention and public safety are an important component of these debates, treating these matters not as free-standing issues but as component elements in thinking about the planning of urban areas. The fact that Section 17 of the Crime and Disorder Act, 1998 imposes a new duty on local planning authorities to exercise their functions with due regard both to the effect on and the need to do all they can to prevent crime and disorder will reinforce this relationship, because it will focus attention on how these matters impact upon design policies and the operation of the development control function. At the time of writing, it is probably fair to say that the full import of this new duty has not yet been fully understood by all local planning authorities; but it is to be hoped that as this process unfolds it will pay particular attention to local circumstances and will not be turned into a set of rigid rules that are applied irrespective of those circumstances and the views and wishes of local people. Much of this experience is likely to be garnered in practice through local initiatives across the country which have an experimental component to them. One such case, for much of the 1990s, was the redevelopment of large parts of Hulme in Manchester, which has received a considerable amount of both critical and uncritical attention and which has played a part in helping to shape some of the ideas discussed above. The story of the 1990s redevelopment of Hulme is one of the detailed case studies in Chapter 8.

REGENERATION, SOCIAL INCLUSION AND THE PARTNERSHIP APPROACH

As has already been indicated through the examples of the Nottingham and the Dearne Valley City Challenge initiatives, the urban regeneration process in Britain in recent years has started to tackle crime and related issues because typically the residents of those areas when asked tend to put such matters at or near the top of the agenda for action. There is some evidence to suggest that this has not always been as effective as was hoped, however, as the final evaluation of the City Challenge Programme (Department of the Environment, Transport and the Regions, 1999b) concludes that crime projects were the least successful of the common types of projects carried out through the programme in terms of delivering targeted outcomes. Perhaps this is a useful cautionary reminder about the limitations of the 'quick-fix' approach all too likely to be adopted in short-term initiatives when dealing with something as endemic as crime.

Another characteristic of the regeneration process in Britain throughout the 1990s has been its emphasis on multi-sectoral partnerships (Bailey, 1995). This approach has been carried through into the Crime and Disorder Act, 1998, which places an equal duty on local authorities and the police to join together and work with others to:

- review crime and disorder problems in their area;
- publish and seek views on their findings; and
- put in place a strategy, taking account of comments, with targets for reducing crime and disorder in the area.

The early experiences of this in Salford, Greater Manchester, constitute one of the detailed case studies developed in Chapter 8. Although this process was the component of the Act that attracted most attention, the fact that Section 17 of the Act also imposed a new duty on local planning authorities to exercise their functions with due regard both to the effect on and the need to do all they can to prevent crime and disorder may also turn out to be of some importance. At the time of writing, this new duty does not appear to have registered very significantly with the British planning community, but since this approach is also followed up in the

Urban Policy White Paper of 2000 (see below) it seems unlikely that it will be left simply as a rhetorical stance by Government.

The most distinctive element that the Labour Government elected in 1997 has brought to all of this is probably the work of the Social Exclusion Unit. In its first major report (Social Exclusion Unit, 1998), the Unit describes the problem of social exclusion[7] as follows:

> Over the last generation, this has become a more divided country. While most areas have benefited from rising living standards, the poorest neighbourhoods have tended to become more rundown, more prone to crime, and more cut off from the labour market. The national picture conceals pockets of intense deprivation where the problems of unemployment and crime are acute and hopelessly tangled up with poor health, housing and education. They have become no go areas for some and no exit zones for others. In England as a whole the evidence we have suggests there are several thousand neighbourhoods and estates whose condition is critical, or soon could be (ibid., page 9).

Social inclusion is therefore the process of tackling the multiplicity of problems exhibited by and in these areas so that they become less separated off from the condition of the rest of the country. The key ideas about tackling crime, as part of a comprehensive attack on this problem, are:

- making crime reduction in the very worst areas a high priority for the police, local authorities and others by, amongst other things, setting targets;
- instituting locally run neighbourhood warden[8] schemes, in cooperation with the police, and empowering such wardens to get involved in a wide range of tasks (such as making environmental improvements) which are relevant to the aim of reducing crime and the fear of crime;
- focusing on anti-social behaviour as a major source of crime and fear of crime;
- tackling racist crimes as a particular subset of anti-social behaviour (Social Exclusion Unit, 2000, paragraphs 6.8–6.18).

The 'National Strategy Action Plan' (Social Exclusion Unit, 2001) that has emerged from this work takes this thinking further. The Foreword by Prime Minister Tony Blair (ibid., page 5) sets out why the approach to the renewal of poor neighbourhoods is different to previous approaches:

> First, the true scale of the problem is being addressed – not the tens but the hundreds of severely deprived neighbourhoods. Second, the focus is not just on housing and the physical fabric of neighbourhoods, but the fundamental

problems of worklessness, crime and poor public services – poor schools, too few GPs and policing. Third, the Strategy harnesses the hundreds of billions of pounds spent by the key Government departments, rather than relying on one-off regeneration spending. Fourth, the Strategy puts in place new ideas including Neighbourhood Management and Local Strategic Partnerships for empowering residents and getting public, private and voluntary organisations to work in partnership.

This approach is translated into two long-term goals (ibid., page 8):

- In all the poorest neighbourhoods, to have common goals of lower worklessness and crime, and better health, skills, housing and physical environment.
- To narrow the gap on these measures between the most deprived neighbourhoods and the rest of the country.

Throughout, the Strategy stresses the holistic nature of the approach that needs to be adopted, emphasising both the need to think about problems and solutions in inter-related ways rather than as the separate prerogatives of individual players, and the need for the processes adopted to be as inclusive as possible in terms of agencies and communities. The key crime reduction target set is that by 2005 domestic burglary will have been reduced by 25 per cent, with no local authority district having a rate more than three times the national average (ibid., page 30), which is also the target contained within the Urban Policy White Paper, 2000 (see below). The specific 'new policies, funding and targets' listed under the heading of 'tackling crime' are as follows (ibid., page 35):

- Use the Crime and Disorder Reduction Partnerships and the Strategies they produce to spearhead action towards ambitious national targets, which include not only the domestic burglary target described above, but also reducing vehicle crime by 30 per cent by 2004 and reducing robbery in the principal cities by 24 per cent by 2005.
- Focus on racist crime and incidents by developing effective solutions to local problems, with appropriate national policy and practice guidance and support.
- Develop youth justice pilot projects, and target re-offending amongst young people and ex-prisoners.

While in specific terms these initiatives do not talk explicitly abut the relationships between crime and the design of the built environment, the emphasis they place upon enabling and supporting action within an appropriate local context involving all the key players, together with the overall emphasis on neighbourhood management and strategic partnership, surely represents a major opportunity for these kinds of initiatives sitting alongside others to be developed as part of a coherent strategy. This sense of opportunity is reinforced by Appendix F of the Strategy (ibid., pages 94–116), which picks out examples of good practice in terms of the common goals of less worklessness, less crime, better skills, less ill-health and better housing and physical environment. Of the fourteen examples listed there under the banner of crime-related initiatives (ibid., pages 98–100), several clearly have a strong environmental component to them, and they demonstrate that it is possible to make significant improvements relatively quickly by a combination of partnership approaches and targeting particular problems. The value of this is not merely that it illustrates the variety of what can be done within the framework that has now been established, but also the commitment that it involves to publicising good practice so that localities can benefit from each other's experience.

The partnership approach, particularly in relation to deprived neighbourhoods with high levels of crime in comparison with national averages, has also been a significant component in recent years of the process of distributing national funding available for local crime prevention work. Partnerships have been able during this period to access both Home Office and Department of the Environment, Transport and the Regions funding for work of this type, and while there have been some difficulties with this in terms of take-up rates it seems likely that this kind of targeted approach will continue to be a feature of practice in this field.

This approach will therefore be a further layer in the accumulation of public policy positions looking at these sorts of issues detailed in this chapter. This ensures that crime and environmental design concerns will be looked at increasingly as part of multi-agency and multi-functional initiatives, working with the local community attempting to tackle the problems of Britain's most deprived areas in holistic ways. This is a challenging agenda; although some experience has been accumulated in relation to some of this, it has to be said that for many ideas there is much pioneering work to be done and hopefully much careful recording of what appears to succeed and what does not, to avoid a process of endless reinvention of the wheel.

THE URBAN POLICY WHITE PAPER, 2000

The Urban Policy White Paper (Department of the Environment, Transport and the Regions, 2000b) provided a major and long-awaited opportunity to pull all this policy material together into an integrated statement showing among other things how crime-reduction initiatives are seen in an urban policy context. It saw the five key issues facing Britain's town and cities as being:

- to accommodate the new homes needed by 2021;
- to encourage people to remain in and move back into urban areas;
- to tackle the poor quality of life and lack of opportunity in certain urban areas;
- to strengthen the factors in all urban areas which will enhance their economic success;
- to make sustainable urban living practical, affordable and attractive (ibid., page 29).

The vision that was presented in response was:

Our vision is of towns, cities and suburbs which offer a high quality of life and opportunity for all, not just the few. We want to see:

- *people shaping the future* of their community, supported by strong and truly representative local leaders;
- people living in *attractive, well kept towns and cities* which use space and buildings well;
- good design and planning which makes it practical to live in a *more environmentally sustainable* way, with less noise, pollution and traffic congestion;
- towns and cities able to *create and share prosperity*, investing to help all their citizens reach their full potential; and
- *good quality services* – health, education, housing, transport, finance, shopping, leisure and protection from crime – that meet the needs of people and businesses wherever they are.

This urban renaissance will benefit everyone, making towns and cities vibrant and successful, and protecting the countryside from development pressure (ibid., page 30).

The White Paper then in effect runs through the action it sees as being necessary in order to deliver against this agenda. Although issues around crime and public perceptions of safety in urban areas could be said to be related to most if not all of these points, little is specifically said about these matters until the consideration of crime under the heading of 'quality services and opportunities for all'. This includes setting the specific target of reducing domestic burglary by 25 per cent by 2005, with no local authority area having more than three times the national average (ibid., page 111). It also includes the specific commitment to make crime prevention a key objective for planning and to review the advice contained in DoE Circular 5/94 (ibid., page 120), although it actually says very little about how this will be done and concentrates instead on summarising and extending existing initiatives. For example, it describes the key elements of a £400 million crime reduction programme which was already under way to support innovative work in local communities, many of which are in high crime urban areas, as follows:

- a national scheme to fund projects in areas containing 2 million homes in crime hot-spots, in order to reduce domestic burglary;
- the biggest-ever expansion of CCTV schemes (in both residential as well as commercial areas);
- programmes to prevent children from becoming involved in crime, and to reduce school truancy and exclusions;
- funding to support the establishment of neighbourhood warden schemes to complement the work of police and local authorities;
- providing drug-arrest referral schemes in all police custody suites, to encourage drug-misusing offenders into treatment and out of crime (ibid.).

Nevertheless, the commitment to making crime prevention a key objective for planning may prove to be a watershed, in the sense that it moves the position from advice given in a Circular (which planners can and do ignore, if they choose) to one where a requirement exists. The changes introduced through the Crime and Disorder Act, 1998 began this process of moving from advice to a degree of compulsion, although as we have noted above in their own terms they do not at the time of writing appear to have had much impact on planners. If this approach is followed up by a re-write of Circular 5/94 which is less 'all things to all men' and much more pointed both in its advice and in its recognition of some of the conflicts that exist in some of the extant policy theorising and guidance in this area, however, this situation could well change quite quickly.

It is clear that the Urban Policy White Paper is placing a considerable amount of reliance on the local partnership mechanisms established under the Crime and Disorder Act 1998, one case study example of which can be found in Chapter 8. It records the position on this at the time of publication as being that 376 crime and disorder reduction partnerships were up and running in England and Wales (ibid.), which means that the vast majority of local authority areas were covered by such a partnership at that time, albeit with variable amounts of progress having been made. One of the key recommendations in the White Paper, however, is the creation of Local Strategic Partnerships to 'bring together the local authority, all service providers (such as schools, the police and health and social services), local businesses, the full range of community groups and the voluntary sector' (ibid., page 34), to:

- develop a Community Strategy to cover the local authority area. This should look at all aspects that contribute to quality of life together; identify strengths and weaknesses; and set out a long-term vision that has been agreed with all the key stakeholders;
- agree priorities for action and monitor local performance against agreed local indicators taking into account national and regional targets; and
- co-ordinate the work of more local or more specific partnerships dealing with particular neighbourhoods or issues (ibid.).

Clearly, therefore, this is another over-arching mechanism to which the work of crime and disorder reduction partnerships will be expected to relate. It remains to be seen whether all of this in the different localities where it will be operational provides an effective local framework, or risks degenerating into a multiplicity of conflicting partnership initiatives which inhibit action, create coordination problems and generate a new bureaucracy of their own.

CONCLUSIONS

This chapter has presented a picture of a national policy framework which has developed considerably over the past decade or so, and may well continue to do so, and also one of a ferment of ideas through which these processes are attempting to steer. Figure 7.3 tries to present this in a simplified form, so that readers can see at a glance the key national policy imperatives that have been impacting upon thinking about crime and the design of the built environment.

Taken together, the range of influences summarised in Figure 7.3 (which is not exhaustive) represents a very significant central government policy push in recent years that marks the British approach out from that of the USA. Indeed, as we have already said, a defining characteristic of the British situation, in comparison with the American situation presented in Chapter 5, is that it has this strong component of central government policy together with a series of mechanisms that to varying degrees of effectiveness ensure that it is followed through at the local level.

At the time of writing, a great deal of work had been done at the national level to put these elements of the approach in place, and at the local level some useful individual initiatives had been taken and the general process of beginning to put into practice the requirements of the Crime and Disorder Act, 1998 had

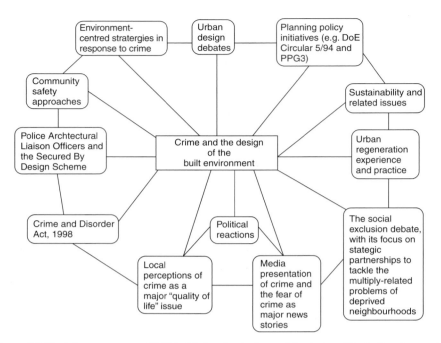

Figure 7.3 Key influences on recent British debates about crime and the design of the built environment

commenced. Thus a framework existed, but a great deal remained to be done to achieve the benefits at the local level that this framework has been assembled in order to seek. Although the planning and environmental design contribution is only a small part of this process, its status is now such that it is acknowledged to be an important component. This suggests both that the opportunities to achieve beneficial changes in these terms over the next few years might be quite considerable and that the expectations that have been raised as a result of setting this up are also on perhaps a greater scale than has been the case in the past. There is undoubtedly still work to be done, however, to set out unambiguously what is actually going to be the 'official' advice about the relationship between environmental design concerns and effective crime prevention. As we have noted, there are some tensions in the range of advice that currently exists, for example between highway layout standards, desires to raise urban densities, the precepts that flow from the Secured By Design scheme and issues around the quality of the urban places we are seeking to create if we are to encourage people to choose to live in cities. The need here is to acknowledge that these tensions exist and then to resolve them, rather than to endorse each of these stances as if they were all automatically comfortable bedfellows. The commitment to revisit the guidance currently provided in DoE Circular 5/94 is clearly an opportunity to do precisely this, which needs to be grasped. That challenge will need to be worked through not just at the (inevitably rather generalised) level of national policy guidance but also all over the country in terms of what is actually done on the ground. If this is not done, and the planning system is expected to deliver beneficial changes as a result of the duties that it acquired under the Crime and Disorder Act, 1998 without this accompanying clarity of strategic thinking, there is a risk that all of this will merely programme the system to achieve less than it would otherwise have been capable of doing.

Chapter 8 has a more local emphasis, at any rate in two of the three case studies that it presents, in order to illustrate contemporary British practice at the local scale in more detail than has been possible in this chapter. The three case studies are the Secured By Design award scheme run by the police, the process of responding to the Crime and Disorder Act, 1998 in Salford through the establishment of a partnership and the preparation of a crime reduction strategy, and the process throughout much of the 1990s of redeveloping Hulme in Manchester in accordance with design guidelines in which concerns about the relationships between crime and environmental design were a major and explicit component. All three of these cases show something of the process of change in British policy and practice in this field that has been taking place in recent years; but all three also show how much still remains to be achieved.

NOTES

1   We have referred in note 2 to Chapter 2 to the terminological and data problems surrounding the use of the expression 'Britain' in some of the literature. Exactly the same issues also arise when discussing policy and practice. For the avoidance of doubt, therefore, when we are discussing British policy and practice in this chapter in terms both of formal legislation and of the work of Government Departments, we mean policy and practice in England and Wales. As far as the remainder of the United Kingdom is concerned, policing in Northern Ireland has been regarded to date as being something of a special case because of the long-standing nature of 'the troubles', with a consequent emphasis in particular upon the fortification of what have been seen as key locations/targets, although hopefully the future will be more normalised in these terms than the immediate past has been. Scotland has not thus far seen much distinctive policy and practice development that would actually mark it out from the initiatives that we describe in this chapter, although the process of devolution with its creation of a separate Scottish Parliament provides an opportunity to do this in future if that is the wish in Scotland. To a lesser extent the same could also be said of Wales, although the remit of the Welsh Assembly is narrower than that of the Scottish Parliament. The title pages of the National Strategy for Neighbourhood Renewal (Social Exclusion Unit, 2001) give expression to this relationship by saying: 'This National Strategy applies to England only,

but will be drawn upon by the administrations in Scotland, Wales and Northern Ireland in compiling their distinctive strategies.'

2   See also the Salford survey in the case study in Chapter 8 on how Salford responded to the requirements of the Crime and Disorder Act, 1998.

3   One of the problems with which we have had to grapple in writing a book seeking to introduce transatlantic perspectives is that terms can take on different meanings in the USA and the UK without those differences being commonly understood. The term 'target-hardening' is a good example of this phenomenon. In the USA, it is usually used to describe one component of a spectrum of action, which is to do with making a building more secure to try to make it more difficult for a criminal to penetrate and to make criminal access and subsequent escape as difficult as possible. In the UK, particularly in recent times, it has come to be used in some quarters as a more all-embracing term for an approach which emphasises physical security at or near potential points of entry to a building, to contrast it with the approach of the 'new urbanists' which emphasises human activity, permeability, and all aspects of natural surveillance as key components of the overall design approach. Thus, the former approach is presented as being narrowly focused on the individual building irrespective of the implications of this for the built environment of the area as a whole, whereas the latter approach is presented as giving primacy to the type of built environment being created. In some such instances, 'target-hardening' appears to have become a term of abuse, seen to be associated with a 'fortress mentality', rather than a recognition that there may be perfectly sensible things that can be done to make a building a harder target for a criminal to penetrate without necessarily sacrificing the quality of the living or the working environment (see Crouch, Shaftoe and Fleming, 1999). Except where otherwise indicated, we use the term 'target-hardening' in the US sense, and not as a term that is intended to have pejorative implications. This particular terminological concern is an issue in some of the literature about the Secured By Design scheme, and so we return to it as part of that case study in Chapter 8.

4   In the view of the authors, this is one of the most striking differences in practice between the USA and the UK. The 'civil liberties' concerns have been much more forcefully and extensively expressed in the USA, which as a consequence has seen nothing like the British large-scale growth of CCTV in public areas and also no equivalent to the volume of public-funding support that has been made available for this in Britain. It should perhaps also be recorded that the concern about the displacement effect of new initiatives in the USA has also generally tended to be more widespread than has been the case in Britain. More generally, there is no real equivalent in the USA to the role played in Britain by police Architectural Liaison Officers, and no equivalent whatsoever to the formal endorsement of this role in the planning system by the Government. We return to this issue in Chapter 9.

5   The reference to 'vertical' here is because many of the outlets referred to operate on the basis of providing standing-room rather than the more traditional sitting-down spaces. This enables more people to be accommodated in a given amount of space but (it is argued) contributes to the tendency for violence to erupt.

6   The primary tasks of 'registered door staff' in Britain are to control access to the premises (for example, to exclude obviously under-aged or already incapacitated drinkers) and to try to deal with any trouble that might arise as swiftly as possible. Thus, they work on behalf of the owners or operators of the establishment in question, and their job is about the smooth operation of that business rather than about any responsibility on behalf of the community as a whole for general issues of public safety in the locality. This can be presented as a form of privatisation of hitherto public functions, although the police arguably never performed these functions on a systematic basis for individual establishments. The scale of this is nothing like the scale of privatisation of security that has been taking place in the USA, however, through developments such as the out-of-town shopping complex and the gated community (see, for example, McLaughlin and Muncie, 1999).

7   While the ideas that sit behind the concept of 'social exclusion' will be relatively well understood in the USA, and perhaps particularly in some of its more socially polarised cities, the term itself is not in common currency. Similarly, while many of the components of the action needed to achieve social inclusion can be found in American political rhetoric and applied policies, it would be hard to argue that a comprehensive approach to this issue driven by the Federal Government exists in a manner that is comparable to that found in Britain. Indeed, it is unlikely that a Federal Government in the USA would find this an easy task to accomplish, even if it were minded to attempt it, because this would tread on jealously guarded territory at State and City levels.

8   Similarly, there is no precise parallel in the USA in terms of national policy prescription to the idea of members of the community working with the police and acting as neighbourhood wardens, although at the local level the USA exhibits a wide range of community-involvement initiatives.

activities, not 'zoned' but integrated, offering a wide variety of uses for people to live, shop, work and relax locally, and bringing new income to the local economy. We want to create a clear urban framework which produces streets, squares and buildings of variety and quality, but within a coherent urban whole, thus welcoming both visitors and residents into and through the area. New developments need to create a density of people and activity sufficient to sustain the local economy and avoid 'dead' and empty streets and public spaces. Particular regard needs to be paid to designing secure and 'self policing' developments, where neighbourliness is encouraged and patterns of life are established which can make the area self-sustaining for generations to come (ibid., page 3).

The contrast between what the SBD scheme is saying and what 'New Urbanist' thinking, as expressed in the Hulme Development Guide, is arguing for should be clear from comparing these two extracts from the latter (respectively, about permeability and about activity) with Table 8.1. It is difficult to see how SBD guidance, for example, would have been likely to have produced the kinds of densities of development in Hulme illustrated in the photographs in Figure 8.3. This perhaps serves to reinforce the point that the SBD scheme is regarded as being controversial in some quarters, notwithstanding its formal commendation in Paragraph 10 of DoE Circular 5/94 (see Chapter 6), and its re-presentation in some aspects to link into the thrust of Government policy in the second half of the 1990s. It is, of course, important to make the point that although there is a clear clash of ideas here, that does not mean that both cannot co-exist. It is simply that they are different, and will result in different kinds of environments. Indeed, it is possible to argue that it is inappropriate to regard one as being 'right' and therefore the other as being 'wrong' (as the protagonists for both sides have from time to time found it convenient to do), and instead to see the approaches as producing a range of choices that people ought to have available to them in or on the edges of our cities if urban/metropolitan living is to be encouraged. In this latter context, there can be no denying the marketing value to developers of the ability to use the SBD logo in their advertising and their promotional literature once they have gained SBD approval for their development, not least because (as Chapter 2 has already shown) there is an association between high crime levels and some urban areas. The 'principles' paper on the SBD website, at paragraph 2, is quick to present this 'marketing opportunity' as a further argument to developers about the value to them of the SBD scheme.

In essence, the way in which the SBD scheme works is straightforward. Guidelines are published which relate to particular types of development; pre-application discussions take place between the Architectural Liaison Officer of the local police force and the intending applicant or agent (at initial sketch plan stage, and before a planning application is submitted to the local planning authority); a formal application is then made with a set of documents specified for this purpose and the specified fee is paid; provisional approval is given once the ALO is satisfied that the necessary standards have been agreed and will be met 'to enable the developer to promote Secured By Design in any marketing strategy' (see 'Applications for SBD' on the Secured by Design website). An SBD certificate will not be issued, however, until a site inspection has taken place upon completion of the building works and has shown them to be of a satisfactory standard.

A key element of this process is clearly the publication of guidelines about particular types of development, and it is also these publications which give the best current indication of what ALO advice is likely to be on development proposals irrespective of whether or not they are being submitted for SBD approval. At the time of preparing this case study, the Secured By Design website contained guidelines in respect of four types of residential development (refurbishments, new homes, multi-storey dwellings and sheltered accommodation), and it also contained SBD application forms for residential development and for commercial development. In addition, guidelines were available for the SBD scheme for secured car parking in a separate publication costing £25, and so these were not on the website. To illustrate the ground covered in guidance of this nature and its level of detail, Tables 8.2 and 8.3 summarise from this material what is being said about sheltered housing and about commercial development.

Table 8.2 SBD guidance – sheltered housing

As well as meeting the general SBD New Homes standard developments must include the following:
1 A good lighting scheme that covers adequately all potential areas of risk with lighting that switches automatically
2 There should be discussions with the ALO to determine whether lockable gates to parking areas/garages are needed
3 The main communal entrance door should be part of an access control system at least linked to the warden's office and ideally linked to each individual unit
4 Other commercial access doors (excluding fire doors) are to be agreed with the ALO, particularly in terms of their locking systems
5 Final communal fire exit doors must meet all the appropriate standards, and must allow residents (bearing in mind their particular characteristics) to escape while being strong enough to keep out intruders
6 The unit front door must have an agreed locking system which provides entry by key only
7 Consideration should be given to a 24-hour monitored help alarm system

Source: Authors' summary of the Sheltered Accommodation SBD guidance on the SBD website, at http://www.securedbydesign.com

Table 8.3 SBD guidance – commercial developments

The ground covered by the application form for commercial developments is as follows:

1   development design, covering issues such as the approach adopted to defensible space, boundary treatments, open views to and from frontages, access and parking arrangements, possible climbing and access points by criminals, mains services and natural surveillance
2   has CCTV been considered and if so of what kind?
3   perimeter treatment is to be agreed with the ALO
4   an illumination scheme is needed for the entire site designed to deny criminals the advantage of being able to operate unobserved during the hours of darkness
5   where cash transfer points are needed, factors about their security are listed for consideration
6   vehicle parking and access arrangements need to be subject to good natural surveillance or inaccessible to intruders, to be controlled, and to have different types separated (visitors, staff and goods, with the latter having a secured compound)
7   outbuildings also need to be covered by the security arrangements
8   the design of the building should have attack-resistance materials, straight sight lines without deep recesses, no features which provide easy access to a roof or to windows, and recessed external pipework
9   a series of detailed specifications are provided about doors
10 a series of detailed specifications are provided about shutters for goods storage areas
11 design principles for roof lights are dealt with
12 sets down a series of tests so as to minimise the likelihood of entry via a roof
13 covers window design, starting from the statement that glazing to industrial units should be kept to a minimum
14 sets down detailed standards for intruder alarms

Source: Authors' summary of the content of the SBD Commercial Development application form on the SBD website, at http://www.securedbydesign.com

It can be seen from Tables 8.2 and 8.3 that some elements of these specifications are detailed and prescriptive, while others offer guidance about the sorts of things that would be acceptable and allow for the exercise of discretion through discussion between the ALO and the applicant. Some of this content would probably be regarded as non-controversial, and indeed as providing common-sense guidance about sensible measures to make premises secure and to avoid intruder access. But some of it may from time to time be more controversial, perhaps especially where it affects a particular design approach so as to change it significantly. For example, the approach in the past has been criticised as reflecting a 'fortress mentality', which pays too much attention to defensive measures that derive from the 'target-hardening' philosophy and not enough attention to the qualities of place that derive from its application or indeed to whether people would actually choose to live and work in such surroundings (Rudlin and Falk, 1995, page 56). Readers might like to test for themselves how they think the guidance summarised in Tables 8.2 and 8.3 stands up against this latter criticism; and they may well conclude, as we have already argued, that a great deal may depend upon how these guidelines are actually interpreted in specific situations by police ALOs. Another example of the more controversial aspects of the guidance might be the bald statement that glazing to industrial units should be kept to a minimum; this might meet security requirements, but might make some industrial buildings aesthetically challenging (as indeed in the real world some of them are), and might also raise questions about what such a building would be like to work in.

Pascoe and Topping (1997), in a review of the basis of the scheme as it stood at that time (and the differences between SBD as it was then and its contemporary form are not particularly significant), saw it as a combination of the thinking derived from the 'situational crime prevention' approach and assumptions about the behaviour of burglars as 'rational opportunists'. Regarding the first of these two elements, they conclude that there was a good degree of fit with the available literature except that the emphasis on 'target-hardening' found in the practical operation of the SBD scheme was greater than could be justified from the published research evidence. This reinforces the conclusion reached by Pascoe (1993b) to the effect that police Architectural Liaison Officers tended to empha- sise the target-hardening elements of the SBD standards rather than the other ele- ments when working on individual schemes. As far as the second element of the scheme is concerned (the assumption that burglars are 'rational opportunists'), Pascoe and Topping argue that while there is a range of views about this and also a range of observable criminal behaviour, the assumption fits broadly with the out- comes of available behavioural research on offender decision-making. This rein- forces the results of previous work by Pascoe (1993a), based upon interviews with burglars, which shows them as typically looking for environmental 'cues' to enable judgments to be made about risk, reward and ease of entry. This work also argues that the decision to attempt a burglary is based upon 'limited rationality', in the sense that the reading of cues is instinctive and the burglar's own previous experi- ences influence his judgement. Thus, Pascoe and Topping conclude that although there is not a perfect fit between the precepts of the SBD model and the available research evidence, the degree of fit was such as to suggest that in its own terms it had a reasonable chance of success. Their plea was for more empirical research to investigate not only what happened over time to SBD schemes but also to look in more detail at the success or otherwise of some of its individual components.

Topping and Pascoe (2000) have subsequently responded to their own challenge by producing an evaluation of the available evidence about the success of
the SBD scheme in countering household burglary. Their broad conclusion is that
the ideas behind SBD are seen as being congruent with the thrust of much policy
development in recent years, and that in various ways the scheme is being more
widely implemented. The (limited) amount of post hoc evaluative evidence that is
available also seems to support the view that in its own terms the scheme is
working: the two recent large-sample studies that have been done do seem to
show statistically significant reductions in the incidence of burglary and in the fear
of crime, and also improvements in residents' perceptions of their quality of life.
Topping and Pascoe's conclusion (ibid., page 77) remains a cautious one,
however, because what remains unclear is which parts of the scheme are having
the desired effects. Critical to this is likely to be an improved appreciation of the
processes of implementation, which unpicks not only the bundle of ideas pulled
together within the SBD template, in order to understand the predictive powers of
each, but also the ways in which the package is applied to the specific circumstances of individual sites, including via the exercise of discretion by the parties to
this process.

Another recent British study which can be seen as making a plea for more
empirical research (Cozens et al., 2000) looks at how different key players (in this
case, burglars, planning professionals and police officers) perceive different types
of housing design in terms of territoriality, surveillance and image. The research
was based upon responses to photographs of five different types of house design
(detached, semi-detached, terraced, low-rise, high-rise), with variations reflecting
maintenance standards (well maintained or poorly maintained). While there were
some differences in the responses obtained in terms of whether the image presented by the house type in question was positive, neutral or negative, there was
also a considerable measure of agreement. So, all three groups perceived
detached housing in positive terms whether well or poorly maintained, and the
same result was also obtained for well maintained semi-detached and terraced
housing. Similarly all three groups saw poorly maintained semi-detached housing,
well maintained high-rise housing and poorly maintained low-rise housing in negative terms. So, the responses to seven of the ten types were identical. The differences were in respect of poorly maintained terraced housing (seen in negative
terms by burglars and planners and as neutral by police respondents), well maintained low-rise housing (seen in positive terms by burglars and in neutral terms by
planners and the police) and poorly maintained high-rise housing (seen in negative
terms by burglars and in neutral terms by planners and the police). Clearly, these
expressed preferences will reflect the different perspectives of the three groups,
but as a generalisation they tend to be more positive towards 'traditional' housing

Table 8.4 Hierarchy of vulnerability to crime of house types

Combined ranking	House type	Burglar rankings	Planner rankings	Police rankings
1	poorly maintained low-rise flats	1	1	3
2	well maintained high-rise flats	4	2	1
3	poorly maintained high-rise flats	2=	5	2
4	poorly maintained terraced houses	2=	4	4
5	poorly maintained semi-detached houses	5	3	5
6	well maintained low-rise flats	7	6	6
7	well maintained terraced houses	6	7	7
8	well maintained detached houses	10	8	8
9	poorly maintained detached houses	8=	9	9
10	well maintained semi-detached houses	8=	10	10

Source: developed from Cozens et al. (2000) Figure 4

types (detached, semi-detached and terraced) than they are towards more 'modern' housing types (low-rise and high-rise multiple-occupation blocks). This appears to be confirmed by the results obtained when respondents were asked to comment on these housing types in terms of their vulnerability to crime. While again there were some differences between the responses of the three groups, the most striking component of the results is that they show a very similar hierarchy in terms of the perceived vulnerability of the various housing types. From most vulnerable (rank order 1) to least vulnerable (rank order 10), the hierarchy this produces is shown in Table 8.4.

As well as suggesting that in terms of their vulnerability to crime 'traditional' housing types are seen in more positive terms than are 'modern' housing types, this hierarchy also reinforces the general importance of maintenance standards in reducing perceptions of risk of being on the receiving end of crime. These results can be seen as being broadly supportive of the kind of thinking that drives the Secured By Design scheme, not just in terms of the views of police and planners (which could perhaps be explained in terms of their pre-existing 'buy-in' to this type of thinking), but also by virtue of the broad similarity of the results achieved from these two groups and from burglars.

Finally, of course, if the developer wants the award (and as has already been said, the marketing advantages of this to the developer are fairly obvious) then the developer has to meet the standard. Since the developer will also need to have in mind the interests of those end-users of the development who will either purchase or rent it – because otherwise the developer's own commercial considerations could be at risk – there could be said to be at least an element of representation of those interests in discussion between the developer and the ALO, with the developer as a proxy; although this argument must get tenuous in cases where, for example, a tenant is several steps away in the chain from a developer. However, other interests (such as, for example, the general public interest in the quality of place that ensues) are not so obviously looked after in this process; while it might be argued that this is properly the job of the planning process there are limitations on the ability of local planning authority development controllers in these terms once they are faced with a planning application that has already been shaped by the SBD process. More generally, there must be a conceptual debate to be had about whether the precepts of SBD will contribute fully to the promotion of higher density urban development in British cities, which is one of the goals of current policy (see Chapter 7), or whether the application of SBD will tend in practice to produce more typically suburban lower density environments. Nevertheless, the SBD scheme has been having an effect on the design of housing developments in particular in Britain for over a decade; Schneider (1996), for example, reports that the rate at which SBD awards were being made to housing estates of various sizes had already exceeded 500 per annum in England and Wales by the middle of the 1990s. Pascoe and Topping (1997) record 35,000 houses on nearly 3,700 estates, involving in excess of 630 builders, as having been built to SBD standards in Britain over the period 1989–1996, which is something like 2–3 per cent of the total number of houses built in Britain over this period.

SALFORD'S CRIME AND DISORDER REDUCTION STRATEGY

The Crime and Disorder Act, 1998, placed a duty jointly on local authorities and on the police working with appropriate partners to carry out an audit and to produce and then implement a crime and disorder reduction strategy for each local authority area. This case study looks at how this task was tackled in one such authority's area. Salford in Greater Manchester is a particularly appropriate authority to choose for this purpose, because it responded quickly to the new duties, as might perhaps have been expected from the local authority that performed lead authority functions on behalf of all ten Greater Manchester District Councils in respect of the Greater Manchester Police Authority.[1] In addition, however, and very much in line with the government policy thinking introduced earlier in Chapter 6, Salford saw issues of crime and of urban regeneration in an holistic manner. Indeed, the work that had already been done in the City in preceding years to pull together partnerships for various purposes gave the City a flying start in terms of assembling a partnership to meet the new requirements of the 1998 Act. The starting point for understanding the approach adopted in Salford should therefore be the City's regeneration strategy.

Salford lies immediately to the west of the City of Manchester, and has just over half of that City's population at just under 228,000 (1996). Like many of the cities of northern England, Salford saw huge changes in its traditional employment base in the latter part of the twentieth century, losing almost one-third of its traditional employment base during the last three decades (Salford Partnership, undated, page 9). This has brought in its wake a series of social, economic and environmental problems, which have made Salford the thirty-first most deprived local authority district in England and fourth in the North West region (ibid.). But, of course, this has also created opportunities; it is this balance of problems and opportunities that the regeneration process in the City has set out to tackle, with some considerable success, from the mid-1980s onwards. This was reinforced in the spring of 1994 by the launch of the Salford Partnership, which was created in order to agree a common and integrated approach to regeneration in the City, to secure the commitment of all partners to this approach, and to ensure that the approach is efficiently and effectively delivered (ibid., page 5). Table 8.5 shows the membership of the Salford Partnership. What is clear from this is how broad-based and multi-sectoral the Partnership is; regeneration here is clearly seen in terms of the broad range of social and economic concerns encompassed by the 'social

Table 8.5 Membership of the Salford Partnership

Salford City Council
Manchester Training and Enterprise Council (which covers the Salford area)
Salford Chamber of Commerce
North West and Merseyside Housing Corporation
Salford and Trafford Health Authority
Greater Manchester Police – Salford Division
Government Office for the North West
Manchester Methodist Housing Association
Salford University
Salford College
Safer Salford[2]
Salford Probation Service
Salford Quays Job Centre (Employment Service)
Cable and Wireless Communication
Speedy Products
Thurnall plc
Greater Manchester Fire Service
Salford Council for Voluntary Service
Salford and Trafford Groundwork Trust
Northern Counties Housing Association

Source: Salford Partnership (n.d.) pages 2 and 3

exclusion' debate introduced in Chapter 7, as well as in terms of the more traditional and often more fully-developed physical development activities. As part of
the analysis of the current position set down in the Partnership's regeneration strategy, it says the following about crime:

- In 1997 Salford Police dealt with over 30,000 key crimes. The incidence of
  these key crimes varied across the City with high rates in Broughton,
  Pendleton, Langworthy[3]/Seedley and Little Hulton.
- They were called out to 9,500 incidents involving juvenile nuisance which
  represents 28 per cent of all incidents. The proportion of juveniles sentenced
  in 1996/97 was 10.9 per cent per 1,000 young people aged 10–17.
- 13 per cent of key incidents involved domestic disputes.
- Over 8,000 burglaries took place in 1997 – 27 per cent of all key crimes.
- Nearly 10,000 car crimes, i.e. theft of, or theft from, vehicles were reported in
  1997, a third of all key crimes (ibid., page 10).

The approach adopted in the regeneration strategy is via three City-wide themes
(economic development, social inclusion, and living environment) applied both
across-the-board and through area-based programmes in areas of need or of
opportunity. Tackling crime is listed as one of five areas of activity falling within the
social inclusion theme, although all of the other areas of activity that make up this
theme (building community capacity, tackling poverty, maximising the potential of
young people and improving health) could be said to be relevant to the objective of
tackling crime, as are areas of activity that form parts of other themes (such as creating clean, safe and healthy local environments under the living environment
theme, for example). Thus the approach being adopted is clearly both multi-agency
via the partnership mechanism and holistic through the breadth of action envisaged
in the strategy. The stated objective for the 'Tackling crime' component, drafted
while what became the Crime and Disorder Act, 1998 was still a Bill, is as follows:

> Tackling Crime – making Salford a safer place by supporting vulnerable
> individuals and communities, creating a safer environment, working to improve
> security and developing innovative, local multi-agency initiatives in response to
> the Crime and Disorder Bill (ibid., page 16).

Perhaps the most important point about this is that it clearly grounds action on
crime in Salford's regeneration agenda, seeing tackling crime not as a free-
standing issue but as something integral to the job of regenerating the City in economic, social and environmental terms. As can be seen from the above quotation,
the Crime and Disorder Bill (which became the 1998 Act) was seen as providing

Table 8.6 Membership of the Salford Crime Reduction Partnership

Salford City Council –	8 members, of which 2 are elected members (respectively, the Chair and Deputy Chair of the City Council's Community Safety Sub-Committee) and 6 are officers who head various parts of the Council's services
Greater Manchester Police –	4 members, all senior officers in the Division of the Greater Manchester Police force ('F' Division) that covers Salford
Salford Victim Support Service	
Safer Salford[2]	
Salford and Trafford Health Authority	
Salford Probation Service	
Greater Manchester Fire Service	
Salford Chamber of Commerce	
Manchester Training and Enterprise Council (which covers Salford)	
Crown Prosecution Service	
Salford Council for Voluntary Services	

Source: Salford Crime Reduction Partnership (1999) page 4

further opportunities to continue this work. The vehicle for this was the Salford Crime Reduction Partnership, which initially came together in 1993 (so actually just before the more broadly based Salford Partnership with its focus on regeneration), but which was clearly given further impetus by the Crime and Disorder Act, 1998. Table 8.6 itemises the membership of the Crime Reduction Partnership, and this can be compared with the information on the Salford Partnership in Table 8.5. This comparison clearly shows a significant overlapping membership between the two in terms of organisations, but it could perhaps be said that the actual membership (in terms of who has formally signed the strategy documents) is at a more operational level for the Crime Reduction Partnership, reflecting its focus on action.

The starting point for the process of producing a crime and disorder strategy for Salford was an audit of the existing situation (Salford Crime Reduction Partnership, 1998). This started from recent survey information that already existed, and notably a recent 'Quality-of-Life' survey commissioned by the City Council which showed amongst other things that 'in answering the question what could be done to improve the quality of the lives of people of Salford, the most common response was for action to be taken to reduce crime in the City'[4] (ibid., page 3). Indeed, the outcome of that particular exercise is interesting in terms of what it says about the views of the people of Salford about the most important actions to be taken to improve the quality of life in the City. Table 8.7 reproduces the results of this survey in priority order.

Table 8.7 1998 Salford Quality-of-Life Survey – Top ten priorities of Salford residents

1   More police about
2   Safe and affordable places for young people to go
3   More discipline in Salford Schools
4   Traffic to be slowed down
5   Improved education standards
6   More training and support to help people into work
7   Somewhere for children to go after school
8   Better healthcare
9   An improved physical environment
10   Better roads and pavements

Source: Salford Crime Reduction Partnership (1999) page 11

The audit then sought to define the key elements of the current situation from existing data (acknowledging the limitations of recorded crime data) both for the City as a whole and on a comparative basis for eleven subdivisions of it. These eleven subareas are called 'service delivery areas', and are the common basis used for the delivery of City Council services in Salford (see Table 8.8). The study of crime and disorder in these eleven service delivery areas concentrated on four key types of crime, which recorded crime statistics showed together to be responsible for 83 per cent of crime in Salford, and also on the area of 'juvenile nuisance' to pick up the 'disorder' part of the audit process because of evidence that suggested that this was responsible for a substantial proportion of anti-social behaviour (ibid., page 6). The four chosen types of crime were:

- *vehicle crime*, which accounted for 31 per cent of recorded crime between the beginning of April and the end of August 1998;
- *criminal damage*, which accounted for 22 per cent of crime on the same basis;
- *burglary other than in a dwelling*, which was responsible for 15 per cent of crime; and
- *burglary in a dwelling*, which was also responsible for 15 per cent of all crimes (ibid.).

A more localised (i.e. at below the level of the service delivery areas) process of mapping crime 'hot spots' was also undertaken, to provide an information base for the Crime Reduction Partnership, but the audit report did not publish information at this level 'so as to safeguard the safety and integrity of local communities'[5] (ibid., page 4); although it was intended to make more information of this kind available as part of the consultation process on the results of the audit.

Table 8.8 Summary of crime level comparison, Salford service delivery areas

Service delivery area	Vehicle crime	Criminal damage	Burglary: non-dwellings	Burglary: dwellings	Juvenile nuisance
Blackfriars/ Broughton	A	A	C	B	B
Charlestown	A	B	B	A	C
Claremont/Weaste	C	C	B	C	C
Eccles	D	C	C	B	C
Irlam	E	E	E	E	C
Kersal	D	D	D	C	D
Little Hulton	E	C	D	B	B
Ordsall	A	A	A	D	C
Precinct	B	B	C	B	B
Swinton	C	C	B	D	C
Worsley/Walkden	D	D	C	D	D
City average (rounded) 1 April–30 August 1998 (incidents per 100 residents)	2.0	1.4	1.0	1.0	1.8

Source: Developed by the authors from information presented in Salford Crime Reduction Partnership (1998) pages 9–13

Notes:
A – more than 50% above City average
B – 20–50% above City average
C – within + or – 20% of City average
D – 20–50% below City average
E – more than 50% below City average

The basic statistics against the five chosen indicators for the eleven service delivery areas were expressed both in real terms and in terms of incident levels per 100 residents, in order to make them more readily comparable with each other. This latter analysis was then compared with the City average. Table 8.8 presents a summary of the complex matrix this would produce. It pulls together into a single table for the convenience of readers information that is presented on several charts in the audit, but shows clearly that this type of information, when taken together with other relevant information available from partners, certainly enables the process of building a picture of the distribution of crime in Salford to begin. While there are very significant variations across the City in relation to several of the indicators (and more localised concentrations still in 'hotspots'), there are also some apparently recurring patterns. Again for the convenience of readers, Table 8.9 presents this in very simplified form.

The analysis in Table 8.9 can be related in very simplistic terms to the socio-

Table 8.9 Analysis of crime level comparisons, Salford service delivery areas

Cluster 1 SDAs with predominantly A and B scores (i.e. at least 20% above City average)	Cluster 2 SDAs with predominantly C scores (i.e. no more than 20% above or below City average)	Cluster 3 SDAs with predominantly D and E scores (i.e. at least 20% below City average)
Blackfriars/Broughton Charlestown Ordsall Precinct	Claremont/Weaste Eccles Swinton	Irlam Kersal Worsley/Walkden

Source: Developed by the authors from Table 8.8

Note: Little Hulton has no clear pattern, since it falls into none of these 3 clusters.

economic geography of Salford by looking at Figure 8.1, which maps this clustering on to the location of the eleven service delivery areas within the City of Salford. What is clear from that comparison is that the four service delivery areas that make up cluster 1 are collected together in the south-eastern part of Salford, which is the area of the City most easily described as 'inner city'. The cluster 2 areas are to be found to the west of this concentration, with the cluster 3 areas to the west of the cluster 2

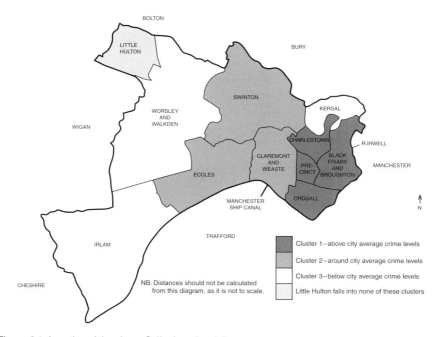

Figure 8.1 Location of the eleven Salford service delivery areas

Source: Developed by the authors

areas and north of the cluster 1 areas forming some of Salford's most affluent suburban areas. This is very simplistic, because a finer-grained breakdown would begin to
show a range within each of these eleven areas, but at this broad level of generalisation it is consistent with the pattern we have already seen in Chapter 2 which shows
the links between levels of crime and levels of relative poverty/deprivation.

Building on this base, the Crime and Disorder Reduction Strategy (Salford
Crime Reduction Partnership, 1999) sets out a statement of intent, a set of strategic objectives and an approach to the management of the process for the period
1999–2002. It is not suggested that crime in Salford can be solved, or anything as
grandiose as that, on this basis. The approach is described as follows:

> Of course it would be unrealistic to believe that we can solve all of the problems
> associated with crime and disorder through this document. A three-year
> timescale will not be enough to radically change some of the deep rooted
> problems which exist and have an impact on criminal behaviour. This strategy is
> the start of what will become a long term programme of crime reduction to
> which all of our key partners are committed (ibid., page 7).

The three principles that are advanced as the basis for tackling the problems
illustrated in the audit are:

- *intervention*, by focusing on young people, communities, and those who are
  the victims and witnesses of crime;
- *prevention*, by making the environment more resistant to crime and preventing further offending behaviour; and
- *detection*, by targeting partnership action and resources at high volume crime
  and at the persistent offenders that commit a high proportion of it.

The ways in which these will be developed are described in the following terms:

> These three principles require us to think more creatively about how we tackle
> crime, so that we can change and tackle the things which have prevented us
> from having the most effective impact within our communities. They also lay the
> foundations for the development and production of effective local action plans.
> It is these local partnership plans which will transform the objectives of the
> strategy into real and tangible action on the ground (ibid.).

The Strategy then proceeds to identify six interrelated themes as the running
agenda for action at both the City-wide and the local action planning scales. The
six are:

- youth and family intervention;
- community mobilisation;
- environmental resistance;
- intimidation, victim and witness support;
- offender targeting and rehabilitation;
- targeting high volume crime and disorder (ibid., page 12).

Of these six, 'environmental resistance' is probably the theme that is most closely related to the interests of this book, but in looking at this in more detail it is important to note that it is intended that action should be taken across the broad range of all six themes rather than be isolated in any one. That having been said, the nine detailed objectives established to guide action under the environmental resistance theme are summarised in Table 8.10.

The connection with the first case study in this chapter (the Secured By Design scheme) will immediately be obvious from Table 8.10: the influence of SBD thinking on its contents is clear among other things from the formal commitment to it in the second objective. It is also clear from Table 8.10, because this is a programme for a limited period of time, that it does not propose the large-scale retro-fitting of existing environments, but takes a very selective approach with an emphasis on managing new development, on town centres and other business areas, on vandalism and graffiti and on street lighting.

In taking forward this strategy, the Crime Reduction Partnership commits itself to five particular sets of actions (on the next page):

Table 8.10 Environmental resistance objectives, Salford crime reduction strategy

• to promote the work of Risk Management Groups across the City (these are groups established to provide local, practical advice and expertise on physical and environmental issues)
• to promote and encourage the adoption of the principles of 'Secured By Design'
• to promote a pre-emptive and a preventative approach to business crime
• to promote safe and secure town centres
• to improve the physical environment by tackling widespread vandalism and graffiti, and by providing opportunities for young people to undertake environmental improvement work within the community
• to review and improve street lighting, particularly in areas of high crime
• to promote Codes of Practice for security services and for Closed Circuit Television (CCTV)
• to explore the expansion and extension of mobile security patrols across the City
• to work with insurance companies to prepare a risk assessment of physical assets within the business community

Source: Salford Crime Reduction Partnership (1999) pages 13, 18 and 19

- ensure that all plans and programmes which impact on this strategy are integrated and closely linked;
- work with Government, and in particular the Home Office, to influence legislation, and to explore whether national rules and regulations need to be amended to enable the most effective and efficient delivery of our objectives;
- secure resources to implement the strategy;
- establish targets and monitor progress, building in evaluation as a key principle of all activity pursued;
- secure real and tangible benefits for local communities, making a real difference to the people living and working in the City (ibid., page 27).

In relation to the environmental resistance theme, the three specific targets set in this first round of strategy making are:

- by 2002, ensure that all local authority contracts comply with the Code of Practice for Security Services and CCTV;
- 30 per cent of all business to be covered by a 'Business Watch' scheme by 2002;
- identify eight nominations for the Secure Car Park Award Scheme by 2000 (ibid., page 31).

It is readily apparent from a comparison of the nine detailed objectives and this short list of specific targets that the process of setting targets that can be used for performance measurement purposes is still in need of further development. This is not entirely surprising in what is, after all, the first cycle of a new process. Without denigrating the three specific targets in themselves, what is probably more import- ant is the commitment established by their definition to the idea that targets need to be set in order to make an assessment of progress possible.

This case study shows the initial steps taken in one City to tackle the new responsibilities established by the Crime and Disorder Act, 1998. This is a locality where there is clear evidence that the local authority and the police were already working closely together, and thus these new responsibilities introduced via the Act were building on existing relationships rather than starting afresh. This will not be the case in every partnership established under the Act, however, and in cases where the pre-existing relationship was a fragile one the process will not be as smooth as it appears to have been in Salford. There may, of course, be longer-term benefits in the development of these relationships where this is needed through the compulsion engendered by statutory partnerships. Over time, of course, the real test will be the effectiveness of a strategy of this nature in the achievement of its objectives, but because the case study was written in the early stages of this process it is still too soon to adopt such an evaluative stance. In any event, the strategy-shaping process will undoubtedly develop further as Salford learns from these experiences, but it is clear from what has been done to date that there are four components of it in particular that are of vital importance:

- the process of ensuring that concerns about crime and disorder are grounded in the broader strategies being developed for the rest of the City, rather than treated in isolation;
- the commitment to a multi-agency and multi-sectoral partnership as the basis for the approach;
- the systematic process adopted of working from an audit through the establishment of principles, objectives and actions, with a commitment to monitoring and review so that this becomes a cyclical and learning process rather than something which is essentially linear in character; and
- the attempt to balance an holistic approach to the problem with a realistic appraisal of what can be achieved in a short period of time.

It should be apparent from the above how this relates to the material presented in Chapter 7 about the approach that is being encouraged nationally to work under the Crime and Disorder Act, 1998.

THE REDEVELOPMENT OF HULME, MANCHESTER

The story of the redevelopment of Hulme has been told in several places (see, for example, Manchester City Planning Department, 1995, pages 37–40; Kitchen, 1997b, pages 153–9; Rudlin and Falk, 1999, pages 207–30), so readers who wish to look at aspects of this particular initiative other than those covered in the case study can readily do so. Essentially it is a story of a part of the inner city of Manchester which had been redeveloped in the 1960s and 1970s as part of Manchester City Council's slum clearance programme, but in a manner which quickly earned the tag of 'failed'. This was mainly because of major difficulties with some of the new housing stock – the notorious 'Hulme Crescents', system-built, walk-up, high-rise blocks which quickly proved unsatisfactory as family housing for a variety of reasons – but also because the kind of place that had been created effectively turned its back on the rest of the City and became isolated, despite its location just south of the City Centre and adjacent to the City's University precinct, and on either side of the main road from the City Centre to Manchester Airport. It had become a place nobody went through to get to anywhere else, and which had little interaction with the main motors of the City's economy (of which the city centre, the universities and the airport were major elements). In addition, although air photographs, if taken from high enough up, made Hulme look like a very green place, in practice much of that was informal public open space that served no particular purpose and quickly became degraded.

On top of these physical difficulties, Hulme was also among the most deprived wards in the inner city of Manchester in socio-economic terms. Figure 8.2, using data from the 1991 Census (i.e. the period just before the redevelopment of Hulme through the City Challenge process commenced), shows where

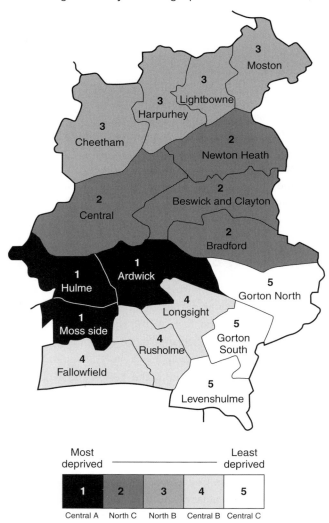

Figure 8.2 Spectrum of deprivation in the wards of inner-city Manchester, 1991

Source: This diagram first appeared as Figure 7.2 in Kitchen (1997b) page 133

Hulme sat at that time in the spectrum of deprivation amongst the inner city wards of Manchester; it also illustrates the point made above about the relative centrality of Hulme's geographical location.

Taking all of these matters together, it was small wonder that Manchester City Council had been grappling for years with the issue of whether it could afford to redevelop Hulme but had regretfully concluded that it could not. The opportunity in public funding terms to do so was presented, however, by the announcement of the Government City Challenge scheme in 1991. Hulme was a first-round winner, and this provided Government funding of £37.5 million for a five-year period as the basis for establishing a public-private partnership to oversee the redevelopment of the area. Hulme Regeneration Ltd became the vehicle for this process.

There was a huge amount of consultation and discussion around the questions of the nature and the form of this redevelopment. Some of that was acrimonious, in the sense that it reflected clashes not merely of ideas but also of personalities. One of the areas of discussion that certainly did turn out to be contentious was the relationship between the design of the built environment and crime; the police (via the Architectural Liaison Officer of the Greater Manchester force) argued for the kinds of principles enshrined in the Secured By Design award scheme, while the group of people who eventually took the lead in drafting the Hulme Development Guide argued much more along 'New Urbanist' lines (Kitchen, 1997b, pages 156 and 157; Rudlin and Falk, 1995, page 56), having already secured the support of leading politicians for this stance. Rudlin and Falk, writing very much from a 'New Urbanist' stance and also from David Rudlin's involvement as one of the group of people working on the Hulme Development Guide, put this clash in the following terms:

> This new urban thinking suggests a different approach to security. There has been a great deal of debate about security in housing promoted largely by the work of Alice Coleman (1990). 'Secure By Design' principles have been used to criticise the emerging approach to urban layouts. In Hulme one of the main critics of the Urban Design Guide has been the police architectural liaison officer. The exponents of secure by design favour an approach of 'target hardening' with respect to individual homes and estate layouts. The aim is to put up barriers to crime and to assist policing by reducing escape routes. The alternative argument is that estates can never be made entirely secure and that the best defence against crime is the activity and informal stewardship which characterises traditional urban areas . . . . [T]he main deterrent to crime is activity so that mixed use development which promotes activity throughout the day is the best way to design out crime. The promise is of more congenial places (or softer cities) rather than the creation of defended enclaves within increasingly hard and hostile urban areas (Rudlin and Falk, 1995, page 56).

In presenting the case study of the Secured By Design initiative earlier in this chapter, we have already used elements of the Hulme Development Guide to point out some of the areas of controversy that can arise from the SBD approach, particularly around the concepts of permeability and of the promotion of activity which are central to New Urbanist thinking. It should also be acknowledged, however, as noted above, that many of the ideas being promoted in relation to the redevelopment of Hulme were seen as controversial by the police in terms of their advocacy of the SBD approach.

The key ideas that drive the Hulme Development Guide (Hulme Regeneration Limited, 1994) are set out in Table 8.11. Of those concepts of the type of place being sought, one that has had a particular impact upon the kinds of new environment that have been emerging is that of 'stewardship'. This concept is important because it makes the claim that the ways in which buildings and spaces are designed and relate to each other can make a real difference to the willingness of people to incorporate responsibility for what goes on in

Table 8.11 Hulme Development Guide – the kind of place it seeks to create

- an emphasis upon the public realm, defined as all the spaces between buildings in which people interact. The intention here is to create outdoor spaces which stimulate the senses but which are comfortable and human in scale, are clearly defined and serve a useful purpose
- an emphasis upon streets and squares. Streets (as distinct from roads) are seen as being not merely about conveying vehicles quickly but also as being 'a self-supervised area of public contact and interaction'
- a rich mix of uses and tenures, rather than the segregation of both that tended to characterise much of the past
- a high enough density both of population and development so as to achieve a sustainable community, including helping to make commercial activity servicing the area viable and achieving the aspiration of security through natural surveillance
- strong links to and through the area, to achieve a high level of permeability
- a strong sense of place, fostered not only by making good use of the public buildings that remain but also by locating major buildings at nodes of activity such as junctions and squares. Such buildings define corners, help to create vistas and contribute to the overall sense of identity of the area
- all spaces should have clearly defined functions which encourage a sense of stewardship on the part of those living and working in the developments overlooking them
- the creation of sustainability through flexible and adaptable developments, high densities, and resource-efficiency

Source: Hulme Regeneration Ltd (1994) pages 10–13 (authors' summary)

those spaces into their daily routines. In essence, this asserts that enough people will feel a sense of responsibility for their immediate environments that they will be willing not merely to act as 'eyes on the street' but will also take appropriate action in relation to criminal activity once they become aware of it, including reporting it to the police.

It should be noted in this context that doubts have been expressed for some time about whether this concomitant of the philosophy of natural surveillance (that people will challenge others when they see behaviour that is apparently wrong or suspicious) will actually be reflected in what people do. Merry (1981), for example, has argued that this is inherently less likely in areas with a high per-ceived risk to personal safety than it is in areas where risks are perceived to be lower; and if this is true, it suggests that approaches based upon creating the concept of 'stewardship' might be more likely to succeed in areas where the fear of crime is less entrenched than in others. This argument can be pushed too far, however. It is not necessary to adopt a wholly deterministic approach (i.e. to conclude that this kind of approach to environmental design will automatically trigger the kind of human behaviour that is desired) to be able to accept that the philosophy of 'eyes on the street' increases the likelihood that anti-social behaviour will be observed and that, as a consequence, the likelihood of an appropriate response is improved, as compared with a situation which does not create these kinds of opportunities in the first place. The Hulme Development Guide puts this as follows:

> Streets, squares and courtyards all have recognisable functions and help to foster stewardship. Carefully designed, they can help to minimise the risk, and fear, of crime, and a high priority will be placed on designing in high levels of natural surveillance. Thus we want to see buildings fronting streets, with pavements well overlooked by windows and doors within frontal elevations close to the pavement edge. We are also keen to see cars parked on the street where they can be easily seen, or in properly secured, private courtyards, rather than within the front curtilage where they break the important relationship between building and street, and also compromise the all-important surveillance of the pavement and street (ibid., page 12).

The translation into practice of this particular component of the guidance can be readily seen several times over in the photographic essay of Hulme included with this case study (Figure 8.3).

These driving ideas are followed up in the 'Design Guide' section of the Hulme Development Guide by a series of more detailed policies under the follow-ing headings:

- the street
- integration
- density
- permeability
- routes and transport
- landmarks, vistas and focal points
- definition of space
- identity
- sustainability
- hierarchy   (ibid., pages 18–36)

We have introduced what the guidance says about permeability earlier in this chapter as a counterpoint to what can be found in the police's Secured By Design scheme. As a further example, Table 8.12 shows the guidance given under the heading 'the street', and the level of prescriptiveness it contains should be clear to the reader. This guidance has also had a direct effect on the kinds of development that have materialised in Hulme, as the photographic essay at Figure 8.3 clearly illustrates. In looking at these photographs to see how the guidance described here has been translated into reality, readers should ask themselves (just as was argued in relation to the Secured By Design scheme) what they think of the quality of the built environment being produced and what they think it would be like to live there.

The twelve photographs that make up the essay cannot hope to do full justice to the new Hulme, but hopefully they will help the reader not familiar with the area to understand the sort of environment being produced as a result of the application of the guidance just described. It should be noted that they were taken on a weekday (i.e. working) afternoon in July 2000: one thing common to all of them is the virtual absence of people from the streets. That does not, of course, mean that there were no 'eyes on the street', since the photographs all show a heavy emphasis on fenestration in the elevations facing the streets. As well as perhaps being a consequence of the photographs being taken during the working day, the apparent lack of street activity might also be a function of the fact that the essay concentrates mainly on housing and therefore under-represents the mixed use component of development in Hulme. It should be remembered that the variety of activities that mixed uses can promote, at different times of the day and night, is an important part of the argument for the mixed use approach.

Readers can obviously make up their own minds about how they view the kind of environment being created in Hulme. It can already be said, however, that people are voting with their feet to live in Hulme, which represents a total reversal

Table 8.12 Hulme Development Guide – urban design guidance – 'The street'

Aspiration
- A variety of streets will define the urban structure of Hulme.
- These streets will serve equitably the needs of all pedestrians, cyclists, public transport and the private car without being dominated by the motor vehicle.
- Streets will be defined and animated by buildings and their occupants.

Buildings of all types should front onto streets, squares or parks
'They should show their public face to the street and spill their activity out onto it. The primary means of access to all buildings should be from the street.'

Streets should be designed to encourage walking and cater for the needs of people with mobility problems
'The street should be a public space which promotes socialisation, and must be attractive and safe for pedestrians. The car should be accommodated but should not dominate the street, and vehicle speed should be severely restricted by design. Devices such as speed tables and pedestrian crossings should be used to maximise pedestrian safety.'

There should be eyes on the street
'It is important that streets are overlooked to promote natural supervision. Blank walls onto streets and excessive distances between the footpath and windows will therefore not be permitted.'

Doors onto streets should be at no more than 15-metre intervals
'This is necessary to ensure that sufficient activity and vitality is generated on the street.'

Ground floors of residential properties can be elevated 450 millimetres above pavement level
'This enables better supervision of the street, as well as increasing the privacy of ground floor rooms. Notwithstanding, convenient access should be provided for people with mobility problems.'

Source: Hulme Regeneration Ltd (1994) page 19

of the experience of the years preceding City Challenge. As a very simple illustration, the housing stock shown in the photographic essay was clearly occupied rather than vacant, and new (private sector in particular) housing was under construction at several locations near to the points from which the photographs were taken, which clearly suggests a positive market response. As far as crime is concerned, the redevelopment of Hulme has had to grapple with its long-term stigmatisation as an area with a high crime rate. There is some evidence (for an area wider than Hulme, but encompassing it) that in recent years reported crime has been

Photograph 1

Photograph 2

Figure 8.3 Hulme Photographic Essay

Photographs 1 and 2: Variety of building forms, heights and tenures in Hulme street scenes. The intended physical relationships between buildings and highways can clearly be seen.

Photograph 3

Photograph 4

Figure 8.3 *Continued*

Photographs 3 and 4: Off-street car parking arrangements in Hulme. The sculpted gate treatment of the main access area can clearly be seen, as can the relationship between the car park and surrounding housing to create multiple overlooking.

Photograph 5

Photograph 6

Figure 8.3 *Continued*

Photographs 5 and 6: The relationships between open spaces of various sizes and built form in Hulme. How many different kinds of 'eyes on the street' can be seen in photograph 6?

Photograph 7

Photograph 8

Figure 8.3 *Continued*

Photographs 7 and 8: Street layout arrangements designed to restrict speed and to promote on-street parking. Note also in photograph 8 that the space between the front elevation of the housing and the back of the pavement is so narrow that its use is virtually restricted to refuse bins.

Photograph 9

Photograph 10

Figure 8.3 *Continued*

Photographs 9 and 10: Variety of detailed housing treatments in Hulme. The housing in photograph 9 appears to be a product of a relatively relaxed view of the guidance, given that it is set back from the street far enough for a drive to be incorporated on which a car could park. Note the strengthened corner treatment in photograph 10.

Photograph 11

Figure 8.3 *Continued*

Photograph 11: The modelling of a corner in this case has been taken to the point of producing a balcony that provides 'eyes on the street' in different directions by overlooking the road junction.

Photograph 12

Figure 8.3 *Continued*

Photograph 12: As well as a front elevation containing nine windows (including the one on the front door) for a three-storey property, the treatment here also includes a corner balcony to provide an opportunity to look down the street. It can be argued that in this case the desire to create "eyes on the street" has actually unbalanced the elevation.

Table 8.13 Reported crime, C2 Division (encompassing Hulme), 1996 and 1997

Type of crime	1996	1997	1996–1997 percentage change
Burglary (dwellings)	1600	1200	−25
Theft from motor vehicle	1200	1100	−9
Theft of motor vehicle	1100	750	−32
Robbery	650	700	+8
Theft from the person	300	200	−33

Source: McLoughlin (1999) page 6. Figures have been rounded because they have been calculated from a chart.

reducing (McLoughlin, 1999), as Table 8.13 shows; it should however be stressed that the long-term monitoring information that would demonstrate more conclusively that crime levels in Hulme are making an effective case for the design approach adopted in its redevelopment does not yet exist.

As readers will be aware from the discussion of this matter in Chapter 2, there are general reasons to be careful about statistics based upon reported crimes, as well as specific ones (the area concerned is wider than Hulme, and the figures only cover a very short period of time) in this particular case. The source paper in question also contains a cautionary note about an apparent increase in car crime in 1998 (ibid., paragraph 4.2), as well as commenting more generally on Hulme's growing population, its changing population structure, apparent improvements in the relationships between the police and the community in the area, and changes in crime reporting procedures, all of which could very well have an effect on crime statistics. There is also a manifest difficulty with the relationship between cause and effect here; even if we could dismiss all of these statistical concerns, could we be sure that the improvement was attributable to the application of the guidelines? All of that having been said, very often these are the only kinds of statistics available at such a localised level for judging whether, in terms of their explicit objectives in relation to crime, the guidelines could be said to be working; to the extent to which these statistics have to be relied upon they are clearly promising.

Perhaps the other thing that can already be said about Hulme is that it is being described as a success in some quarters well before it is complete and long before any longitudinal studies of people's reactions to living in it have been done. The Government's Urban Task Force (1999, page 135), for example, praises the 'integrated approach which has been crucial to the prospects for long term sustainable regeneration'. Rudlin and Falk, writing from an unequivocally committed standpoint, go so far as to ask whether Hulme should be seen as a 'model neighbourhood', and quickly jettison their question mark as their text unfolds (Rudlin and

Falk, 1999, pages 207–30). While understanding why people would want to look for successful models of urban development, our standpoint of wanting to see claims backed up by authoritative research demands a note of caution. It is vital in a case like this that the experience of living in the kind of environment being created in Hulme should be carefully monitored over a period of time, so that we know what ordinary people think about this and about the problems (if any) that they find, and so that we do not have to rely solely on arguments from either supporters or opponents of the driving ideas. It is also important to remember that Hulme is not like many other parts not just of Manchester (Kitchen, 1997b, pages 158 and 159) but also of many other British cities, in that their immediate urban futures will not be in terms of large-scale redevelopment. There are therefore some clear difficulties with presenting Hulme as a generally applicable urban model, as is being done in some quarters. We see Hulme as an interesting story with valuable lessons to offer, and as a development which ought to be carefully monitored as the process continues and as the experience of living in it accumulates; but it is far too early as yet to describe it as a panacea.

CONCLUSIONS

It is impossible to draw general conclusions from these three case studies because it is very difficult to say how representative they actually are of the extent and variety of British practice. It is more helpful to see them as current slices of what is taking place in contemporary Britain in the field of crime and the design of the built environment, and as illustrating some of the issues, debates and processes to be found there.

The Secured By Design scheme is part of current practice; although it has been criticised in some quarters (and, as we have shown, is in some ways very different from the 'New Urbanist' approach being adopted in Hulme) it continues to affect the quality of what gets submitted to local planning authorities and what gets built all over the country. It also influences the police contribution to the Crime and Disorder Partnerships that are everywhere grappling with the new responsibilities imposed by the Crime and Disorder Act, 1998, and the approach described in Salford illustrates one way of tackling this new set of responsibilities and structures. The redevelopment of Hulme has turned into a high-profile regeneration initiative, within which 'New Urbanism' principles with their explicit views about the relationship between crime and the design of the built environment are being applied; and whatever view one takes about the theory, it is certainly a very interesting case from the point of view of this book, with the potential to offer a variety of lessons if properly researched.

The approach being adopted in Hulme is probably found much less frequently in British practice than the introduction of SBD ideas and principles through local Crime and Disorder Partnerships and Strategies. Depending upon one's perspective, one can either attribute that to how the battle of ideas is panning out or to the practicality of the situation on the ground, where Hulme-type experiences of large-scale demolition and redevelopment are likely to be infrequent but where the police are always major players in the local Crime and Disorder Partnership. Our preferred explanation tends towards this latter view, although we have noted in Chapter 7 that many of the contemporary concepts that are to be found in key policy documents are consistent with 'New Urbanist' ideology but are not always wholly consistent with SBD thinking. Our hope in presenting these cases is that they give at least a flavour of some of the contemporary initiatives that are taking place in Britain in this field, and help readers to reflect on some of the important practice questions raised by these initiatives.

NOTES

1   In England, when the former Metropolitan County Councils were abolished in 1986 and local government in these areas became single-tier rather than two-tier, one of the issues that had to be resolved in each metropolitan area was which of the Metropolitan District Councils would take lead responsibility on behalf of all of the others for administrative functions still operated on a County-wide basis. The police authority function was one such activity, and Salford City Council performed this function in Greater Manchester on behalf of all ten District Councils.

2   'Safer Salford' is the Community Safety Unit for the City of Salford, and is responsible for the coordination of crime and disorder issues for the City Council and its partners. It is a continuation of an initiative that first began with the Home Office's Safer Cities Programme in 1989, and is now part of the Chief Executive's Department in the City Council. Strictly, therefore, for the purposes of Tables 8.5 and 8.6 it should be counted as part of the Salford City Council membership, but it has been treated as a separate entity because of this particular role and history.

3   The Langworthy area was one of the forty-seven crime 'hot spots' in England and Wales identified by the Government in July 2000 as a location for an initiative under the Youth Inclusion Programme, targeting the fifty youngsters aged 13–16 seen as representing the greatest risk of criminal activity (The Independent, 26 July 2000). Langworthy is in the Claremont and Weaste SDA as defined in Table 8.8.

4   This mirrors the findings of research from elsewhere, reported in Chapter 7, about resident perceptions of quality of life issues. Both the large study of Greater Manchester, Merseyside and Tyne and Wear, and the smaller studies in the Dearne Valley and Nottingham as part of the City Challenge process, show essentially the same public views.

5   This reflects the tension which frequently exists between the desire to publish informa-
     tion both to demonstrate the thoroughness of the work that has been done and to
     encourage discussion, and the desire in so doing not to stigmatise an area and perhaps
     as a result run the risk of making the problems worse. The compromise recorded here
     (of saying that more localised information would be available for certain purposes only)
     is quite a common response to this problem.

COMPARISONS AND KEY ISSUES

CHAPTER 9

SOME ANGLO-AMERICAN COMPARISONS

INTRODUCTION

In this chapter, we revisit much of the ground that we have already covered in this book, but this time with the explicit objective of making some more formal Anglo-American comparisons. We want to do this not merely for its intrinsic interest, but also because we are conscious that ideas and practices in the contemporary world can flow very quickly between locations and cultures. Unless, however, these ideas and practices are understood in the contexts in which they have been developed and/or applied, there is a risk that they will be transplanted without consideration of the contextual elements which may be of critical importance to their success or failure. Further, it would be helpful if those considering adopting ideas and practices used in other locations would check whether any careful evaluation studies have been undertaken, to try to understand in what ways and to what extent particular initiatives actually succeeded in achieving their stated objectives. Sadly, in far too few cases will such an evaluation exist, so people will be forced to rely on the inherent attractiveness of an idea (which may well be a function of how effectively it has been sold by its progenitors and supporters) rather than on reliable evidence about what its application has achieved. Our ideal would be that moving ideas around the world, which is becoming ever easier with modern information technology, is done in full knowledge both of context and outcome, because we believe that this is the most successful way to take policy ideas from one society and culture to another. Since many of the major ideas in the field covered by this book emanate from either the USA or Britain, an Anglo-American comparison is clearly important in terms of understanding how portable this material might be (Kitchen and Schneider, 2000).

To this end, we revisit the relationships between crime and the fear of crime, crime trends in both societies, the history of place-based crime prevention, the intellectual heritage that supports our current understandings of the relationships between crime and the design of the built environment, and the policy and practice frameworks in the two countries. Our broad overview of this is that the major differences are to be found in crime trajectories (although not, we think, in terms of some of the issues of the geography and the demography of crime that sit behind these trends) and in the policy and practice frameworks in each country. There are also some significant differences in the ways in which individual ideas are conceived and used and in the cultural reactions to certain kinds of initiatives, particularly in the examination of the history of place-based crime prevention, and we touch on these as we work through this analysis. As far as other areas are concerned, the similarities seem to us to be more important than the differences and, indeed, we believe that what we have described as the intellectual heritage that supports work in this field, would be accurately described as common. We return to this broad overview in the concluding section of this chapter.

CRIME AND THE FEAR OF CRIME

Both the USA and Britain clearly face major problems in terms of fear of crime; in both countries, the available research evidence suggests that it is either at the top of or very high up community lists of what concerns people the most in terms of quality of life in the contemporary world. While it is almost counter-intuitive to say this, we have come to the conclusion from looking at the ways in which these issues emerge and are dealt with in both societies that treating crime and the fear of crime as two separate but related concerns is more helpful than thinking of them as two sides of the same coin. The large literature about the fear of crime (Pain, 2000) points to a complex range of social phenomena as factors which influence it rather than a simple linear connection with extant or recent crime rates. It also needs to be acknowledged that sometimes fear of crime may be an acceptable expression of an underlying social attitude that may be less acceptable in contemporary society, which is really fear of differences (which might be socio-economic, cultural, ethnic, religious or indeed other elements as well (Sandercock, 2000)); this makes for obvious difficulties in the use of expressed fear of crime as a precise indicator. This does not, in our judgment, suggest that fear of crime should be regarded as anything other than a very real public concern in most urban areas; it is simply a measure that should be used carefully. This is reinforced by the observation that we have made in Chapter 2 to the effect that crime rates in the USA were falling throughout much of the 1990s, yet social surveys were not showing Americans to be much less concerned about crime or less fearful of its potential impact upon their lives, their family's lives and their homes. In public policy terms, this suggests that we cannot expect that initiatives designed to achieve crime reduction in a particular locality will automatically bring down the fear of crime in that locality. Even when crime incidents reduce, or people's experiences of crime recede into the past, there appears, as we have argued in Chapter 1, to be a residual fear of crime (perhaps analogous to the imprint that a strong light can leave on the eye after it has been switched off) which must be counted as part of the 'hidden' costs of crime because of its impact upon the quality of life that we are only now beginning to assess. All of this suggests that what is likely to be necessary is a separate (but, hopefully, linked) set of initiatives which seek to tackle each problem, rather than the undifferentiated assumption that both will be addressed by a single set of actions. We think that this confusion of objectives (is something designed to tackle the incidence of crime? the fear of crime? or both?) has sometimes been visible in initiatives in both the USA and Britain, and may well have contributed to the difficulties sometimes experienced by those initiatives.

It is almost certainly the case that we do not fully understand the sets of relationships that are involved here. It is also almost certainly the case that it is essential to talk about this in the plural form, in the sense that we are talking about sets of relationships in particular circumstances rather than one particular view with universal explanatory value; it is very doubtful that a single model could have such value other than at a very high level of generality. In this very general sense, however, we can probably say that there are links between crime rates, public perceptions of the fear of crime, the ways crime-related issues are reported in the media, and political and managerial responses to crime concerns, but that we are unsure about the causality elements of these relationships. What we can almost certainly also say is that, in their different ways, each of these elements is acted upon by a wide range of cultural, economic, social and physical/environmental factors, rather than that the four elements described above constitute a closed system. In turn, we think that these 'crime-specific' elements contribute to this cultural, economic, social and physical/environmental milieu in both negative and positive ways, which are very imperfectly understood. We try to give expression on a very simplified basis to this probable set of relationships in Figure 9.1, but in doing so we want to stress that we think that in the real world this is likely to operate in very complex ways that will vary very greatly from locality to locality and from culture to culture. In other words, we do not think that there are in principle significant differences between the USA and Britain, but we do believe that in these terms both countries are likely to exhibit a wide range of circumstances, many of which will be very different from each other. The variety visible in the USA may well actually be greater than the variety visible in Britain, however, because as we will go on to show Britain has been experiencing in recent years the strong imposition of policy frameworks and processes on the part of its central government which may well have brought about a degree of uniformity in local responses. The USA, on the other hand, has experienced no comparable equivalent, and is indeed characterised by a diversity of approaches at the local level in the absence of a strong and uni-directional central push.

Figure 9.1 is not meant to imply that all of these elements are in play or indeed are necessarily filtered by all of the other components in each instance. A very simple illustration of this would be a woman in fear of violence in the domestic

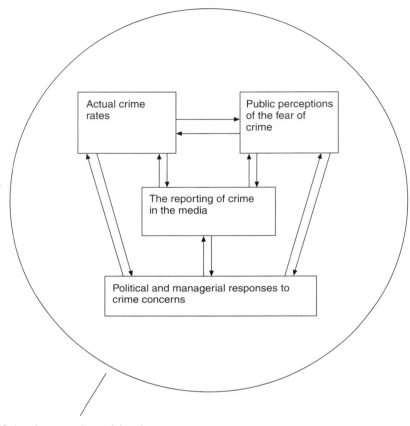

Cultural, economic, social and
physical/environmental milieu within
which (and with which) these 'crime-
specific' elements interact

Figure 9.1 How might crime and the fear of crime be linked?

arena from a partner who on previous occasions has been violent towards her. It is
entirely understandable in this situation that her fear derives from her previous
experience, rather than being related either to the ways in which domestic violence
is reported in the media or conceived of as a problem requiring their attention by
politicians or managers of agencies or facilities. But even here, the other factors
may influence what she does as a consequence of her experiences and her fears;
for example, women today may now be much more willing than was the case thirty
or forty years ago to talk about such matters with other people rather than simply
endure them, or even to report them to the police, or indeed to take direct action
themselves and seek both physical and legal refuge. Or, to take an environmental

example, someone needing to withdraw money from their bank account late at night via an ATM may be afraid of doing this if the facility is badly lit or has dark places immediately around it where others might hide, simply because this situation is inherently intimidating; that person's instinctive fear is likely to be a more important component of this judgement than what they can recall of what has been said about this problem in the media, by politicians or by managers. Even here, however, it is possible to argue that these other elements are absorbed by people throughout their lives on an ongoing basis and thus contribute, albeit subliminally, to people's fears. The other relevant point to make about these two examples for the purposes of this book, of course, is that they illustrate the point that not all types of crime are equally amenable to amelioration through environmental action, with the first case (the problem of domestic violence) being primarily non-environmental in terms of societal action to deal with the problem, whereas the second case (the location of an ATM) ought to be amenable to action in terms of the visibility of its location, the quality of lighting in the immediately surrounding area, and the avoidance of the creation of hiding places.

The reporting of crime in the media may have a particular effect on the fear of crime if it emphasises as if they were commonplace crimes that are in fact relatively scarce. As we have already shown, crimes of violence are not evenly distributed by age and by gender throughout society, but the ways in which these types of crime are reported may not reflect this distribution. For example, young men are the social group most at risk from physical attack (usually by other young men), but unless its consequences are very serious a fight between two groups of young men is not usually deemed to be worthy of media attention or, if it is, that reporting is usually very low key. On the other hand, elderly women are typically the social group least at risk from attack, but if an elderly women is attacked and beaten press photographers are likely to visit her hospital bed and photographs are likely to accompany screaming headlines. In one sense, of course, this is affirming the point that such an event is atypical; it is news because it is unusual. In another sense, the event is in its own right a deeply shocking thing, and thus is absolutely legitimate territory for media attention. But the cumulative effect of all of this can be very distorting, particularly in terms of the messages it sends out to elderly people about their safety. Both authors, during their preparation of this book, have had the experience of talking to public officials about the adverse consequences which a single story of this nature given prominence in the local media can have for careful and long-term campaigns about public safety; but equally, these officials tend not to believe that it would be legitimate to ask the local media to give such a story less prominence when it occurs. Perhaps the main point to be taken from these experiences is that campaigns dealing with public perceptions about safety need to include a strong media dimension, but also need to anticipate, no matter how cooperative the general attitude of the local media, the likelihood of individual stories with a negative impact on that campaign.

It is probably also the case that the media have a much more general effect on crime and public perceptions of safety than in the fairly specific terms set out above, and that is in terms of the host of media images with which we are confronted every day in the western world. It is not the purpose of this book to go into the arguments about the extent to which this directly influences human behaviour, although we are aware that a wide range of views exists about this. But it seems inherently implausible to argue that human beings in the contemporary world are likely to go through their lives completely unaffected by this barrage of images, since the whole point of media portrayal is that we should take some sort of notice of what is being portrayed. Crimes of all kinds play a large role in some parts of the popular media in Britain and the USA, such as the film industry, and thus it seems likely that the experience of absorption in this particular culture will have some sorts of effects (probably widely varying) upon people. In this sense, it is probably helpful to see the impact of the contemporary media on public fears of crime as not just being in the specific box assigned to it in Figure 9.1 by virtue of the ways in which crime gets reported, but also to see the more general contribution of the media of popular culture as part of the cultural, economic, social and physical/environmental milieu shown in Figure 9.1 as the frame within which the more specific variables interact.

Political and managerial reactions to problems of crime and of public perceptions of safety are significant both because of their mutually reinforcing nature and because they create the opportunity for experiment and for participation. It could be argued, for example, that media coverage creates the impression that 'something needs to be done'; in turn, once politicians and managers have decided what that 'something' is, they will certainly be interested in securing media coverage of their actions; and so crime issues remain in the headlines throughout this process. It is not necessary to adopt a cynical stance towards the motivation of politicians and of managers to see that, if crime and safety are major issues of public concern, then they would both want to do something about them and want to be seen to be doing something about them. While one of the great virtues of place-based crime prevention is that it has the potential to be adopted as 'self-help', many of the practical things that need to be done to kick-start initiatives of this kind (particularly when public funding is involved) require authorisations in the first instance from politicians and managers, and so their roles are vitally important in this sense as well.

For managers of facilities and agencies, a further pressure to take action is bound to come from the vested interest in running an efficient business within budget. Public transport operators, for example, tend to be very interested in action to combat vandalism and graffiti because these things cost them money and adversely affect the quality of the service they offer; and if the public impression is that the service is unsafe for passengers (as, for example, has been said about some late night bus services in British cities), then the response of those passengers and of others whose actions are affected by this adverse publicity may be to ignore the service altogether, resulting ultimately in its withdrawal. This can relate both to problems of safety within vehicles (where 'environmental' responses may be limited) and to safety at transit stops (where environmental responses may be very significant; see Loukaitou-Sideris, 1999). Similarly, the success of car parking facilities may well be a function of how safe from crime potential patrons feel their car would be; environmental responses may have a large part to play here in taking action that in reducing the perceived risks on the part of customers also makes the operation a commercial success (Smith, 1996).

Our plea would be for more effective monitoring and evaluation of initiatives that are taken to deal with these problems, and a greater willingness to report this type of work in publicly available locations so that others can learn from the experience. This really should include both successes and failures, because it is possible to learn from both, although organisations are often more reticent about publicising their failures than they are their successes. To repeat what we have previously said in this book, we agree with the rather dispiriting judgement of a recent review of crime prevention programmes in the USA for its Department of Justice (Sherman et al., 1997):

> Many crime prevention initiatives work. Others don't. Most programs have not
> yet been evaluated with enough scientific evidence to draw conclusions (ibid.,
> page 1).

This is a situation that really does need to change in future, not only in Britain and the USA, but also in many other parts of the world[1] if we are to do better.

At the level of the individual property and the individual householder, we suspect that while advice from bodies such as the police is occasionally sought, most decisions about the emphasis to place on security are the result of individual views about fear of crime rather than any real knowledge of crime opportunities. The photographic essay that constitutes Figure 9.2 uses an Australian example to demonstrate this point, by showing how four rather different treatments of essentially the same situation in nearby properties on the same street in the same Perth suburb have materialised over the years as a result of decisions by the individual property owners.

The situation here is that single storey (and in this case middle-income) houses have been built on common plot sizes on an area of land which was

Photograph 1

Photograph 2

Figure 9.2 Suburban residential units in Perth, Western Australia

Photographs 1 and 2 show the property largely hidden from view to and from the street by a combination of walls/fences and vegetation.

Photograph 3

Photograph 4

Figure 9.2 *Continued*

Photographs 3 and 4 show much more open fronts with a much higher level of visibility to and from the street than is the case with photographs 1 and 2.

cleared and subdivided for residential purposes. Over the years, residents have made their own decisions about elements such as constructing walls or fences, about the nature and scale of landscaping, about window treatments and about the sitting-out area at the front of the house. Their individual reasons for manipulating these various elements in the ways in which they have done this will be many and varied, and will in all probability be about the amenity value they get or hope to get from their property at least as much as about safety considerations. These decisions result in very different outcomes from what is in each case essentially the same situation, which of course is the right of the individual householder but which, as far as these decisions are based upon perceptions of safety, may be misinformed. For example, does a large front wall mean that the occupant is safer, or does it merely create the illusion of safety? If the 'eyes on the street' philosophy has any meaning at all, it must be in a two-way sense; in other words, a property owner contributes to community safety through their own eyes on the street, but in turn their safety is contributed to by the ability of others to watch what is going on at the front of their property. So a large wall, while giving an owner privacy and perhaps a sense of safety, might mean that a burglar who has scaled it is actually less at risk of being caught because they will not be able to be seen from the street. Similar issues arise in respect of different types of fencing, of how luxuriant landscaping is allowed to become, and of how individuals choose to make use of the front parts of their houses. Readers are invited, having thought about this discussion, to place the four photographs that make up Figure 9.2 in rank order in terms of both apparent resident perceptions of safety and what they think actual safety might be, and then to reflect on the differences (if any) between these two analyses and their implications.[2] It is also worth reflecting on the quite limited extent to which the actions taken in these cases over the years by property owners actually involved any formal planning controls on the part of the local authority.

Our overall conclusion about the relationship between crime and the fear of crime is that, as we said at the outset, both USA and British experience suggests that it is more helpful to think of them as two separate but linked issues than it is to think of them as being two sides of the same coin. The fear of crime is a hugely complex phenomenon (probably more so than is crime itself, which in one sense can actually be seen as a relatively straightforward matter), which does not appear in either of the two societies to be closely related to what happens year on year to crime rates. Indeed, this point is well expressed by recent US experience, where the fact that crime has been falling in recent years (which we discuss in more detail below) does not appear to have resulted in much diminution of the fear of crime. In turn, this suggests to us that programmes designed to tackle crime problems ought to be very clear about their objectives, rather than simply assume that in tackling crime they are also tackling fear of crime, and indeed should often adopt a twin-track approach; a programme to tackle a crime problem, and a linked programme to tackle associated issues of public perception.

CRIME TRENDS IN THE USA AND IN BRITAIN

As Chapter 2 has illustrated, the USA in recent times has seen generally falling crime rates, whereas until recently Britain has seen a continuation of a long-term rise to the point at which, for many individual types of crime, rates in Britain by the mid-1990s were well ahead of those in the USA. The most recent British data do suggest that a downturn occurred in the late 1990s, although it is too soon on the basis of two data sets (the British Crime Surveys of 1998 and 2000) to declare this to be the permanent reversal of the long-term upwards trend. This is almost certainly not consistent with many of the images of popular culture, which typically present the USA as a lawless society and Britain as being essentially law-abiding – although there is evidence to suggest that this image is more accurate in terms of violent crime as measured by comparative murder rates and the use of firearms in crimes. Even here, however, the position in the USA appears to have been improving in recent years, although in terms of these particular types of crime the USA remains well ahead of Britain. It is possible that these trajectories have in turn affected the attitudes both within the two societies and in their governments towards the need for new policy frameworks within which crime issues should be understood and tackled: the policy framework within the USA in recent years has been relatively stable (and largely local in its nature) whereas in Britain there appears to have been an ever-broadening approach in search of a solution to what appeared to be an intractable problem. The British approach may produce a great deal of innovation, but what it cannot claim (at least yet) is that it has been successful over any period of time. Indeed, it would be hard to argue convincingly that the downturns recorded in the 1998 and 2000 British Crime Surveys were mainly a function of the specific policy innovations taken by the Blair Government since its election to office in 1997, simply because insufficient time had been available to enable initiatives such as those introduced via the Crime and Disorder Act, 1998 to have much effect.[3] The USA approach, on the other hand, allows scope for local innovation within a broadly stable national framework, and it can be argued that this balance has actually contributed to the successes in containing and reducing crime.

We have not attempted to explain why we think these divergent trends have occurred in the two societies, nor do we think that a single explanation would in all probability be accurate. We suspect that in both societies the explanations are multiple and complex, within which national and local economic circumstances, cultural norms and behaviour patterns, the ways in which issues concerned with crime are dealt with in the media, approaches to punishment upon conviction, patterns and styles of policing, and public attitudes to the police all play a part; and there may be many other elements in there as well. In a sense, for the purposes of this book the broad explanations do not matter all that much, except in the sense that they influence decisions about policy and practice. What really matters is that crime continues to exist on a large scale; it is clearly perceived as a major problem both by society at large and by governments; it is clearly also a major problem to those who are on the receiving end of it; and because much of it is place-specific it raises issues about the kinds of place-related activities that might make a difference both to the opportunities to commit certain kinds of crimes and citizens' fears that they will be the victims of such an attempt. While we have not attempted to enter this debate about why crime trends in the two societies until very recently have followed divergent paths, we have pointed out on several occasions throughout this book that many others have made claims about this. We have also shown in Chapter 2 that these matters are frequently the stuff of media and political exchanges. Readers should be aware, therefore, that this is heavily contested territory.

These large differences between the scale and the trajectory of crime trends in the USA and Britain should not hide the point (as they can easily do) that the patterns of crime in each country tend to be largely similar. Crime is a particularly urban phenomenon in both countries; many types of crimes appear to impact particularly upon the poorest people in those societies; these concerns seem to be linked to issues of housing tenure and of race; and there are important differences between geographical locations within the two countries which exhibit broadly the same characteristics. The concept of 'unequal risks' used in recent British Crime Surveys can just as easily be applied in the USA, and it can be applied in broadly predictable ways. So, without wanting to suggest that the experience of the two societies in these terms is identical, we believe that the broad similarities here are at least as important as the relatively detailed differences that could readily be enumerated in a comparative study. The importance of this, of course, is that, as we have already argued, one of the critical needs when seeking to adapt an innovation that has been attempted in one location to another is the need to understand the context within which that initiative has been applied. While there are important societal and cultural differences between Britain and the USA at the local or neighbourhood level (Bennett, 1997, pages 3–24), it is also possible to find broadly comparable situations in these terms that might suggest that what has worked in one location could work in another, and which at the very least would facilitate comparative studies.

THE HISTORY OF PLACE-BASED CRIME PREVENTION

In terms of urban settlement, Britain is a much older country than the USA, and thus has a longer history of settlement form being influenced by considerations such as the ability to defend (in the military sense) key buildings or locations, in the manner described in Chapter 3. Because British settlements are often influenced by historic layout patterns even where no or few artefacts remain, this can have a direct effect on contemporary urban form; an example would be the centre of a town or city where the medieval street plan and associated building layout still dominate, even though few if any original medieval buildings remain. Large areas of British cities face major decisions about the re-use of land rather than decisions about further outward expansion; and as we have seen from Chapter 7 this is now reflected in British Government policy, with its requirement for at least 60 per cent of development to meet the needs of anticipated new household formation over the next few years to be on previously used urban land. Even some British suburbs are by now becoming quite venerable, although this should not be taken as implying that no new development is taking place on greenfield sites; a target of 60 per cent of development on previously used urban land still implies that 40 per cent of development will take place on land that does not fall into this category.

By contrast, the USA has a shorter urban history, and although many of its cities are quite old a much larger proportion of development in the USA is through further suburbanisation (and, indeed, the use of more remote locations) than is the case in Britain. In an absolute sense, land is not generally perceived to be in short supply in the USA, although its value varies hugely by location, and in comparison to Britain there are simply not the same pressures to redevelop in urban areas to prevent further rural encroachment. Very high car ownership levels, and in some areas poor or non-existent public transport services, have exacerbated this trend. The USA also saw major inter-regional shifts in the twentieth century, with large-scale movements of population to sun-belt states such as California, Arizona, Texas, Georgia and Florida as the economy of the USA reduced its dependence on the manufacturing activities mainly located further north. That has left major urban regeneration (in the USA, 'urban revitalization'; Wagner, Joder and Mumphrey, 1995) issues to be tackled in cities such as Pittsburgh and Detroit, but it has also meant that cities such as Miami, Los Angeles and Atlanta experienced growth in the twentieth century on a massive scale.

These pen-pictures immediately indicate that, in terms of the relationships between crime and the design of the built environment, we would expect to see some quite major differences not merely between the two countries but also inside each of them as well. The USA is still a growing country, where in general terms land is not treated as a commodity in short supply, and the likelihood is that the

vast majority of development will continue to be on land being used for urban purposes for the first time. Britain, on the other hand, is a country where the overall
population (as distinct from the number of households) is growing very little, and
where there is considerable policy pressure to see urban land re-used to prevent
the further spread of suburban and rural development. Despite the building of a
relatively small number of New Urbanist developments in the USA, one of the consequences of this difference is that planners dealing with further suburban development in America will usually be dealing with relatively low density layouts where
the car is the only means of transport; whereas in Britain densities will often be
higher, public transport considerations may apply to the development, and one of
the important issues will be fitting it as well as possible into the existing urban
fabric.

We believe that only a small proportion of the development we have been
talking about above over the last 25 years or so has given much explicit consideration to place-based crime prevention issues, not in the military sense (which has
affected settlement structure on a long-term basis in many locations) but in the
sense for which Oscar Newman coined the term 'defensible space'. We estimated
in Chapter 8 that some 2–3 per cent of British houses over the period 1989–1996
had been built in accordance with Secured By Design standards, and of course
another way of putting this same figure is that 97–98 per cent had not explicitly
met these standards. That figure probably underestimates the effect of defensible
space and related ideas on new house-building in Britain over this period, of
course, because Oscar Newman's ideas will have influenced many architects, irrespective of whether the house-builders for whom they were working wished to
advertise their products as Secured By Design. Nonetheless, it is probably true to
say that in both countries explicit consideration of the desire to reduce the
opportunity for crime through environmental design, and within this the use of
defensible space ideas as a major design parameter, has not been a major feature
of most house-building in recent times. One of the consequences of this, certainly
experienced in both countries, is that where problems of particular types of crime
are subsequently encountered this is often tackled by 'retro-fitting' (adapting what
already exists); this is by definition a constrained process which probably tends to
emphasise target-hardening actions at the level of the individual property, simply
because these are much easier to carry out than a major revision of the layout of
the wider area which might entail a considerable amount of demolition.

Having suggested that probably only a small minority of the housing stock
built both in the USA and in Britain over the past twenty-five years has been
explicitly influenced by these sorts of ideas as a means of discouraging criminal
activity, we believe that there have been some significant differences between the
two societies in some of the derivatives of these ideas that have made an impact

over this period. The three on which we wish to concentrate here are the privatisation of space and facilities and the approach to security that goes with it, the notion of the gated community, and the spread of closed circuit television (CCTV). We take each of these in turn below.

Although both the USA and Britain have seen the privatisation of security operations on a large scale, our impression is that this has been taken much further in the USA than it has in Britain. Out-of-town shopping malls, for example, which have proliferated in the USA, will typically have their own security systems in place, including both cameras and their own security staff, and the anathema towards CCTV cameras in public places in the USA (which we discuss in more detail below) has not stopped their widespread use in what are formally private places. The approach that is adopted essentially seems to be that people are invited into these private places (which is necessary if they are to succeed commercially) provided that they abide by the rules established by the operators, with these rules being enforced not usually by the police but usually by the operators' security staff. The phenomenon of gated communities (which we discuss in more detail below) can be seen as a further example of this process of private security operation, in the sense that people use their purchasing power to opt into a security system that is designed to keep others out, or at the very least to screen them carefully. Since in these cases we are talking about enclosed spaces (the walls and gates of a gated community, the internal environment of a shopping mall), the approach to the relationship between the opportunity for crime and environmental design is also an internalised approach; crime is contained within a space, and the hope is that the security system can become aware of it and deal with it quickly while it remains within that space.

The American notion of the gated community finds no real parallel in contemporary Britain, although of course it can be argued that it is the modern equivalent of the walled cities common in Europe up to the medieval period and in some cases beyond, as discussed in Chapter 3. Where the similarity ends is that the modern gated communities, which have been springing up particularly in California, Texas and Florida, can be seen as being anti-urban. The thrust of this argument is that the phenomenon represents people voting with their feet and their wallets against the things they dislike in the American city, including crime and the fear of crime, and instead establishing themselves in a secure enclave outside it, particularly in America's 'sunbelt' states which have in any event been experiencing in-migration in recent years (Blakely and Snyder in Ellin, 1996, pages 85–7). This can be seen as people explicitly turning their backs on the notion of cities as 'communities of difference' which need to be managed as such (Sandercock, 2000), because they have sufficient purchasing power to be able to make a choice of this nature. It is thus an exclusive concept, and is deliberately marketed as such;

and it is clearly a powerful image, as is instanced by the growth in the metropolitan area of Orlando in Florida during the 1990s from virtually no inhabitants to an anticipated population of 100,000 in gated communities by the year 2000 (Haynes, 1997, page 52). These people are far from being a random cross-section of the population of the city; they are overwhelmingly from its wealthiest sectors. The clear sense of this as turning away from the city, and indeed of sending a message about not wishing to associate with the remaining city dwellers, is import-ant to the 'parent' city not just in a psychological sense but also in a community sense, because many of these people would otherwise have been among the natural leaders in the urban community and as such would have played an import-ant part in trying to make the city a better place. As an approach, this would be anathema to current British public policy, with its emphasis on regenerating cities through housing the majority of development needs on previously developed urban land; and by the year 2000 very little of this kind of development could be found in Britain. But it is often said that Britain experiences USA urban trends some ten to twenty years later; it will therefore be interesting to see whether the clear US market interest in gated communities crosses the Atlantic and is able to overcome British planning policy resistance during this period.

The experience with CCTV appears to be the complete reversal of the experience with gated communities; British cities have taken CCTV as an import-ant component of their strategies both for protecting public places and for encour-aging people to believe that public places are safe. As a consequence the 1990s in particular saw not only the mushrooming of CCTV schemes in British cities but also the development of public funding regimes in order to encourage further schemes to come forward. The available research seems to suggest that this initi-ative is working; public acceptance of CCTV seems to be at quite a high level; and it is now regarded as a vital component of British policy both towards commercial areas and also increasingly towards other types of areas (Oc and Tiesdell, 1997). Other societies seem to have followed a similar route, as became very evident for example during a visit by one of the authors to Perth, Western Australia in August and September, 2000. This has simply not happened on this scale in public places in the USA, where civil liberties concerns and the fear of 'big brother' have consid-erably restricted the use of CCTV. This has not been such a problem in relation to private places, however, where as we have noted above acceptance of CCTV seems in effect to be part of the 'rules' which govern admission. Thus, while CCTV is part of the approach to security adopted in many shopping malls in the USA, it is much less common in the public parts of the downtown areas of many American cities, many of which of course have been losing retail floorspace to out-of-town or suburban malls over a long period. There may well be a relationship between these two phenomena, in the sense that retailers may have relocated not just because they sensed that that was the way the market was moving but also because they felt that the security package on offer in the malls (of which CCTV was often a component) was more attractive to their business than a perceived lack of security in a downtown location.

A final comment under this broad heading may be of some significance: evidence is starting to accumulate that in the USA, a society where litigiousness may have been taken further than in most other parts of the world, landlords could conceivably be at risk of successful civil actions by tenants if it can be argued that they have failed to take advantage of current best practice in terms of Crime Prevention Through Environmental Design (CPTED) and a crime has taken place as a result of which the tenant has sustained losses (Gordon and Brill, 1996). So far at any rate this line of argument has not really surfaced in Britain; in any event it seems to us to be a difficult line of argument, since it carries with it the assumption, which we would dispute, that thinking about CPTED has been developed to the point at which for many situations there is clearly a right and a wrong answer which can be backed up by research findings. However, if this line of argument were to become fully established, it would clearly be a powerful force pushing landlords towards taking their crime prevention responsibilities more seriously.

We think that it is possible to argue, when looking at this comparative survey of the use of place-based crime prevention ideas in both societies, that the same basic principles have been around in discussions (both professional and lay) about the form of urban development in each, but that they have been applied in different ways (where this has happened at all) primarily as a result of cultural factors. So, it would certainly be possible both in the USA and in the UK, when analysing the forms that development has taken over the past 20 years or so in the context of crime prevention, to find examples in both cases of the situational crime prevention principles of opportunity, reward, risk and effort and of the defensible space principles of territoriality, surveillance, access control and activity generation that we introduced in Chapter 4; but these are likely to have been differently applied in the two societies for cultural reasons. To illustrate this by returning to the example of gated communities that we discussed above (see also the discussion by McLaughlin and Muncie in Pile et al., 1999, pages 117–22), they can be seen as perhaps fairly extreme attempts to minimise the opportunity and maximise the risks and efforts involved in crime through harnessing the principles of territoriality, surveillance and access control. We think that the likeliest explanation as to why gated communities have occurred on a large scale in recent years in parts of the USA and in some other parts of the world, but not on any scale in the UK and some other societies, is because of the cultural endorsement of the view in the former group that if people can afford to pay to live in developments of this nature then they should have the opportunity to do so. Perhaps what this particular example reflects is the cultural view that what really matters most in the USA is what choices individuals make in respect of their private and semi-private spaces, whereas in countries like Britain the public purpose and public policies seem to count for more. If this is true, it suggests that we will make real progress in developing our ideas about crime prevention and environmental design through improving our understandings about how these broadly common principles or ideas interact with the cultural values and norms of particular societies.

Our overall conclusion about the history of place-based crime prevention measures when looked at comparatively, however, is that it seems unlikely that this idea has dominated contemporary thinking either in the USA or in Britain in terms of the deliberate manipulation of the physical environment in order to reduce crime opportunities. Both societies have seen huge volumes of new residences constructed since Oscar Newman's ideas were first published and, while the latter have been part of the intellectual capital that the development professions have drawn on in the intervening period, the available evidence suggests that only a small minority of these houses have been constructed with this relationship uppermost in the minds either of the house-builder or of the design team. This view is shared by Richard Peiser (in Felson and Peiser, 1998, pages x–xi) in commenting on the lack of impact that crime prevention measures through development and management approaches had yet had in the USA on the real estate community:

> NIJ's (National Institute of Justice) CPTED program (Crime Prevention Through Environmental Design) is virtually unknown to the real estate community.... . Real Estate owners and developers have considerable experience in dealing with different types of crime, but the major organisations whose members are property owners and developers had little formal contact with the principal institutions involved in research on criminology – until the policy forum in Washington D.C. in June 1995.

Clearly, even if designers and house-builders as communities had taken fully on-board the messages of place-based crime prevention (and the evidence suggests that at the time Peiser was writing this was not the case), they would have found putting these messages into practice an uphill struggle given the absence of understanding of these matters by the owners, developers and financial institutions who tend to hold the purse-strings of the property development process.

Several of the other elements that we have examined under this heading have taken different forms in each of the two societies, and we see this mainly as an expression of cultural differences. So, for example, the gated community idea has taken hold in the USA because it is seen as relating to individuals' rights if they have the financial resources to purchase their way into a secure and exclusive environment, whereas the more collective ethos of Britain would (at least for the present) reject this approach because of its inconsistency with current public policy. Similarly, CCTV has been both relatively popular and successful in many British public places because it is seen as dealing with an overriding public good (perceptions of safety in a major public place such as a city centre, which in turn affects the continuing economic viability of such places), whereas in the USA this has been seen to be less important than concerns over the civil liberties of individuals; although we have noted in passing that these concerns seem to be less significant in private places in the USA, where a different ethos reigns. These differences certainly remind us of the importance of cultural considerations when looking at transatlantic comparisons of this nature.

THE INTELLECTUAL HERITAGE IN THE AVAILABLE LITERATURE

We can deal with this subheading briefly, because in our view the transatlantic comparison is a straightforward matter in this instance. The intellectual heritage in terms of what the available literature has to say about the relationship between crime and the design of the built environment is a common one. There is not one identifiable American strand and another identifiable British strand containing different sets of ideas. Rather, ideas have moved back and forth across the Atlantic with contributions on an ongoing basis from both American and British authors, with each building on the work already done irrespective of nationality. Interestingly, formal comparisons to see whether cultural, social, economic or physical/environmental contexts are sufficiently similar to warrant such a ready transfer are quite rare in the literature, and it therefore seems clear that the majority of the authors who borrow from work done on both sides of the Atlantic do not regard these issues as being of particular significance. Similarly also, the available literature, irrespective of its source, remains open to the charge that it is fairly thin on careful post hoc evaluations of what has been done, and particularly so in terms of the absence of many longitudinal studies; although an interesting exception is the longitudinal study of Baltimore over the period 1981/82–1994 by Taylor (1999) which does stress the importance of the wider social, political and economic environment. Nonetheless, it is clear that the field has been developing and will continue to develop in this multi-national manner, and the advantages of a common intellectual tradition will in our view outweigh the disadvantages, as long as these points about context and about outcomes identified via careful research receive more attention than has been the case hitherto.

The most important points about this common intellectual heritage are that it should be used, and that its users should in turn accept a responsibility to con-tribute to it via their own experiences. It is easy, as indeed we have done above, to criticise the literature for what it does not contain, but this should not obscure the fact that there is some solid evidence that some place-based crime initiatives do appear to have worked. As we have said, most of this evidence appears to be relat-ively short-term in its nature, and the absence of much evidence about what the longer-term consequences of measures have been is one of the reasons why we are sceptical about some of the claims made to the effect that it is possible to 'design out crime' or to 'plan out crime' (to paraphrase titles of key texts that can be found in the contemporary literature). We would say, on the basis of the avail-able evidence, that it is possible in some instances through place-based approaches to crime problems to 'make a difference'. We would also argue that this more limited claim is nevertheless a worthwhile objective, which can be achieved without necessarily endorsing some of the more controversial extensions of defensible space thinking, such as gated communities or some of the aspects of target-hardening.[4] We also believe that it is possible in the future to do better than we often have in the past and on a more consistent basis, through learning from the successes and failures that are experienced as a result of taking initiatives. If we are to achieve this, it will require a greater commitment from the relevant practi-tioner and academic communities to monitoring, critical evaluation, and reporting both in the immediate aftermath of an experiment and longitudinally. What we hope as a result is that in the future the available literature will be more helpful to intend-ing takers of initiatives than it is today, and that the cycle of overblown hype and public relations followed by let-down which has accompanied too many initiatives in the past will as a consequence be less common.

POLICY AND PRACTICE FRAMEWORKS

There are clearly major differences in the policy and practice frameworks to be found in the USA and in Britain. To take the organisational structure first, the USA simply has no equivalent to the British system of Architectural Liaison Officers (or equivalent title) throughout British police forces, nor is there any equivalent to the formal link between this and the planning system of the kind forged by DoE Circu-lar 5/94, with its commendation to local planning authorities of the value of working in this manner. Some USA police forces have CPTED trained staff and in some localities the working relationships between police and planners are good through the personal contacts that have been forged; but there is no explicit route for the police into the process of influencing development control decisions in these situ-ations of a kind that compares with the formal status in this process granted to their British ALO opposite numbers by Circular 5/94. In the United States, probably the best known endorsement of place-based crime prevention measures (and specifically defensible space), which is also the statement which by virtue of its source is closest to being an equivalent of the British Circular 5/94, was the essay by former HUD Secretary Henry Cisneros published in 1995, which lauded Oscar Newman's work at Clason Point Gardens in New York's South Bronx (Cisneros, 1995). More recently in Britain, Section 17 of the Crime and Disorder Act, 1998 has gone still further in placing a statutory duty on local planning authorities to have regard to crime and disorder issues in carrying out their statutory functions, although it is as yet far from clear what this new duty will actually mean in terms of everyday planning practice at the local level.[5] This has reinforced the sense that the British planning system at the local level is at least beginning to incorporate these concerns into its activities, even if as yet this is often not very well thought through, and there is no near equivalent to this in the USA.

At the time of writing, work on local crime reduction strategies is also getting under way throughout England and Wales, via the partnership approach required under the Crime and Disorder Act, 1998 (Crime Concern, undated). The critical point about this is not merely its emphasis upon a partnership approach, and not even its requirement that a crime audit should precede work on the strategy, but the fact that it places equal responsibility on the local planning authority and the police to take this approach forward. It is too soon to say how well this new approach is working in England and Wales, and in any event it is almost certain that, when looked at across the board, performance particularly in the early years will be patchy. But the Salford case study described in Chapter 8 certainly showed the approach to be promising. There is no formal equivalent in the USA in the sense of legislation mandating this as a requirement in every locality, but the idea of multi-agency partnerships to tackle crime is not a new one. Thus, several roughly analogous initiatives will be found in the USA, albeit without the explicit statutory backing of the British case; a recent study (Rohe *et al.*, 2001) has calculated, for example, that about half of local American police departments had adopted by 1994 various forms of community policing strategies involving multi-agency community planning, law enforcement and development partnerships. This suggests that cross-national comparisons may have a role to play in looking at the contributions such approaches can make: a study restricted to Britain looking at several partnerships all operating within the same legislation might struggle to see difficulties arising from the framework itself, as distinct from the ways in which it is being applied in various localities, whereas a comparative element looking at aspects of the approach without this legislative support might provide some useful insights. It will also be interesting to see over the next few years what impact these new arrangements have in Britain upon mainstream planning activities, and in turn what effects planning systems and processes have on work under the 1998 Act, especially in the context of its Section 17.

At the national level, as Chapter 7 has indicated, British policy in the past decade has gone through a series of ever-widening discourses in the apparent search for answers, and now locates the relationship between crime and the design of the built environment in amongst a large number of policy drivers in a manner that we have tried to encapsulate in Figure 7.3. There is undoubtedly an intellectual rationale for this in the sense that it is possible to argue for all these policy connections without too much difficulty. The problem is that so far this framework has delivered very little; it has been characterised in recent years by further policy initiatives being added on a regular basis to the 'ferris wheel' represented by Figure 7.3, rather than by very much in the way of effective implementation that is starting to change things on the ground. This is not to be dismissive of all of this, so it is not claiming that the framework is inappropriate or is incapable of delivering. Simply, it is not yet possible to demonstrate the effectiveness of this approach, whatever its intellectual attractions might be, through solid achievements on the ground, and this must be its real test. Throughout this period until very recently, the phenomenon of apparently ever-rising crime rates in Britain has been a more or less continuous presence, and indeed it is possible to argue that there is a relationship between this continuing central problem and the apparent process of thrashing around ever more broadly looking for solutions.

The position in the USA, by contrast, has been considerably more calm, although this does not necessarily mean that it will stay that way, especially if the American economy experiences a period of prolonged turbulence. Without suggesting that the crime problem can be regarded as 'solved' in the face of a set of falling crime statistics, there has certainly not been the ferment of policy searches that has characterised the British situation. Indeed, it is possible to argue that it would in any event be very difficult for both constitutional and political reasons for a US Federal Government to adopt a stance similar to that of the British Government, even if it felt that this was an appropriate thing to do, because so much of the policy responsibility taken by the British Government falls in the USA to state or more local levels, and indeed is jealously guarded as such. So, while the Federal Government can (and does) support local initiatives through competitive bidding processes for grant-aid, it would find it very difficult to adopt the more holistic stances seen in Britain because of the limitations of Federal responsibility. At the same time, it could be argued that this creates more scope for the exercise of local initiative in the USA, simply because it does not impose the kind of local uniformity that can be a characteristic of strong central initiatives. It should be pointed out, of course, that there have been no particular signs in recent times of the political will in the USA to follow the British pattern; this could be argued to be a rational stance in the sense that the trajectory of crime statistics in the USA does not seem to be indicating the need for more radical policy actions. All of this might suggest that the existence of a strong central policy push is not a necessary precondition of successful action in this field, but is a function of the political constitution and character of the society in question. So, we would expect to see such a phenomenon in Britain but we would not expect to see its equivalent in the USA. We suspect that both approaches are capable in their different ways of achieving successful crime reduction strategies, with neither necessarily being better than the other; they are simply different.

We conclude from the foregoing that in the next few years Britain is likely to exhibit more uniformity of practice than the USA. In the former case this will be driven by a strongly top-down (i.e. central government-led) approach, whereas the USA will see more diversity arising from a range of initiatives at the local scale characterised by a much more bottom-up approach. This range is likely to be very broad, from virtually nothing in some cases to a very considerable set of actions in others; but what happens in individual instances will be determined predominately by local people (citizens, professionals and politicians) and local situations rather than by any particularly strong Federal push. Indeed (writing at the start of the administration headed by George W. Bush), given what is known about its likely philosophical orientation as compared with that of the preceding Clinton administration, we would expect to see more of an emphasis in Federal policy on punitive crime policies in the immediate future and relatively less emphasis on prevention, whether through treatment of offenders or of environments.

To repeat our regular pleas, our hope is that this range of actions on both sides of the Atlantic, whatever it turns out to be, is accompanied by careful monitoring work which is made widely available so that we learn what appears to be succeeding in what circumstances and why, as well as what appears to be failing. The mix of approaches that we have described may also lend itself to careful cross-national comparisons, in particular to try to understand the importance of some of the contextual issues that are always part of any initiative but which are very difficult to separate out from the specific variables being studied. We return to this matter in our final chapter which looks at some of the further research that we think is necessary in this field.

CONCLUSIONS

As we said at the outset, our main conclusion is that the most visible differences between the USA and Britain are their opposite experiences in recent years of crime levels and trajectories and the very different policy and practice frameworks that have arisen in each country. We also believe that there are some important cultural and societal differences in the ways in which individual concepts or policy ideas are handled, and we have discussed most of these under the broad heading of 'the history of place-based crime prevention'. In spite of this, there are also several similarities. Notable amongst these are the common intellectual tradition, with ideas and literature essentially being shared (as is also the habit of often not bothering to evaluate properly the initiatives that are taken), which is simply not a respecter of national boundaries and clearly is not about to become so. Another major similarity is the broad pattern of the incidence of crime problems and the phenomenon of 'unequal risk', despite the overall differences in the scale and the trajectory of the crime figures themselves. So, for example, crime in the inner cities of Britain is likely in practice to have many features in common with crime in the inner cities of America, and in many ways the geography and the sociology of both criminal activity and the propensity to become a victim of crime tend to be fairly similar. This suggests that there is scope for the USA and Britain to learn from each others' experiences, to try initiatives in one that appear to have worked in the other provided that there is a sophisticated understanding of the contextual differences that are bound to be encountered, and to participate in joint studies which use these similarities and differences as learning devices. But this analysis also suggests that seizing on something from the one culture in the hope that it will provide a 'quick fix' in the other without understanding the contextual differences and in advance of any careful analysis of whether or not it actually works in situ is a recipe with a high potential for failure.

A particular similarity which we have been struck by in carrying out the work for this book has been the experience of the fear of crime in both societies. Although the scales and the trajectories of crime in the USA and in Britain are very different, the evidence we have cited (although it is very difficult to compare it directly) suggests that fear of crime is embedded in both societies as a major issue. At the simplest of levels, we have tried to model both this and its relationship with actual crime levels in Figure 9.1, although we stress again that this is a very complex set of relationships which we would expect to see vary very considerably according to local circumstances. But this very general conclusion has led us to suggest that we think that the most helpful way of looking at this phenomenon in terms of public policy initiatives is to see actual crime types and rates and public perceptions of the fear of crime as two separate but related areas requiring separate but related policy attention. We think it very likely that initiatives which fail to make this distinction, or which implicitly assume that by dealing with the one issue they are automatically dealing with the other, are increasing very considerably the probability that they will not succeed. Similarly, initiatives which fail to set clear objectives which recognise this distinction, or which confuse the two sets of objectives, are also likely to struggle. We believe that parallel and mutually reinforcing initiatives, with clear and distinctive sets of objectives, are most likely to succeed in these terms, especially where major efforts have been made both to win community support for and then to enrol community partnership in those initiatives. We believe that this is such a significant conclusion that we return to it again in Chapter 10.

NOTES

1   For example, one of Ted Kitchen's conclusions from a review of practice in this field in the metropolitan area of Perth in Western Australia undertaken as part of a Visiting Fellowship at Curtin University in the late summer of 2000 was that this judgement by Sherman *et al.* could certainly be applied to the Australian situation as well.

2   For what it is worth (because there is no right or wrong answer here), our view about this is that each of these adaptations is probably regarded as being safe by the property owner because that is what they have deliberately chosen to do, but we suspect that in terms of actual safety the rank order may actually be the reverse of the order in which the photographs are presented, i.e. the property in photograph 1 may be the least safe because that high fence once penetrated provides perfect screening for an intruder, and the property in photograph 4 may be the safest because it offers a good example of 'eyes on the street'.

3   We are conscious of stepping out into deep water here, because we are aware of the extent to which this is contested political territory, with parties quick to blame others and claim credit for themselves. For the avoidance of doubt, therefore, we are not criticising the specific policies of the Blair Government when commenting that we think it unlikely that they are the main reasons for the improving crime figures recorded in the 1998 and 2000 British Crime Surveys; we are merely saying that there is probably not much of a relationship between these two because there has been insufficient time for such relationships to develop with any strength. The 2000 British Crime Survey does begin to offer some explanations for falling property crime in recent years, mainly around improved security on the part of property owners, local crime reduction initiatives, and a general improvement in economic circumstances (Home Office, 2000b, pages 56 and 57), and it also makes the point that this trend is visible in many other countries such as the USA (ibid, page 57).

4   Our discussion in Chapter 4 raises some of the issues that surround the notion of defensible space and some of the questions that have arisen over the years about the extent to which and the consistency with which the idea is capable of being successfully applied. A further useful discussion of some of the issues and concerns here can be found in McLaughlin and Muncie (in Pile *et al.*, 1999, pages 119–22); and we would want to associate ourselves with the view expressed there to the effect that some of the products of this thinking can be socially repressive, whether this is intended or not (our

paraphrase). We would also agree with the view expressed in the same book by its editors (ibid, page 354) to the effect that while this certainly makes it possible to criticise the argument that social problems (if that is ultimately what crime is seen as being) can be solved through physical means, it would be unwise to dismiss both this line of argument and the impact that it has had and will continue to have in decisions about the future of our cities. We see this as being consistent with our formulation that the available evidence does not (at least, not yet) support the idea that it is possible to 'design out crime', but that place-based responses to crime problems are capable of 'making a difference'.

5   At the time of writing, the British Government has still to spell out what changes in planning practice it thinks need to flow from this new duty placed on local planning authorities to have regard to crime and disorder issues, although as we have shown in Chapter 7 the Urban Policy White Paper (Department of the Environment, Transport and the Regions, 2000b, page 120) does contain a commitment to review the extant guidance. Key examples where attention may need to be focused in this context are:-

(a)   the policies contained in development plans, which inter alia may need to contain more explicit statements in support of appropriate urban design policies;

(b)   a greater emphasis upon crime prevention measures in the development control process, both through the reasons that local planning authorities might use to refuse planning applications or the conditions they might impose upon consents and through the guidance material that they might prepare and disseminate; and

(c)   the contents of environmental improvement programmes, which could be seen through the partnerships promoted via the Crime and Disorder Act, 1998 as contributory public sector components to a range of crime prevention measures.

CHAPTER 10

THE WAY FORWARD

INTRODUCTION

This chapter tries to pull together some of the most important threads that have been emerging throughout this book. To do this, we have divided it into three broad sections. The first deals with general stances, and discusses some of the most significant perspectives which in our view should determine the way forward for the broad field of planning for crime prevention. The second looks at some key propositions which we feel able to advance with a degree of confidence as useful elements to help with this journey. And the third section deals with what we consider the way forward for research in this field to be, given that we have placed emphasis throughout on the importance of knowledge accumulation rather than polemic if the field is going to develop and if practice decisions are to benefit from effective guidance from the record to date. Our conclusions reiterate the key messages that we hope readers will take from this book.

We should say straight away that we do not feel able to advance an approach to 'the way forward' which people can simply take away and apply to whatever cases they are dealing with in the full expectation that the outcome will be successful. Nothing would give us greater pleasure than to be able to do this: to produce the equivalent of a Mrs Beeton's cookery book (or, for American readers, a 'Joy of Cooking') for the field of planning for crime prevention which could stand the test of time would be an achievement indeed. But, as we have said on many occasions throughout this book, the level of what we can claim to know in this field which is backed up by reliable research or by post-hoc evaluation is simply insufficient to support a cook-book approach of this kind. This may well be an appropriate long-term objective, but were we to attempt this for the present this would simply put another piece of polemic alongside the considerable volume of material of this kind which already exists. This is so despite the fact that there is indeed a growing body of evidence collected on both sides of the Atlantic to the effect that some place-based crime prevention strategies do work or are at least promising. Nevertheless, the tripartite approach that we have outlined (general stances, key propositions and further research) is as far as we think we can reasonably go at this stage; and we hope it contributes not merely to current understandings but also to the process of shaping future work agendas. To readers who have come thus far with us and who were expecting a conclusion replete with more fireworks than this, we can only ask that they reflect on what we have said.

GENERAL STANCES

A recent review for the US Department of Justice of place-based crime prevention in the USA (Feins *et al.*, 1997) summarises its findings in terms that we would strongly support:

> The most effective place-specific crime prevention strategies are those that take into account the geographic, cultural, economic, and social characteristics of the target community. Thus, the selection of place-specific crime prevention strategies and tactics should be made in close collaboration with the community, after sustained observation of its current patterns of use. The experiences of the study sites reveal two major lessons:
>
> - Physical design modifications, management changes, and changes in use should be tailored to specific locations and co-ordinated in their planning and implementation.
> - The most effective security and crime prevention efforts are those that involve a coalition of different players working together to define the problem and then seek solutions.
>
> By emphasising that crime prevention is not a 'one-size fits all' effort, and that some communities may require more attention and ingenuity than others in crafting effective strategies, this report stresses the importance of a thorough analysis of the problems and needs of a given community, as well as ongoing monitoring and evaluation of the place-specific strategies selected (ibid., pages xi and xii).

We believe that this encapsulates many of the ideas in the field that really do matter quite considerably. Key amongst these are:

- Different strategies are likely to be successful in different places because of differences in localities, in the people who live, work in or use them in other ways, and in the relationship between these two.[1]
- There cannot as a consequence be a strong argument for proceeding to determine what is likely to work in a given locality without a careful study of that locality and the characteristics of how it is used by people.

- Ideas gleaned from elsewhere may be very useful as a source of starting points for thinking about solutions, but they should not be imported irrespective of the results of careful and detailed local study.
- All of this should be done in partnership with local communities and with the key agencies operating in the area, because it is likely to be the case that their knowledge will help shape appropriate solutions in the first instance and it is almost certain that over the long term their behaviour will make a considerable difference to whether or not success is achieved. This latter point simply acknowledges the unavoidable observation that there are very often intervening variables in the relationships between crime and environmental design, and many of these are about people, about cultural and social norms and forces, and about the operational behaviour of agencies.
- There are no reliable sets of standard solutions here, because there often are no standard problems and there are certainly no standard communities. In reviewing the various theories, ideas and practices that are to be found in the literature, we have been careful not to pick on a small number and argue that they are to be preferred, because at this stage of our knowledge we simply do not believe that it is possible to do this with confidence; and we consider it inherently implausible in any event in such a varied world that standardised approaches could possibly be appropriate as anything other than starting points for careful and detailed local consideration.
- Careful monitoring of what is happening with any initiative, including a willingness to make changes if that is what the monitoring information is pointing to, plus a vigorous post hoc evaluation of what has worked and why (and what has not worked and why not), offer the best prospects of building up the pool of knowledge we need in order to take major strides forward. They are also of vital importance in helping those initiatives and the people committed to them to adapt to the changing circumstances that they must expect to have to face during the life of a project.

This is a strongly empirical approach, which perhaps of itself represents something of a departure from the history of work in the field which has tended to be dominated by ideas and propositions which are largely untested but which happen for various reasons to have become fashionable. Perhaps a good example at the time of writing is the strong support that exists in certain quarters for the ideas of 'New Urbanism', which have not only been influential in some projects in the USA but have travelled across the world and have also influenced projects as diverse as the redevelopment of Hulme in Britain (which is one of the case studies in Chapter 8) and the regeneration of East Perth in Western Australia. The photographs in Figure 10.1 show some aspects of this latter project, and readers might like to

Photograph 1

Photograph 2

Figure 10.1 'New Urbanism' in the up-market regeneration of East Perth, Western Australia

Note the importance of water as a key element in the design approach.

Photograph 3

Photograph 4

Note also the application of the 'eyes on the street' philosophy both to significant vehicular access streets (photograph 3) and to off-street pedestrian walkways (photograph 4).

compare and contrast the more 'up market' application of these ideas in East Perth with the illustrations of Hulme in Chapter 8, where design and layout principles were also heavily influenced by 'New Urbanist' thinking. Our views about this are that 'New Urbanism' represents an interesting and potentially fruitful contribution to the spectrum of ideas, albeit one that needs to be applied across a broader spectrum of house-price ranges and tenures than the relatively expensive owner-occupied housing that has dominated to date; that its emphasis upon human activity, natural surveillance and permeability rather than physical barriers as the basis of crime prevention is intellectually attractive; but that it is not the universal panacea that some of its advocates come close to presenting it as being (see, for example, Rudlin and Falk, 1999) and could not be at least until a considerable amount of post hoc and long-term evaluative research looking at New Urbanist projects has accumulated. We want to emphasise in particular the importance of long-term perspectives here, because most of the post hoc evaluation studies that have been done to date have been relatively short-term in their focus; they have, in effect, looked at the immediate aftermath of an initiative, rather than at what has happened to an area and to the quality of life it affords its users over subsequent years. As we have said, the field to date has been dominated to too great an extent by the trumpeting of ideas both before and beyond their demonstrated worth, which has not only done few favours for the field itself but may also result in individual ideas riding the roller-coaster of fashion and then being dismissed rather than finding a worthwhile place among the pantheon of possibilities. A more empirical and a less adversarial approach is exactly what the field now needs, in our judgement, together with a greater sense of those things that can achieve lasting and positive impacts.

This does not prevent us from advancing some key propositions which we think may well be reliable as a set of starting points for the endeavour over the next few years that we have described above. We do this in the next section of this chapter, together with some comments on their policy and practice implications which we hope readers will find helpful. These also include some cautionary words about the possibility that the process of accumulating knowledge which we are arguing for here might in future cause us (or others) to want to modify some or all of these propositions.

KEY PROPOSITIONS

Acknowledging the present stage of work in the field, and based upon the things that we have said throughout this book, there are nine broad propositions that we wish to advance as concepts that we believe are likely to prove to be reliable contributory elements to future work.[2] These are as follows:

- Issues related to crime and the fear of crime matter very much to local people in their communities, and if planning is to address the 'quality-of-life' issues that local people identify then it must address this concern more effectively than it has done to date. Place-based crime prevention is far too important to be left to the police alone or to any other agency that does not have a grasp of comprehensive design, planning and development issues. Thus, while as societies we may be content to have police playing their traditional role of keeping places safe, we need far broader participation in the processes of making them *safer*.

- The design of the built environment does impact both upon opportunities for crime and the fear of crime, but it does this in complex ways often involving a range of intervening variables rather than in ways that generate universal rules about what works. It is not the only factor that needs to be taken into account when seeking to understand these issues in localities, and for some (perhaps many) types of crime it may not be the most important explanatory element; but environmental design needs to take its place as one of the significant factors to think about when considering opportunities for crime and the fear of crime in localities.

- While crime and the fear of crime intuitively ought to be related to each other, in practice this relationship appears to be very complex. As a consequence, rather than assume that action in the one area will automatically bring benefits in the other area as well (as many contemporary initiatives do) it is better to see these as two separate but related problems which each need to be tackled via tailored programmes with clear objectives which are coordinated with each other.

- There needs to be a much more rigorous approach to the careful evaluation of initiatives in this field so that we learn what works well where and why, rather than the over-reliance that we have seen to date on sets of ideas often advanced by true believers in the absence of such a research base.

- Approaches need to be tailored to specific local circumstances and to the people whose daily lives are framed by those circumstances, because the likelihood that there are standard formulae that can be universally applied with a guarantee of success is remote. This is so despite the fact that there are now some increasingly accepted principles that link crime prevention with human behaviour and the physical environment. The role of theoretical ideas and of experiences from elsewhere is to provide some starting points for this process, rather than to predetermine it.

- Issues around crime and the design of the built environment do not exist in isolation, but are intimately bound up with all the other cultural, social, economic and physical forces that impinge upon people's lives. Whether or not the formal approach to this is the very structured one to be found in Britain or the rather less structured one to be found in the USA, the intellectual approach to the task ought to be an holistic one rather than one that sees crime prevention measures as free standing.

- In turn, this inevitably means that planners have to work closely not just with the police but also with many other professionals in developing possible solutions to these sorts of problems. This process must also be one of working with local communities to this end, rather than believing that solutions can be imposed on local communities. This represents a real challenge to planning professionals not just to improve their inter-professional working skills but also to improve the ways in which they work with local communities over the long term, to shape, implement, monitor and if necessary modify initiatives.

- Statistically at least, some of the greatest potential gains to be had from initiatives to reduce crime and the fear of crime by environmental measures sitting alongside other types of initiatives are in some of the poorest and most deprived communities in our urban areas, simply because these are the areas where crime rates and victimisation are likely to be the highest. They may also, of course, be the hardest initiatives to mount and to sustain, as compared for example with initiatives in suburban areas with very active local communities.

- When looking at ideas from other places that may appear to be attractive, it is important to understand the context in which they have been applied and also whether or not robust evaluation has taken place. The failure to study both context and outcome can all-too-easily lead to ideas being imported which are imperfectly understood from the outset, and as a consequence can increase significantly the likelihood of failure when they are attempted elsewhere. In a world where knowledge in all its forms is not only constantly growing but is able to be moved around ever more rapidly, the risk of this is probably growing, especially where a 'quick fix' or 'something different' is being sought.

We take each of these in turn below, using in each case a shorthand title to summarise the essence of the concept.

CRIME AND THE FEAR OF CRIME MATTER GREATLY TO THE INTENDED BENEFICIARIES OF PLANNING

As we have seen, issues to do with crime and the fear of crime are very high both on political horizons and on the results of surveys which ask citizens about the things that matter to them about their lives; and, indeed, we think these two things are intimately related. This seems to be true irrespective of the trajectory of crime statistics in recent years; the evidence that public concerns about crime in the USA are fading along with continually declining crime levels is still somewhat limited, and in Britain the roller-coaster of recent crime statistics seems to make very little difference to public attitudes. Further, concerns about crime are clearly not just about global statistics; what matters to people is what is happening in their locality and what they perceive to be their risk of being on the receiving end of crime. Planning (in the sense of urban planning, to use a phrase that would be recognised throughout the world), with its concerns to improve the quality of people's lives through the ways in which they engage with and relate to their localities and to involve citizens in decisions about these processes, ought, therefore, to be deeply involved with this agenda as well. It would be an odd kind of planning given this central thrust that only concerned itself with the issues that planners felt were important, and did not address (and, indeed, give a measure of priority to) the views of the intended beneficiaries of its activities.

And yet, without wishing to deny the value of some local initiatives in which planners have been deeply involved, it would be broadly true to say that planning has not to date made anything like the impact upon the relationship between crime and the design of the built environment that it could potentially have done. We believe that planning needs to embrace this concern much more fully and much more effectively than it has done to date; and we are encouraged to note (as we have done in Chapter 7) that the British Government, among its welter of policy initiatives in recent years, has acknowledged the need for crime prevention to become one of the central concerns of planning. In so doing, planners will need to see their contributions as being complementary to those of other professions, notably those of the police; place-based crime prevention initiatives should be seen as arenas of multi-professional activity rather than largely being left to the police who, with the best will in the world (and without denying the potential value of their contribution), are not well equipped to shoulder this responsibility largely alone because they do not have a comprehensive grasp of design, planning and development issues. Planners will need to learn to respect the knowledge and experience of the police in these matters, recognising that just because these come from a different epistemology they are not inferior. This is about planners and the police (and indeed other environmental professionals as well) working together in partnership to add value, and not merely the one substituting for the other.

THERE ARE COMPLEX RELATIONSHIPS BETWEEN CRIME, THE FEAR OF CRIME AND ENVIRONMENTAL DESIGN

Of course, if planners are to engage more effectively in the kinds of initiatives we have outlined above, a prerequisite is for them to understand and to accept the nature of the relationships that exist between crime, the fear of crime and environmental design. Perhaps in the past this understanding and acceptance has not been helped by the swings of fashion (for example, promoting initiatives as panaceas and then having them dismissed as environmental determinism), and also by the overly simplistic nature of some of the prescriptions that have been offered.

The starting point in rectifying this might be two very simple assertions. The first is that it is self-evidently the case that certain kinds of crimes and certain kinds of fears have an environmental component to them. For example, whether or not a property is seen as a potential target by a burglar is likely to be a function among other things of whether that individual sees in the immediate environment of that property opportunities to break into it and to escape from it without being seen; or whether a woman feels comfortable walking along a footpath late at night is likely among other things to be related to how well lit the footpath is and how overgrown (and therefore possibly providing hiding places for aggressors) the surrounding landscaping appears to be. Environmental issues will not be the only concerns at work here and in many other kinds of examples that could have been cited, but in these cases and in others they are highly likely to be an important part of the mix. It is therefore inappropriate (and flying in the face of experience) to dismiss this as 'environmental determinism'.

The second assertion is simply that these relationships are likely to be both very complex and very variable, and as yet we know far too little about them. One of the reasons why we have argued throughout this book for a much more systematic approach to the monitoring and evaluation of local initiatives is because this is one of the most important ways in which we will begin to build up our knowledge about these relationships. Another very promising way in which we can expand our knowledge about these matters appears to be through the use of GIS technology, which can look in increasingly sophisticated ways and at a wide range of spatial scales at geographical patterns of crime to contribute not only to our understanding of what has been happening in localities but also to our knowledge of risk and of what sorts of responses might be effective (Craglia *et al.*, 2000). But while this accumulation of knowledge is an essential endeavour, it is not a substitute for planners getting involved in local initiatives, taking as few preconceptions into them as they possibly can, and immersing themselves in the local situation, working alongside the other people and organisations involved, and tailoring what they and their colleagues do to this growing local understanding.

CRIME AND THE FEAR OF CRIME ARE DIFFERENT BUT LINKED PHENOMENA WHICH BOTH NEED TO BE TACKLED

We have talked on several occasions throughout this book about the extent to which 'objective' knowledge about crime and 'subjective' perceptions about fear of crime, although clearly linked in the broadest of senses, cannot be relied upon to operate as mutually supportive concepts. So, for example, clear evidence from published crime statistics does not appear to result in a reduction in people's fear of crime, and statistical assessments of risk experienced by various kinds of groups in the population are often not closely related to the perceptions of risk recorded by members of those groups when asked. What is equally clear is that it is not practically possible to focus on one of these phenomena to the exclusion of the other. In many ways, fear of crime is as potent a problem as crime itself, because, as the evidence from both Britain and the USA demonstrates, fear changes people's behaviour and can condition their expectations of political and organisational responses to problems of crime. Initiatives are thus almost inevitably forced both into tackling problems of crime as it has been experienced and managing people's expectations or fears, and there is clearly a risk that those that only tackle the first of these concerns (as many have in the past) will fail in respect of the second, especially if they make the explicit or implicit assumption that tackling crime successfully will automatically change people's fears in positive ways. We believe that initiatives are much more likely to be successful if they acknowledge explicitly right from the outset that they have to be addressing both of these phenomena, but that because they are different they require different objectives and strategies. These need to be linked; for example, successes in terms of the incidence of crime can be used as 'good news' stories to try to relate to local fears of crime, especially if as part of the process local communities have been heavily involved from the outset and the local media have played a role as a supportive partner.

Good communication with local people as intended beneficiaries before, during and after a specific initiative has been embarked upon is likely to be absolutely fundamental to the process of trying to tackle fear of crime, but so is an understanding of what local fears actually are and a deliberate attempt as part of the process of crafting an initiative to address these issues. The 'we know best' attitude, or the purchase of a standard solution from an external consultant likely to depart the local scene shortly after he/she arrives, will in all probability not work well in these terms; and there have been a large number of both of these in the past. It is likely also that during the life of an initiative there will be setbacks, which are likely to be reported in the local media (because that is their job, irrespective of whether they are playing the role of supportive partner in the initiative); and it is probably best at the planning stage to assume that this is likely to happen and to prepare contingency plans accordingly. Moreover, the media tend to report short-term improvements as if they were permanent. We know, however, that modern crime-deterrence measures can decay, much as the defensive designs of medieval and renaissance cities noted in Chapter 3 did under the onslaught of new technologies; and quite probably over much shorter time-scales in the contemporary world. Criminals and predators adapt to changed environments and criteria as bacteria do to antibiotics. So, this must be foreseen and planned for as well (Ekblom, 1997).

   This twin-tracking approach, which treats both the initiative itself and local fears about crime to which the initiative relates as being equally important, has not always been a prominent feature of local actions in this field in the past, but we believe that it has a great deal to offer.

THE CAREFUL EVALUATION OF INITIATIVES

We have said so much about this in the book already that further repetition here at any length is probably unnecessary. We will content ourselves by repeating the points that far too few of the initiatives in this field that have been embarked upon in the past have been properly evaluated, and that it is difficult to see how we can build up any collective knowledge about what works well where and why without a much more systematic approach to this issue in the future, combined with a greater willingness to make such results available. Modern information technology should make this latter point much more straightforward than has ever been the case in the past. One particularly important proviso that we would add is that it is often possible to learn at least as much from what does not appear to work as from what does. Publicising negative results of this nature can be particularly problematic for organisations, however, because they can often see their own credibility as being at risk in these circumstances. This can be particularly true in respect of initiatives launched amidst a fanfare of publicity where individual politicians are seen as being closely associated with them, since (generally speaking) politicians want to be associated with success rather than with failure, especially when there are likely to be many subsequent reminders to the voting public of that association. On the other hand, we would argue that this is a field where there can be no certainty about the outcome of an initiative, and that this simple recognition might warrant a degree of caution at the outset rather than the creation of a situation where an initiative cannot in practice be seen or allowed to fail. A recognition that there must inevitably be an experimental element to a local initiative, even where something is being attempted which has worked well elsewhere, would help considerably in this kind of situation.

   This makes the role of the planner (and associated professionals) all the more important, since evaluations should be made at short-, mid- and long-term intervals if we are to be able to understand as fully as possible the outcomes of crime prevention initiatives and particularly those acknowledged to be 'experiments'. Both politicians and managers tend to be orientated, for understandable reasons, to short- or at best mid-term horizons in this respect, whereas planners are taught and need to fly the flag for thinking in the longer-term, with horizons extending beyond the next election or term of office of an individual politician or manager.

Indeed, planners often clash with politicians and managers over these differences in perspectives, but long-term vision is an essential part of the planning armoury and should be used for the public's benefit in relation to place-based crime prevention initiatives just as much as in other fields of planning activity.

APPROACHES SHOULD BE TAILORED TO LOCAL CIRCUMSTANCES AND PEOPLE

In the end, most initiatives are by definition applied within a particular local situation. That situation is not just about the characteristics of physical space, but is also about the people and organisations that own, use or relate to that space. This introduces a potentially infinite variety of local circumstances into what might apparently be a commonly occurring problem, and these local circumstances are likely to make a considerable difference to whether or not something works in that particular instance irrespective of the record achieved by similar approaches elsewhere. That record may well be the reason why a particular approach is being suggested in a particular locality, and that is a perfectly proper use of knowledge or experience gained from elsewhere. But that knowledge or experience is not a substitute for careful consideration of how to relate to local circumstances; and the people who know most about those local circumstances in all their manifold variety are the local people and organisations who regard the locality as 'theirs'. So, we believe that the application of standard formulae or prescriptions without very careful consideration of local circumstances and the full involvement of local people in this process is much more likely to result in failure or at any rate under-achievement than is an approach in which these are strong characteristics. There is simply no substitute for a careful study of the local situation drawing on detailed local knowledge, and then for an approach tailored to the specifics of the situation.

ISSUES AROUND CRIME AND THE DESIGN OF THE BUILT ENVIRONMENT DO NOT EXIST IN ISOLATION

Perhaps one of the reasons why some views about the relationship between crime and the design of the built environment have been criticised in the past as 'environmental determinism' is because they suggested a simple, linear, causal relationship between the two. In other words, the impression they gave was that attending to a particular environmental deficiency or adopting a particular view about what needed to be done based upon an environmental stance would of itself solve the crime problem being encountered. We think that this will turn out to be the case in the real world relatively rarely. In most cases, there will be a complex set of cultural, social, economic and physical forces at work, and while environmental concerns will in some cases be of considerable significance, in many others they will simply be one amongst several factors that need to be understood. This suggests that usually environmental initiatives should be seen as part of a multi-headed attack on the problem of crime rather than something attempted in isolation. The approach needs to be both holistic and sustained if it is to maximise the chances of success, rather than to be based upon the starting proposition that a quick piece of environmental adjustment is all that is needed; although it is of course possible that, after the careful examination of a range of solutions studied as part of this holistic approach, all that is deemed to be necessary in a particular situation is a particular programme of environmental change. The critical point here is that the approach should be holistic, and if the outcome is a relatively simple programme of action that should be as a result of such a process and not something that was pre-determined. There is no evidence from our comparison of the USA and Britain, incidentally, which suggests that the formal framework within which decisions of this kind are taken should preferably be either the very highly structured one now to be found in Britain or the very loose one providing considerable room for local initiatives to be found in the USA. These things appear to be more a product of the particular characteristics of governance in the two societies than they are requirements of success.

LOCAL CRIME-PREVENTION INITIATIVES REQUIRE PARTNERSHIP WORKING, BOTH BETWEEN PROFESSIONALS AND WITH LOCAL COMMUNITIES

It follows from all we have said about the nature of the process of setting up local crime prevention initiatives with the maximum prospects of success that the approach needs to be not only a multi-professional partnership but also a partnership which fully embraces local people. This will require planners to work alongside professionals of several types, some of whom will be very familiar as professional partners (for example, architects or highway engineers) but others of whom may often be less familiar (for example, police officers). Professionals often tend to place considerable emphasis on solutions that fall within their own jurisdictions because these are the things they know best and often want to do; but the need here is not to build programmes that necessarily give something to each professional group but rather to assemble programmes which address the problems that have been identified in ways that command the support of local people. A particular issue with this kind of approach can be the extent to which the nature of a programme is determined by the types of funding that are available rather than by local needs, so that some things can be done readily because funding is available for them but others cannot be done, no matter how desirable they might appear to be, because funding is not specified as being available for them. Professionals can often do a great deal in terms of the presence or absence of flexibility between funding areas either to make sure that programmes are tailored to local needs or follow pre-determined formulae, both through their control over and influence upon programme criteria or because they are well placed to lobby for flexibility. This requires genuine multi-professional partnership-working towards common ends, and this can be a challenge in terms of inter-professional working, not least because communication across professional boundaries with other professionals is not always as good as it might be. This has been particularly evident in relations between planners and the police in both Britain and the USA, where there is manifest scope for improvement.

This approach also requires a willingness to work with local people as equals, acknowledging that the detailed local knowledge they bring to the table is at least as valuable in its own way as are the different kinds of professional knowledge that the non-local members of the team bring with them.[3] The processes of shaping, implementing, monitoring and (if necessary in the light of evidence provided by the monitoring process) modifying programmes are time-consuming and complex, but working with local communities throughout these processes and communicating effectively with local people so that they understand the issues involved and have the opportunity to play a major role in decision-making about the programme are of critical importance to success. Planners, with their traditions of public participation and their beliefs in 'planning for people', can make a very significant contribution to processes of this nature.

SOME OF THE MOST EXTREME PROBLEM AREAS ALSO OFFER THE GREATEST POTENTIAL FOR POSITIVE ACHIEVEMENT

We have shown in this book that in both Britain and the USA crime tends to be a particularly urban phenomenon, and that within major urban areas there are often sizeable differences between localities in these terms. Some of the heaviest concentrations of urban crime are in some of the urban areas which experience a range of symptoms of multiple deprivation, with crime being part of that process of deprivation. It follows logically from this that these are among the areas where crime prevention initiatives may be most needed (at any rate in a statistical sense) and may also have the greatest potential to bring about improvements (again in a statistical sense). They may also be among the areas where community-based initiatives can be particularly difficult to start and to maintain, not least because there can be considerable suspicion both of professionals such as planners and of the police on the part of local people. For example, the study by Sherman *et al.* (1997, page 8) lists under the heading 'What doesn't work?':

> Community mobilization of residents' efforts against crime in high-crime, inner city areas of concentrated poverty fails to reduce crime in those areas.

It can often be easier to start and to maintain anti-crime programmes in more middle-income suburban areas, not only because the problems of suspicion of (similarly middle-income) professionals and of the police may be less, but also because the cultural pattern of members of the community participating in initiatives designed to benefit that community at large may well be more established. While areas of this latter type may appear to be more promising as a location for initiatives for these reasons, and while their citizens will of course have the right in a democratic society to benefit from initiatives of this kind, it is important that the more apparently intractable areas are not dismissed as being 'too hard'. They may offer some of the most complex challenges because of the mix of elements that determines their deprived status, but they also offer scope for real achievement in terms of improving the quality of the lives of the very many honest and hard-working citizens who live there, and who can all too easily become stigmatised by virtue of the circumstances that have created their surroundings. As we have shown, surveys frequently find that citizens of a wide range of types of urban area cite crime as one of their major problems. Thus, if urban crime is to be tackled successfully initiatives need to be taken in the most difficult areas (even if they prove to be long and hard and to experience many setbacks along the way) as well as in other areas where fear of crime might be more vocally expressed. If this is going to be done successfully, however, the things that we have said above about winning the support and trust of local people, about multi-professional team working, and about the full involvement of local people in the process making full use of their local knowledge are likely to be of particular significance. We do not wish to underestimate the challenge here, and we know that the record to date in these kinds of areas is not particularly encouraging, but we believe that this real opportunity to do better in future needs to be grasped.

THE IMPORTANCE OF CONTEXT AND OUTCOME WHEN TRANSPLANTING IDEAS FROM ONE PLACE TO OTHERS

Modern information technology makes the process of moving ideas around the world easier than it has ever been. There is, of course, a great deal of advantage to be gained from this situation, but we think that a word of caution is also appropriate in terms of the field that is the subject of this book. We believe that whether or not something actually works is not just a function of the inherent characteristics of the idea, but is also very dependent upon the context (cultural, economic, social and physical) in which it is applied. A failure to understand this can easily lead to a belief that something which appears to have worked in one location is likely to work in another, notwithstanding the very different context in which it will inevitably be applied, and we believe that this failure of understanding will increase the probability of project failure quite significantly. Similarly, it is important to test the extent to which claims about success can be justified on the basis of objective assessment, rather than to rely on what can be self-serving claims to this effect often well before any such evaluation has been competed (and even, in some cases, in the complete absence of any measurement of this kind). It is wholly understandable that people will want to import apparently successful ideas and apply them to situations where previous initiatives have not solved problems,[4] but there is a real risk that if this is done without understanding the context and the outcome of the initial application of the ideas people are simply programming themselves to fail. This would be particularly unfortunate if, for example, it was to result in the opportunity being missed through an awareness of context and outcome to suggest how an idea could be adapted to improve its likelihood of success when applied in different circumstances. We say this particularly because we think it very likely that in this field there is very considerable scope for learning from initiatives elsewhere and for adapting them to differing circumstances, but we believe that this has to be a conscious process of adaptation based upon know-ledge rather than blind copying in the hope of achieving a 'quick fix'. Thus the last of our nine key propositions is an emphasis upon context and outcome as vital ele-ments of the knowledge needed to borrow ideas successfully from elsewhere and apply them in particular situations, because all situations are particular.

Our emphasis upon the importance of the accumulation of knowledge in the field through understanding the context in which initiatives are taken and through careful post-hoc evaluation of outcomes inevitably leads us to conclude this section by observing that these processes may over time cause us (and others) to modify what we have said above about these nine key propositions, although we believe that there is a good chance that this material will stand the test of time. Our hope would also be that this process of accumulation of knowledge would lead us (and others) to want to add to these propositions over time. We would prefer to see the field develop in this manner than to see a continuation of past patterns where fashion and exhortation have played a fuller part in the development of ideas than they should have done.

FURTHER RESEARCH

We have already discussed at some length two of the areas where further research is necessary, namely in the development of the careful post-hoc evalu-ation of initiatives and in the improvement of the understanding of the cultural, social, economic and physical contexts in which they are applied. Related to these, a third area in which further research is vitally necessary is in relation to the most effective processes of making information about these matters available in ways that are readily understandable to a wide range of potential end-users, both professional groups and interested citizens. Within this general framework, we agree very much with the conclusions reached by Taylor and Harrell (1996, pages 22 and 23) after a careful review of the extant literature for the US Department of Justice National Institute of Justice of the major areas of research that were still needed:

- *the sequence of relationships between physical change, crime events, fear of crime and perceptions of place vulnerability.* We know that these areas are inter-related, but we know very little about the causal or the sequential elements in these relationships. More understanding of these complex relationships ought to improve our ability to identify points at which it is possible to intervene to maximum effect.

- *the contribution of social, cultural and organisational features to the success of crime reduction through physical environment modifications.* As we have said, physical environmental changes in relation to crime can rarely be seen to be truly stand-alone, but usually are affected or filtered by a whole series of other aspects which together constitute the context within which initiatives are applied. We need to know much more about these relationships, not least because this will help us to develop a much more sophisticated understanding of the contribution that environmental initiatives can make alongside other kinds of initiatives and of the sorts of factors that need to be taken into account if initiatives of a predominantly environmental character are to be successful (see also Fleissner and Heinzelmann, 1996).

- *the effects of the larger social, political and economic environment on the risk of crime, and the relationships between these broader issues and the process of modifying the physical environment.* If the previous point was mainly about the immediate context affecting the implementation of environmental initiatives, this one is about the very broad societal context. Much of this work may well involve studying changes in places over the long term and relating these local changes to much broader societal changes; as yet there has been relatively little longitudinal work of this nature in this field (but see Taylor, 1999 for an interesting longitudinal study of Baltimore between 1981/82 and 1994 which raises some of these issues).

- *the relative importance of key variables such as housing disrepair and vacancy, land use patterns, vandalism, physical layout, and patterns of traffic and pedestrian circulation.* At a very general level we can say that these elements are likely to have some sorts of effects on local crime patterns and to be amongst the kinds of variables which local initiatives are likely to attempt to manipulate. But we actually know relatively little about how these elements relate to each other in understanding crime patterns, different types of crime, or people's perceptions of risk. Trying to improve our understanding of these elements, while continuing to accept the huge variety in these terms likely to be found in the real world, would produce some very useful and strongly policy-oriented research.

We think in turn that all of this implies a fifth major area of research:

- *the need for more cross-national studies.* Given that, as we have said, ideas and approaches will increasingly flow around the world irrespective of national boundaries, we need to know much more about how they are capable of being successfully transplanted from one culture to another. This will involve in particular an attempt to understand the significance of cultural factors in the successful application of initiatives, and of the processes of adaptation that are likely to be necessary to enable similar levels of success to be achieved with broadly the same ideas in very different cultures. What hopefully would come out of this would be a better understanding of those elements of the relationships between criminal behaviour, the physical environment and planning to prevent crime that may prove to have the status of general principles rather than being essentially determined by particular local circumstances.

Finally, we think it is very important that there is a continuing willingness to explore ideas, to try them out in different situations, and to report on them not just in terms of whether they were successful in their own terms but also in the sense of what potential for development and wider application they may have. An important piece of work in this context was a 1998 study for the US Department of Justice National Institute of Justice which looked at more than 500 (mainly American) crime prevention practices which had been the subject of systematic review to try to determine '... what works, what doesn't, (and) what is promising' (Sherman *et al.*, 1997). Although most of the initiatives examined there could not be described as environmental initiatives per se, many certainly have environmental components. This kind of research stock-taking from time to time is extremely valuable, not least because it helps to shape public policy (it is better to concentrate public money on things that appear to work or may have a chance of working rather than things that do not) as well as to focus future research effort, particularly in terms of developing those initiatives described as 'promising'. If we are to see the field develop in the kind of knowledge-driven manner that we have argued for throughout this book, this kind of systematic appraisal from time to time of the knowledge that is constantly accumulating via individual pieces of research is going to be needed as a critical piece of support.

CONCLUSIONS

The basic messages that we hope that our readers have taken from this book are as follows:

- Improving crime prevention in localities really matters to local people, and can make a big difference to the quality of life in those areas. So it is worthy of much more planner attention than it has achieved to date because it is capable of 'making a difference' to the quality of life available in our urban areas.

- The organisation and management of the physical environment is one of the components that is capable of being manipulated in order to improve crime prevention in localities. It is not a universal panacea for crime prevention; it is much more significant in relation to some kinds of crimes than others; and rarely will environmental solutions be able to prevent crime in complete isolation from other types of considerations. But place-based crime prevention when seen in these lights can contribute to successful local crime prevention efforts, and needs to take its place alongside other measures as an important and in some cases powerful weapon in the armoury.

- There are no 'cook book' approaches to this task that can be recommended with certainty, although there are advocates for many such approaches who will speak with zeal about them. Rather, there are some broad concepts that appear to have some validity and that can be applied with very considerable care to particular local circumstances, taking into account not merely the physical situations to be found in those areas but also the human behaviour patterns to be observed and the views of the users of those localities.

- To do this, planners need to work in partnership with the police, other environmental professionals and people and organisations in the communities where crime prevention initiatives are to be taken. This is a team task, where the contribution of each of these elements that will constitute the team needs to be respected alongside the views and knowledge of local people. It is also a task that needs to be seen in terms of a long-term commitment to improving the quality of life in the locality rather than a 'quick fix'.

- To this end, we need to improve our knowledge and understanding of what works and what does not, where and why, in its short-, mid- and long-term senses. And we need the willingness both to record our successes and failures and to communicate this kind of information in accessible ways to increase considerably, if the future in these terms is to be much more knowledge-driven than has often been the case in the past.

Our hope is that readers will share these aspirations, and will see their own work not just as helping to tackle pressing local problems but also as contributing to the development of this broader knowledge base for which we are arguing. If we have helped readers through this book to understand the need for and to adopt these perspectives, we will be well pleased.

NOTES

1   This is not merely a result of the cultural differences between the USA and the UK that we have emphasised in Chapter 9, important though these are. The cases that we have presented in Part 2 of this book show that, although general principles such as opportunity blocking, surveillance, access control, boundary definition and regular main-tenance are to be found throughout that range and remain relatively constant, the effec-tiveness of their application in different places is likely to be different because of differences in micro-environments and in the people who live, work or use these places as well as in the cultural context that surrounds such applications. So, for instance, the cases of Pruitt-Igoe in the USA (see Chapter 5) and of the Hulme Crescents in the UK (see Chapter 8) provide evidence that high-rise apartment living can be far more of a crime problem for low-income residents because of the particular combinations of cir-cumstances to be found in each of these situations than for middle or upper income residents; but the responses to these two situations (apart from the fact that they both involved demolition) were somewhat different.

2   This list first appeared in summary form in Kitchen and Schneider, 2000.

3   Local people can often be the source of ideas which are completely different from those being pursued in political and official quarters. An interesting example of a community originating initiative of this kind that is beginning to attract media attention in Australia is a scheme called 'Camwatch', begun by a local group in Perth, Western Australia, led by Roger Broinowski. This takes as its starting basic principle that residents are encour-aged to have cheap but reliable portable small cameras available at all times in their homes and in their cars to take photographs of apparent criminal activity that they see around them, in order to provide evidence. Camwatch stickers are produced to put on places such as letterboxes and front windows, to show to intending criminals as well as to the local community that Camwatch activities of this kind are taking place in the neighbourhood. Community groups sharing this basic approach then get together to exchange information and to discuss what other actions they can take to encourage crime prevention, such as photographing valuable possessions, planting thorny plants such as roses, making fences and gates as secure as possible, and taking action as community groups to identify and report anti-social behaviour in public places. Some of this, of course, has clear commercial potential, and this is one of the issues now being explored to develop from this basic idea. Further details of Camwatch can be found from its website http://www/camwatch.org.

4   As an example, some of the claims that the authors have heard advocates of 'new urban-
     ism' make about what it is capable of achieving could be said to be of this type. Apart
     from the fact that such claims may not succeed in their own right, they scarcely do 'new
     urbanism' itself many favours, because instead of it settling down amongst the range of
     available ideas about urban design, exaggerated claims carry the risks of tarnishing its
     reputation and then of generating a subsequent negative backlash.

BIBLIOGRAPHY

Ajoc S. (1996) *CPTED (Crime Prevention Through Environmental Design): Providing a Framework for Safer Communities Through Environmental Design and Planning*, unpublished Masters Terminal Project, Department of Urban and Regional Planning, University of Florida.

Alexander C. (1964) *Notes on the Synthesis of Form*, Harvard University Press: Cambridge, MA.

Alexander E. A. (1992) *Approaches to Planning*, Gordon and Breach: Philadelphia.

American Institute of Certified Planners/American Planning Association (1992) *Ethical Principles in Planning*, http://www.planning.org.

Anderson D. (1999) *New Research Shows that Crime Costs in the U.S. Have Passed the Trillion-Dollar Mark*, http://www.centre.edu/web/news/andersoncr.html.

Angel S. (1967) 'Combating crime', *The Annals of the American Academy of Political and Social Science*, November, vol. 374.

Angel S. (1968) *Discouraging Crime Through City Planning*, Working Paper Number 75, Center for Planning and Development Research, University of California: Berkeley.

Ardrey R. (1966) *The Territorial Imperative*, Dell: NY.

Association of British Insurers (1998) *Crime Costs Average Household 31 Pounds per Week*, http://www.abi.org.uk.

Atlas R. and LeBlanc, W. G. (1994) 'Environmental barriers to crime', *Ergonomics in Design*, October, 9–16.

Bailey N. (1995) *Partnership Agencies in British Urban Policy*, UCL Press: London.

Barclay G. C. and Tavares C. (2000) *International Comparisons of Criminal Justice Statistics, 1998*, HOSB 04/00, Home Office: London.

Barr R. and Pease K. (1992) 'The problem of displacement', in Evans D. J., Fyfe N. R. and Herbert D. T. (eds), *Crime, Policing and Place: Essays in Environmental Criminology*, Routledge & Kegan Paul: London, pp. 138–50.

Bennett L. (1997) *Neighborhood Politics: Chicago and Sheffield*, Garland: NY.

Bentham J. (1962) *The Works of Jeremy Bentham* (published under the superintendence of his executor, John Bowring), Russell and Russell: NY.

Bichler G. and Clarke R. V. (1996) 'Eliminating pay phone fraud at the Port Authority bus terminal in Manhattan', in Clarke R. V. (ed.), *Preventing Mass Transit Crime*, Crime Prevention Studies, vol. 6, Criminal Justice Press: Monsey, NJ, pp. 98–112.

Blakely E. J. and Snyder M. G. (1999) *Fortress America: Gated Communities in the United States*, Brookings Institution Press: Washington, D.C.

Booth C. (1888) 'Conditions and occupations of the people of East London and Hackney', *Journal of the Royal Statistical Society*, 51, 326–91.

Booth P. (1996) *Controlling Development: Certainty and Discretion in Europe, the USA and Hong Kong*, UCL Press: London.

Bottoms A. E. (1990) 'Crime prevention facing the 1990s', *Policing and Society*, 1, 1, 3–22.

Bradford Metropolitan District Council (2000) *Crime and Disorder Act Audit*, http://www.bradford.gov.uk/council/crimeaudit/titlepage.html.

Branch M. C. (1985) *Comprehensive City Planning*, American Planning Association: Washington, D.C.

Brand S. and Price R. (2000) *The Economic and Social Costs of Crime*, Home Office Research Study 217, Home Office: London.

Brantingham P. J. and Brantingham P. L. (1981) *Environmental Criminology*, Sage: Beverly Hills, CA.

Brantingham P. L. and Brantingham P. J. (1993) 'Paths, nodes, edges: considerations on the complexity of crime and the physical environment', *Journal of Environmental Psychology*, 13, 3–28.

Brantingham P. L., Brantingham P. J. and Wong P. (1990) 'Malls and crime: a first look', *Security Journal*, 1, 3, 175–81.

Brantingham P. J. and Jeffrey C. R. (1981) 'Crime space and criminological theory', in Brantingham P. J. and Brantingham P. L. (eds), *Environmental Criminology*, Sage: Beverly Hills, CA pp. 227–45.

Brantingham P. L., Rondeau M. B. and Brantingham P. J. (1997) *The Value of Environmental Criminology for the Design Professions of Architecture, Landscape Architecture and Planning*, Draft Paper, Second Annual International Crime Prevention Through Environmental Design Conference, ICA: Orlando, FL.

Breheny M. and Ross A. (1998) *Urban Housing Capacity: What Can Be Done?*, Town and Country Planning Association: London.

Bronowski J. (1973) *The Ascent of Man*, Little, Brown & Company: Boston, MA.

Brown B. (1995) *CCTV in Town Centres: Three Case Studies*, Crime Detection and Prevention Series Paper 68, Police Research Group, Home Office: London.

Brown B. B. and Altman I. (1981) 'Territoriality and residential crime: a conceptual framework', in Brantingham P. J. and Brantingham P. L. (eds), *Environmental Criminology*, Sage: Beverly Hills, CA, pp. 55–76.

Brugmann J. (1999) 'Is there method in our measurement? The use of indicators in local sustainable development planning', in Satterthwaite D. (ed.), *The Earthscan Reader in Sustainable Cities*, Earthscan: London, pp. 394–407.

Bureau of Justice Statistics (2000) *National Crime Victimization Survey: Criminal Victimization 1999, Changes 1998–99 with Trends 1993–99*, US Department of Justice, NCJ 182734, Office of Justice Programs: Washington, D.C.

Burgess E. W. (1916) 'Juvenile delinquency in a small city', *Journal of the American Institute of Criminal Law and Criminology*, 6, 724–8.

Burgess E. W. (1925) 'The growth of the city', in Park R. E., Burgess E. W. and McKenzie M. (eds), *The City*, University of Chicago Press: Chicago, IL, pp. 47–62.

Calhoun J. A. (2000) *Crime Prevention in the New Millennium*, NCPC: Washington, D.C., http://www.ncpc.org//millennium/1-7.html.

Campbell B. C. (1996) 'The system of 1896 and policy performance in the American states', notes prepared for a panel sponsored by the Society of Historians of the Gilded Age and Progressive Era at the annual meeting of the American Historical Association, Atlanta, January 5 1996, at http://www2.h-net.msu.edu/~shgape/papers/sys96.html.

Carter S. P. (1997) *Sarasota, Florida, CPTED City*, paper presented at the Second International CPTED Conference, December 1997, Orlando, FL.

Catchpole T. (1996) 'Book that changed my life: Zen and the Art of Motorcycle Maintenance', *Review of Urban Design Quarterly*, 59.

Charter of New Urbanism (n.d.) at http://www.cnv.org/charter.html.

Childe V. G. (1964) *What Happened in History*, Penguin Books: Harmondsworth.

Cisneros H. G. (1995) *Defensible Space: Deterring Crime and Building Community*, US Department of Housing and Urban Development: Washington, D.C.

Citizens Crime Commission of New York City (1985) *Downtown Safety, Security and Economic Development*, NCJ Document 103411, US Dept of Justice: Washington, D.C.

City of St. Petersburg (1999) *Neighborhood Revitalization in St. Petersburg, Florida: A Case Study, Part IV*, City of St. Petersburg: St. Petersburg, FL.

Clarke R. V. (1980) '"Situational" Crime Prevention: Theory and Practice', *British Journal of Criminology*, 20, 2, 136–47.

Clarke R. V. (ed.) (1992) *Situational Crime Prevention: Successful Case Studies*, Harrow and Heston: Albany, NY.

Clarke R. V. (ed.) (1997) *Situational Crime Prevention: Successful Case Studies*, second edition, Harrrow and Heston: Albany, NY.

Clarke R. V. and Cornish D. B. (1985) 'Modeling offenders' decisions: A framework for policy and research', in Tonry M. and Morris N. (eds), *Crime and Justice: An Annual Review of Research, Volume 6*, University of Chicago Press: Chicago, pp. 147–85.

Clarke R. V., Field S. and McGrath G. (1991) 'Target hardening of banks in Australia and displacement of robberies', *Security Journal*, 2, 84–90.

Clarke R. V. and Homel R. (1997) 'A revised classification of situational crime prevention techniques', in Lab S. P. (ed.), *Crime Prevention at a Crossroads*, Anderson: Cincinnati, Ohio, pp. 17–27.

Clarke R. V. and Mayhew P. (1980) *Designing Out Crime*, HMSO: London.

Clarke R. V. and Wersburd D. (1994) 'Diffusion of crime control benefits: Observations on the reverse of displacement', in Clarke R. V. (ed.), *Crime Prevention Studies*, vol. 2, Criminal Justice Press: Monsey, N.Y.

Clifton W. (1993) *Convenience Store Robberies in Gainesville, Florida: An Intervention Strategy by the Gainesville Police Department*, Gainesville Police Department: Gainesville, FL.

Cohen L. E. and Felson M. (1979) 'Social change and crime rate trends: A routine activity approach', *American Sociological Review*, 44, 588–608.

Coleman A. (1985) *Utopia on Trial: Vision and Reality in Planned Housing*, Hilary Shipman: London.

Coleman A. (1990) *Utopia on Trial*, revised edition, Hilary Shipman: London.

Coleman C. and Moynihan J. (1996) *Understanding Crime Data: Haunted by the Dark Figure*, Open University Press: Buckingham.

Cornish D. B. and Clarke R. V. (1986) *The Reasoning Criminal: Rational Choice Perspectives on Offending*, Springer-Verlag: N.Y.

Coupland A. (1997) *Reclaiming the City: Mixed Use Development*, Spon: London.

Cozens P., Hillier D. and Prescott G. (2000) *Perceptions of Residential Space in the British City. Insights from Planners, Police and Burglars, Decoding the Criminogenic Capacity of Characteristic Housing Designs*, paper to the Habitus 2000 Conference: Perth, Western Australia.

Craglia M., Haining R. and Wiles P. (2000) 'A comparative evaluation of approaches to urban crime pattern analysis', *Urban Studies*, 37, 4, 711–29.

Crime Analysis Unit, City of Gainesville, Florida (2001) *Crime Analysis Suspect Actions*, Internal Document, City of Gainesville Police Department: Gainesville, FL.

Crime Concern (n.d.) *Reducing Neighbourhood Crime: a Manual for Action*, Crime Concern for the Home Office's Crime Prevention Agency: Swindon.

Crouch S., Shaftoe H. and Fleming R. (1999) *Design for Secure Residential Environments*, Longman: Harlow.

Crow W. J. and Bull J. L. (1975) *Robbery Deterrence: An Applied Behavioral Science Demonstration – Final Report*, Western Behavioral Sciences Institute: La Jolla, CA.

Crowe T. (1991) *Crime Prevention Through Environmental Design*, Butterworth-Heinemann: Boston, MA.

Crowe T. (1997) '*Crime prevention through environmental design strategies and applications*', in Fennelly L. J. *Effective Physical Security*, second edition, Butterworth-Heinemann: Boston, MA, pp. 35–88.

Crowe T. (2000) '*Crime Prevention Through Environmental Design*', second edition, Butterworth-Heinemann, Boston, MA.

Cullen J. B. and Levitt S. D. (1996) *Crime, Urban Flight and the Consequences for Cities*, NBER Working Paper 5737, National Bureau of Economic Research: Boston, MA.

Dawson T. (1994) 'Framing the villain', *New Statesman and Society*, 28 January, 12–13.

Dearne Valley Partnership (1996) *City Challenge: Final Review*, Dearne Valley Partnership: Wath-upon-Dearne.

Dechert M. S. A. (1983) *City and Fortress in the Works of Francesco Di Giorgio: The*

Theory and Practice of Defensive Architecture and Town Planning, University Micro-films International: Ann Arbor, MI.

DeFrances, C. and Titus, R. (1993) 'Urban planning and residential burglary outcomes', *Landscape and Urban Planning*, 26, 179–91.

DeLong J. (2000) *Mayor Brown Announces Operation Renaissance Cleanup Program*, US Mayor Article, US Conference of Mayors, www.usmayors.org/uscm/us_mayor_newspaper/documents/03_brown_article.htm.

Department of Defense (1993) *Protection of DOD Personnel and Activities Against Acts of Terrorism and Political Turbulence*, DOD 0-2000.12-H, Government Printing Office: Washington, D.C.

Department of Justice, Canada (1998) *Backgrounder: National Strategy on Community Safety and Crime Prevention*, at http://canada.justice.gc.ca/en/news/nr/1998/nrcavback.html.

Department of the Environment (1994) *Planning Out Crime*, DoE Circular 5/94, HMSO: London.

Department of the Environment, Transport and the Regions (1998a) *Planning for the Communities of the Future*, DETR: London.

Department of the Environment, Transport and the Regions (1998b) *Places, Streets and Movements: a Companion Guide to Design Bulletin 32: Residential Roads and Footpaths*, DETR: London.

Department of the Environment, Transport and the Regions (1999a) *Revision of Planning Policy Guidance Note 3: Housing*, DETR: London.

Department of the Environment, Transport and the Regions (1999b) *Regeneration Research Summary: City Challenge, Final Evaluation*, 27, DETR: London.

Department of the Environment, Transport and the Regions (2000a) *Planning Policy Guidance Note No. 3: Housing*, DETR: London.

Department of the Environment, Transport and the Regions (2000b) *Our Towns and Cities: the Future: Delivering an Urban Renaissance*, Cm 4911, HMSO: London.

Devon County Council (2000) *Indicators for Devon*, http://www.devon.gov.uk.

de Waal F. B. M., Aureli F. and Judge P. G. (2000) 'Coping with crowding', *Scientific American*, 282, 5 (May), 76–81.

DiLonardo R. L. and Clarke R. V. (1996) 'Reducing the rewards of shoplifting: An evaluation of ink tags', *Security Journal*, 7, 11–14.

Donnell C. (2000) *The Maginot Line*, www.geocities.com/Athens/Forum/1491/index.html.

Duffy C. (1975) *Fire and Stone: The Science of Fortress Warfare 1660–1860*, David & Charles: Newton Abbot.

Duffy C. (1979) *Siege Warfare: The Fortress in the Early Modern World 1494–1660*, Routledge & Kegan Paul: London.

Dunlop B. (1997) 'The new urbanists: The second generation', *Architectural Record*, January, 132–7.

Eck J. E. (1997) 'Preventing crime at places', in Sherman L. W. *et al.* (eds), *Preventing Crime: What Works, What Doesn't, What's Promising*, US Department of Justice, Office of Justice Programs: Washington, D.C.

Eck J. E. and Wartell J. (1996) *Reducing Crime and Drug Dealing by Improving Place Management: A Randomized Experiment*, Report to the San Diego Police Department, Crime Control Institute: Washington, D.C.

Eck J. E. and Weisburd D. (1995) 'Crime places in crime theory', in Eck J. E. and Weisburd D. (eds), *Crime and Place Crime Prevention Studies, Volume 4*, Criminal Justice Press: Monsey, N.Y, pp. 1–33.

Edgar D., Earle L. and Fopp R. (1993) *Introduction to Australian Society*, Prentice Hall: Sydney.

Ehrenhalt A. (1998) *The Dilemma of the New Urbanists*, reprinted at http://fcn.state.fl.us/ Fdi/edesign/news/9801/urbnst1.htm.

Ekblom P. (1997) 'Gearing up against crime: A dynamic framework to help designers keep up with the adaptive criminal in a changing world', *International Journal of Risk, Security and Crime Prevention*, 2, 4, 249–65.

Ellin N. (1996) *Architecture of Fear*, Princeton Architectural Press: Princeton, NJ.

Feins J. D., Epstein J. C. and Widom R. (1997) *Solving Crime Problems in Residential Neighborhoods: Comprehensive Changes in Design, Management and Use*, US Department of Justice, Office of Justice Programs, National Institute of Justice: Washington, D.C.

Felson M. (1986) 'Linking criminal choices, routine activities, informal control, and criminal outcomes', in Cornish D. B. and Clarke R. V. (eds), *The Reasoning Criminal*, Springer Verlag: NY, pp. 119–28.

Felson M. (1992) 'Routine activities and crime prevention: Armchair concepts and practical action', *Studies on Crime and Crime Prevention*, 1, 31–4.

Felson M. (1995) 'Those who discourage crime', in Eck J. E. and Weisburd D. (eds), *Crime and Place*, Vol. 4, Criminal Justice Press: Monsey, NY, pp. 53–66.

Felson M. and Peiser R. (1998) *Reducing Crime Through Real Estate Development and Management*, Urban Land Institute: Washington, D.C.

Fennelly L. J. (1997) *Effective Physical Security*, second edition, Butterworth-Heinemann: Boston, MA.

Fisher B. and Nasar J. (1992) 'Fear of crime in relation to three exterior site features: prospect, refuge and escape', *Environment and Behavior*, 24, 35–65.

Fleissner D. and Heinzelmann F. (1996) *Crime Prevention Through Environmental Design and Community Policing*, US Department of Justice, Office of Justice Programs, National Institute of Justice: Washington, D.C.

Franck K. A. and Mostoller M. (1995) 'From courts to open spaces to streets: changes in the site design of US public housing', *Journal of Architectural And Planning Research*, 12, 3, 186–220.

Friedmann J. (1987) *Planning in the Public Domain: From Knowledge to Action*, Princeton University Press: Princeton, NJ.

Friedmann J. and Hudson B. (1974) 'Knowledge and action: A guide to planning theory', *AIP Journal,* January, 2–16.

Gardiner R. (1978) *Design for Safe Neighborhoods: The Environmental Security Planning and Design Process*, National Institute of Law Enforcement and Criminal Justice: Washington, D.C.

Gelfand D. M., Hartmen D. P., Walder P. and Page B. (1973) 'Who reports shoplifting? A field experimental study', *Journal of Personality and Social Psychology*, 23, 276–85.

Gerckens L. C. (1979) 'Historical development of American city planning', in So F. (ed.), *The Practice of Local Government Planning*, ICMA: Washington, D.C., pp. 21–57.

Gilling D. (1999) 'Community safety: a critique', *British Criminology Conferences: Selected Proceedings*, vol. 2, British Society of Criminology: Loughborough.

Glazer, Nathan (1979) *On Subway Graffiti in New York*, Public Interest: Winter.

Goodman W. I. and Freund E. C. (1968) *Principles and Practices of Urban Planning*, ICMA: Washington, D.C.

Gordon C. L. and Brill W. (1996) *The Expanding Role of Crime Prevention Through Environmental Design in Premises Liability*, US Department of Justice, Office of Justice Programs, National Institute of Justice: Washington, D.C.

Gore R. (1997) 'The dawn of humans – the first steps', *National Geographic Magazine*, 191, 2, 72–99.

Gore R. (2000) 'The dawn of humans – people like us', *National Geographic Magazine*, 198, 1, 91–117.

Graham S. and Marvin S. (1996) *Telecommunications and the City*, Routledge: London.

Greene J. R. (2000) 'Community policing in America: Changing the nature, structure and function of the police. The Nature of Crime: Continuity and Change', *Criminal Justice 2000*, 3 (July), 299–371, NCJ 182408, at http://www.ojp.usdoj.gor/nij/criminal-justice2000/vol3-2000.html.

Griswold D. B. (1984) 'Crime prevention and commercial burglary: A time series analysis', *Journal of Criminal Justice*, 12, 493–501.

Grayson L. and Young K. (1994) *Quality of Life in Cities: An Overview and Guide to the Literature*, British Library and London Research Centre: London.

Guerry A. M. (1833) *Essai sur la Statistique Morale de la France*, Crochard: Paris.

Hall E. T. (1959) *The Silent Language*, Fawcett: NY.

Hall E. T. (1966) *The Hidden Dimension*, Doubleday: Garden City, NY.

Hall P. (1988) *Cities of Tomorrow: An Intellectual History of Urban Planning and Design in the Twentieth Century*, Blackwell: Oxford.

Hamermesh D. S. (1998) *Crime and the Timing of Work*, Working Paper 6613, National Bureau of Economic Research: Boston, MA.

Hart H. L. A. (1968) *Punishment and Responsibility*, Oxford University Press: NY.

Haynes M. C. (1997) *Private Gated Communities: A Case Study of Metropolitan Orlando*, unpublished MA Dissertation, University of Florida Graduate School: Gainesville, FL.

Hebel J. W. (ed.) (1933) *The Works of Michael Drayton, Volume IV, Poly-Olbion*, Shakespeare Head Press: St Aldates, Basil Blackwell: Oxford.

Herbert D. T. and Smith D. M. (1989) *Social Problems and the City*, Oxford University Press: Oxford.

Hesseling R. B. P. (1994) 'Displacement: a review of the empirical literature', in Clarke R. V. (ed.), *Crime Prevention Studies*, vol. 3, Criminal Justice Press: Monsey, NY.

Hoare S. (1995) "Safe as houses?", Construction News Interconnect Supplement, 7 September, in RICS 1996, *The Real Costs of Poor Homes*, The Royal Institution of Chartered Surveyors: London, p. 5.

Hogg I. V. (1975) *Fortress: A History of Military Defense*, St. Martin's Press: NY.

Hollinger R. C. and Dabney D. A. (1998) 'Crime in shopping centers', in Felson M. and Peiser R. B. (eds), *Reducing Crime Through Real Estate Development and Management*, Urban Land Institute: Washington, D.C., pp. 91–101.

Hollinger R. C. and Dabney D. A. (1999) 'Motor vehicle theft at the shopping centre: An application of the routine activities approach', *Security Journal*, 12, 1, 63–78.

Home Office (1993) *Police Reform*, CM 2281, HMSO: London.

Home Office (1998) *The 1998 British Crime Survey*, Statistical Bulletin 21/98, Home Office: London.

Home Office (2000a) *The Government's Crime Reduction Strategy*, http://homeoffice. gov.uk.

Home Office (2000b) *The 2000 British Crime Survey: England and Wales*, Home Office Statistical Bulletin 18/00, Government Statistical Service: London.

Home Office Crime Prevention Centre (1994) *Police Architectural Liaison Manual of Guidance*, Home Office Crime Prevention Centre: Stafford.

Honess T. and Charman E. (1992) *Closed Circuit Television in Public Places: Its Acceptability and Perceived Effectiveness*, Crime Prevention Unit Series Paper 35, Police Research Group, Home Office: London.

Hughes Q. (1974) *Military Architecture*, St. Martin's Press: NY.

Hulme Regeneration Limited (1994) *Rebuilding the City: A Guide to Development in Hulme*, Manchester City Council: Manchester.

Jacobs J. (1961) *The Death and Life of Great American Cities*, Vintage Books: NY.

Jeffrey C. R. (1971) *Crime Prevention Through Environmental Design*, Sage: Beverly Hills, CA.

Jeffrey C. R. (1977) *Crime Prevention Through Environmental Design*, second edition, Sage: Beverly Hills, CA.

Jewson N. and MacGregor S. (1997) *Transforming Cities: Contested Government and New Spatial Divisions*, Routledge: London.

Kaufmann J. E. and Kaufmann H. W. (1997) *The Maginot Line: None Shall Pass*, Praeger Publishers: Westford, CT.

Kelling G. L. and Coles C. M. (1996) *Fixing Broken Windows*, Touchstone: N.Y.

Kelso W. A. (1994) *Poverty and the Underclass: Changing Perceptions of the Poor in America*, New York University Press: N.Y.

Kempster N. and Meisler S. (1998) 'Secure Embassies Protect Diplomats but Make their Jobs Harder', *Los Angeles Times*, 7 August, http:/forums.mercurycenter.com/world/bombing/embassy 0808h.htm.

Kennedy D. B. (1993) 'Architectural concerns regarding security and premises liability', *Journal of Architectural and Planning Research*, 10, 2, Summer, 105–29.

Kenyon J. R. (1990) *Medieval Fortifications*, Leicester University Press: Leicester.

Kenyon K. M. (1957) *Digging Up Jericho*, Ernest Benn: London and Frederick A. Praeger: N.Y.

Kitchen T. (1997a) *CPTED and the British Planning System: Some Reflections from Experience*, paper delivered at the International CPTED Association Conference: Orlando, FL.

Kitchen T. (1997b) *People, Politics, Policies and Plans*, Paul Chapman: London.

Kitchen T. (2001) 'Planning in response to terrorism: The case of Manchester, England', *Journal of Architectural and Planning Research*, forthcoming.

Kitchen T. and Schneider R. H. (2000) *Crime and the Design of the Built Environment: Anglo-American Comparisons of Policy and Practice*, paper to the Habitus 2000 Conference, Perth, Western Australia, scheduled to be published as Chapter 13 of Hillier J. and Rooksby E. (eds) (2001) *Habitus: A Sense of Place*, Ashgate: Australia.

Knights B. and Pascoe T. (2000) *Burglaries Reduced by Cost Effective Target Hardening*, DETR Contract Number cc1675, Building Research Establishment, Garston: Watford.

Kostof S. (1991) *The City Shaped*, Little, Brown & Company: Boston, MA.

Kostof S. (1992) *The City Assembled*, Little, Brown & Company: Boston, MA.

Kuhn T. (1962) *The Structure of Scientific Revolutions*, University of Chicago Press: Chicago, IL.

Kulash W. M. (1997) *Don't Even Think of Closing that Street*, presentation to the Second Annual International CPTED Conference, 3–5 December 1997: Orlando, FL.

Kunstler J. H. (1998) *Home from Nowhere*, Touchstone: NY.

Kushmuk J. and Whittemore S. L. (1981) *Re-Evaluation of Crime Prevention Through Environmental Design in Portland, Oregon*, US Dept of Justice, NCJ Document 80573: Washington, D.C.

Kuykendall L. (1999) *A Guide to Developing and Implementing Crime Prevention through Environmental Design Ordinances*, unpublished Masters Terminal Project, Department of Urban and Regional Planning, University of Florida: Gainesville, FL.

LaGrange T. C. (1999) 'Impact of neighborhoods, schools, and malls on the spatial distribution of property damage', *Journal of Research in Crime and Delinquency*, 36, 4, 393–422.

Langan P. and Farrington D. (1998) *Crime and Justice in the United States and in England and Wales, 1981–96*, US Department of Justice, Office of Justice Programs, Bureau of Justice Statistics: Washington, D.C.

Latane B. and Darley J. M. (1970) *The Unresponsive Bystander: Why Doesn't He Help?*, Appleton-Century-Crofts: NY.

La Vigne N. (1997) 'Security by design on the Washington Metro', in Clarke R. V. (ed.), *Situational Crime Prevention: Successful Case Studies*, Harrow and Heston: NY, pp. 283–99.

Lea J. and Young J. (1993) *What Is To Be Done about Law and Order?*, Pluto Press: London.

Leakey M. (1995) 'The dawn of humans – the farthest horizon', *National Geographic Magazine*, 188, 3, 38–51.

Leary R. M. (1968) 'Zoning', in Goodman W. I. and Freund E. C. (eds), *Principles and Practice of Urban Planning*, ICMA: Washington, D.C., 403–42.

Leistner D. (1999) *Convenience Stores and Crime: Design and Locational Issues*, unpublished Masters' Degree Terminal Report, University of Florida, Department of Urban and Regional Planning: Gainesville, FL.

Liddle A. M. and Gelsthorpe L. R. (1994) *Crime Prevention and Inter-Agency Co-operation*, Crime Prevention Unit Series: Paper No. 53, Home Office Police Department: London.

Locke T. (1990) *New Approaches to Crime in the 1990s*, Longman: Harlow.

Loukaitou-Sideris (1999) 'Hot spots of bus stop crime: The importance of environmental attributes', *Journal of the American Planning Association*, 65, 4, 395–411.

Lucy W. H. (2000) 'Watch out: It's dangerous in exurbia', *Planning*, November, American Planning Association, 66, 11, 14–7.

Lundqvist L. J. (1986) *Housing Policy and Equality: A Comparative Study of Tenure Conversions and Their Effects*, Croom Helm: NH.

Lynch K. (1960) *The Image of the City*, MIT Press: Cambridge, MA.

Lynch K. (1981) *A Theory of Good City Form*, MIT Press: Cambridge, MA.

Maguire M. (1982) *Burglary in a Dwelling*, Heinemann: London.

Maltz M. (1999) *Bridging Gaps in Police Crime Data*, discussion paper from the BJS Fellows Program, Washington, D.C., NCJ 176365, http://www.ojp.usdoj.gov/bjs/pub/ascii/bgpcd.txt.

Manchester City Council (1997) *A Guide to Development in Manchester*, Manchester City Council: Manchester.

Manchester City Planning Department (1995) *Manchester: 50 Years of Change*, HMSO: London.

Marcuse P. (1997) 'Walls of fear', in Ellin N. (ed.), *Architecture of Fear*, Princeton Architectural Press: Princeton, NJ.

Marcuse P. and van Kempen R. (2000) *Globalising Cities: A New Spatial Order?*, Blackwell: Oxford.

Marshall H. and O'Flaherty K. (1987) 'Suburbanization in the seventies: The "push-pull" hypothesis revisited', *Journal of Urban Affairs*, 9, 249–62.

Matthews R. (1990) 'Developing more effective strategies for curbing prostitution', *Security Journal*, 1, 182–7.

Matthews R. (1993) *Kerb-Crawling, Prostitution and Multi-Agency Policing*, Crime Prevention Unit Paper 43, Home Office: London.

Mawby R. I. (1977) 'Kiosk vandalism: A Sheffield study', *British Journal of Criminology*, 17, 30–46.

Mayhew P. (1979) 'Defensible space: The status of a crime prevention theory', *The Howard Journal of Penology and Crime Prevention*, 18, 150–9.

Mayhew P. (1981) 'Crime in public view: Surveillance and crime prevention', in Brantingham P. J. and Brantingham P. L. (eds), *Environmental Criminology*, Sage: Beverly Hills, CA, pp. 119–34.

Mayhew P., Clarke R. V. G., Burrows J. N., Hough J. M. and Winchester S. W. C. (1979) *Crime in Public View*, HMSO: London.

McKay T. (1997) *CPTED Tried, Tested & Proved*, paper presented at the Second Annual International Crime Prevention Through Environmental Design Conference, Orlando, FL. See also the Peel website at www.peelpolice.on.ca/council.html.

McLaughlin E. and Muncie J. (1996) *Controlling Crime*, Sage: London.

McLaughlin E. and Muncie J. (1999) 'Walled cities: Surveillance, regulation and segregation', in Pike S., Brook C. and Mooney G. (eds), *Unruly Cities?*, Routledge: London, pp. 103–48.

McLoughlin B. (1999) *The Development of Sustainable Communities in Moss Side and Hulme, Manchester*, paper delivered at the Tokyo LANPO conference by the Director of the Moss Side and Hulme Partnership (available from that organisation).

Merry S. (1981) 'Defensible space undefended: Social factors in crime control through environmental design', *Urban Affairs Quarterly*, 16, 397–422.

Michelson W. H. (1976) *Man and His Urban Environment*, Addison-Wesley: Reading, MA.

Miethe T. D. (1991) 'Citizen based crime control activity and victimization risks: An examination of displacement and free-rider effects', *Criminology*, 29, 419–40.

Miller D. L. (ed.) (1986) *The Lewis Mumford Reader*, Pantheon Books: NY.

Minneapolis–St. Paul Metropolitan Council (1997) *Twin City Residents Appear Less Certain About Region's Quality of Life: Crime Remains Top Regional Concern According to Metro Area Survey*, http://www.metrocouncil.org/news/news48.htm.

Montgomery R. (1965) 'Improving the design process in urban renewal', *Journal of the American Institute of Planners*, 31, 7–20.

Morris A. E. J. (1979) *History of Urban Form Before the Industrial Revolutions*, second edition, Longman Scientific and Technical: Burnt Mill, Harlow.

Motoyama T., Rubenstein H. and Hartjens P. (1980) 'Link between crime and the built environment – methodological reviews of individual crime', *Environment Studies*, Volume 2, US Development of Justice, National Institute of Justice: Washington, D.C.

MVA Ltd (2000) *The 2000 Scottish Crime Survey: First Results*, Crime and Criminal Justice Research Findings No. 51, Scottish Executive Central Research Unit: Edinburgh.

Nando (1996) *Computer Crime Cost Britain 1.5 Billion a Year*, http://nando.net/news-room/ntn/info/012469/info4013296.html.

National Institute of Justice (1996) *Victim Costs and Consequences: A New Look*, US Government Printing Office: Washington, D.C.

National League of Cities (2000) at http://www.nlc.org/Mem-cat.htm.

NCPC (National Crime Prevention Council) (1997) *Designing Safer Communities: A Crime Prevention Through Environmental Design Handbook*, NCPC: Washington, D.C.

NCPC (National Crime Prevention Council) (1999) *Are We Safe? National Crime Prevention Survey*, NCPC: Washington, D.C.

NCPC (National Crime Prevention Council) (2000) at http://www.ncpc.org/.

NCPI (National Crime Prevention Institute) (1986) *Understanding Crime Prevention*, Butterworth: Boston, MA.

Newark Redevelopment and Housing Authority (1984) *Public Housing Master Plan*. Newark, NJ.

Newman G. (1999) *Global Report on Crime and Justice*, United Nations Office for Drug Control and Crime Prevention, Centre for International Crime Prevention, Oxford University Press: NY.

Newman G., Clarke R. V. and Shoham S. G. (1997) *Rational Choice and Situational Crime Prevention*, Ashgate Publishing: Aldershot.

Newman O. (1971) *Architectural Design for Crime Prevention*, National Institute of Law Enforcement and Criminal Justice, Law Enforcement Assistance Administration: Washington, D.C.

Newman O. (1973) *Defensible Space: Crime Prevention Through Urban Design*, Macmillan: N.Y.

Newman O. (1976) *Design Guidelines for Creating Defensible Space*, National Institute of Law Enforcement and Criminal Justice: Washington, D.C.

Newman O. (1981) *Community of Interest*, Anchor Press/Doubleday: Garden City, NY.

Newman O. (1995) 'Defensible space: A new physical planning tool for urban revitalization', *Journal of the American Planning Association*, 61, 2, 149–55.

Newman O. (1996) *Creating Defensible Space*, US Department of Housing and Urban Development: Washington, D.C.

New Urban News (2001) 'The new urbanism is the most important trend in land use planning and development in 50 years', promotional letter for *New Urban News*, Ithaca: NY.

Nieto M. (1997) *Public Video Surveillance: Is It An Effective Crime Prevention Tool?*, California Research Bureau, Paper 97-005, at http://www.library,ca.gar/CRB/97/05/.

NILECJ (National Institute of Law Enforcement and Criminal Justice) (1976) *CPTED Program Report*, US Department of Justice: Washington, D.C.

Nottingham City Council (n.d.) *Nottingham City Challenge, 1992–1997: a Story of Renewal*, Nottingham City Council, Nottingham.

Oc T. and Tiesdell S. (1997) *Safer City Centres: Reviving the Public Realm*, Paul Chapman: London.

Osborn S. and Bright J. (1989) *Crime Prevention and Community Safety*, National Association for the Care and Resettlement of Offenders (NACRO): London.

Pacione M. (1997) *Britain's Cities: Geographies of Division in Urban Britain*, Routledge: London.

Pain R. (2000) 'Place, social relations and the fear of crime: A review', *Progress in Human Geography*, 24, 3, 365–87.

Painter K. and Farrington D. P. (1997) 'The crime reducing effect of improved street lighting: the Dudley project', in Clarke R. V. (ed.), *Situational Crime Prevention: Successful Case Studies*, second edition, Harrow and Heston: Albany, NY, pp. 209–26.

Park R. E., Burgess E. W. and McKenzie M. (1925) *The City*, University of Chicago Press: Chicago, IL.

Pascoe T. (1993a) *Domestic Burglaries: the Burglar's View*, BRE Information Paper 19/93, Building Research Establishment, Garston: Watford.

Pascoe T. (1993b) *Domestic Burglaries: the Police View*, BRE Information Paper 20/93, Building Research Establishment, Garston: Watford.

Pascoe T. and Harrison M. (1997) *CPTED a Risk Management Tool for the Future?*, paper presented at the Second Annual International Crime Prevention Through Environmental Design Conference at Orlando, FL.

Pascoe T. and Topping P. (1997) 'Secured by design: Assessing the basis of the scheme', *International Journal of Risk, Security and Crime Prevention*, 2, 3, 161–73.

Pearson G. (1996) *City Security: Designing for Safety and Crime Prevention*, Proceedings of the Town and Country Planning Summer School 1996, 81 and 82, Royal Town Planning Institute: London.

Pease K. (1991) 'The Kirkholt project: Preventing burglary on a British public housing estate', *Security Journal*, 2, 73–7.

Pease K. and Laycock G. (1996) *Revictimization: Reducing the Heat on Hot Victims*, National Institute of Justice: Washington, D.C.

Peiser R. B. and Chang A. (1998) 'Situational crime prevention in Cerritos and Paramount Industrial Parks', in Felson M. and Peiser R. B. (eds), *Reducing Crime Through Real Estate Development and Management*, Urban Land Institute: Washington, D.C., pp. 91–101.

Pettersson G. (1997) 'Crime and mixed use development', in Coupland A. (ed.), *Reclaiming the City: Mixed use Development*, Spon: London, pp. 179–202.

Pile S., Brook C. and Mooney G. (1999) *Unruly Cities?*, Routledge in association with the Open University: London.

Pirenne H. (1969) *Medieval Cities: Their Origins and the Revival of Trade*, Princeton University Press: Princeton, N.J.

Plint T. (1851) *Crime in England*, Charles Gilpin: London.

Povey K. (2000) *On the Record*, Her Majesty's Inspectorate of Constabulary, Home Office: London.

Poyner B. (1983) *Design Against Crime: Beyond Defensible Space*, Butterworth: London.

Poyner B. (1991) 'Situational crime prevention in two car parks', *Security Journal*, 2, 96–101.

Poyner B. and Webb B. (1991) *Crime Free Housing*, Butterworth: Oxford.

Poyner B. and Webb B. (1992) 'Reducing theft from shopping bags in city center markets', in Clarke R. V. (ed.), *Situational Crime Prevention: Successful Case Studies*, Harrow and Heston: Albany, NY, pp. 83–9.

Rainwater L. (1966) (ed.) 'Fear and the house as haven in the lower class', *Journal of the American Institute of Planners*, 32, 23–7.

Ramsay M. and Newton R. (1991) *The Effects of Better Street Lighting on Crime and Fear: A Review*, Crime Prevention Unit Paper 29, Home Office: London.

Reiss A. J. and Roth J. A. (1993) 'Perspective on violence', in *Understanding and Preventing Violence*, Research Council: Washington, D.C., p. 148.

Reps J. (1965) *The Making of Urban America*, Princeton University Press: Princeton, NJ.

Riis J. (1890) *How the Other Half Lives: Studies Among the Tenaments of New York*, Scribner's Sons: NY.

Robson B., Bradford M., Deas I., Hall E., Harrison E., Parkinson M., Evans R., Garside P. and Robinson F. (1994) *Assessing the Impact of Urban Policy*, HMSO: London.

Rohe W. M., Adams R. E. and Arcury T. A. (2001) 'Community policing and planning', *Journal of the American Planning Association*, 67, 1, 78–90.

Rosenthal A. (1964) *Thirty Eight Witnesses*, McGraw Hill: NY.

Rosenthal G. A. (1995) *Housing and Community Development*, Wallace Roberts & Todd: Philadelphia, PA.

Royal Town Planning Institute (2000) *News in 'Planning'*, http://www.rtpi.org.uk/eandp/planning/index.html.

Royal Town Planning Institute (2000) *Code of Professional Conduct*, http://www.rtpi.org.uk/about/codeofconduct2000.pdfct.

Royal Town Planning Institute (2000) *RTPI News* http://www.rtpi.org.uk.

Rudlin D. and Falk N. (1995) *21st Century Homes: Building to Last*, URBED: London.

Rudlin D. and Falk N. (1999) *Building the 21st Century Home: the Sustainable Urban Neighbourhood*, Architectural Press: Oxford.

Salford Crime Reduction Partnership (1998) *Crime and Disorder – An Audit for Salford*, Salford City Council: Salford.

Salford Crime Reduction Partnership (1999) S*alford's Crime and Disorder Reduction Strategy, 1999–2002*, Salford City Council: Salford.

Salford Partnership (n.d.) *Building Sustainable Communities: a Regeneration Strategy for Salford*, Salford City Council: Salford.

Sampson R. J. and Wooldredge J. D. (1986) 'Evidence that high crime rates encourage migration away from central cities', *Sociology and Social Research*, 90, 310–14.

Sandercock L. (2000) 'When strangers become neighbours: Managing cities of difference', *Planning Theory and Practice*, 1, 1, 13–30.

Saville G. (1997) *Displacement: A Problem for CPTED Practitioners*, paper presented at the Second Annual International CPTED Conference, December, Orlando, FL.

Scherdin M. J. (1986) 'The halo effect: Psychological deterrence of electronic security systems', *Information Technology and Libraries*, September, 232–5.

Schneider R. H. (1981) *Local Construction Regulatory Process Innovation: A Comparative Analysis of Florida Building Inspection Agencies*, doctoral dissertation, University of Florida: Gainesville, Florida.

Schneider R. H. (1996) *Comparison of Defensible Space and Crime Prevention Through Environmental Design (CPTED) Approaches and Applications in the United States and Britain*, Draft Working Paper, Department of Urban and Regional Planning, University of FL.

Schneider R. H. (1998) *Survey of Florida Police Use of CPTED*, Florida CPTED Network, Department of Urban and Regional Planning, University of Florida: Gainesville, FL.

Scott L., Crow W. J. and Erickson M. A. (1984) 'Robbery as robbers see it', in Clifton W. (ed.), *Convenience Store Robberies in Gainesville, Florida: an Intervention Strategy by the Gainesville Police Department*, Gainesville Police Department: Gainesville, FL.

Shaw C. R. (1969) *Juvenile Delinquency and Urban Areas*, revised edition, University of Chicago Press: Chicago, IL.

Shaw C. R. and McKay H. D. (1931) *Social Factors in Juvenile Delinquency*, Government Printing Office: Washington, D.C.

Sheffield First Partnership (n.d.) *Sheffield Trends 1999*, Sheffield First: Sheffield.

Sherman L. W. (1990) 'Police crackdowns: initial and residual deterrence', in Tonry M. and Morris N. (eds), *Crime and Justice: a Review of Research*, vol. 12, University of Chicago Press: Chicago, IL.

Sherman L. W. (1995) 'Hot spots of crime and criminal careers of places', in Eck J. E. and Wisburd D. (eds), *Crime and Place*, Criminal Justice Press: Monsey, N.Y.

Sherman L. W., Gottfredson D. C., Mackenzie D. C., Eck J., Reuter P. and Bushway S. D. (1997) *Preventing Crime: What Works, What Doesn't, What's Promising*, National Institute of Justice Research in Brief, US Department of Justice: Washington, D.C.

Sherman L. W. and Klein J. (1984) *Major Lawsuits Over Crime and Security: Trends and Patterns, 1958–1982*, University of Maryland Institute of Criminal Justice and Criminology: College Park, Maryland.

Simpson D. (2000) http://www.thenortheast.fsnet.co.uk/Hadrians.htm.

Sloan-Howitt M. and Kelling G. L. (1990) 'Subway graffiti in New York City: "Getting up" vs. "Meaning it and Cleanin" it', *Security Journal*, 1, 3, 131.

Smith M. F. and Clarke R. V. (2000) 'Crime and public transport', in Tonry M. (ed.), *Crime and Justice: A Review of the Research*, vol. 27, The University of Chicago Press: Chicago, IL pp. 169–233.

Smith M. S. (1996) *Crime Prevention Through Environmental Design in Parking Facilities*, National Institute of Justice Research in Brief, US Department of Justice: Washington, D.C.

Social Exclusion Unit (1998) *Bringing Britain Together: A National Strategy for Neighbourhood Renewal*, Cm 4045, HMSO: London.

Social Exclusion Unit (2000) *National Strategy for Neighbourhood Renewal: A Framework for Consultation*, HMSO: London.

Social Exclusion Unit (2001) *A New Commitment to Neighbourhood Renewal: National Strategy Action Plan*, HMSO: London.

Sommer R. (1969) *Personal Space: The Behavioral Basis of Design*, Prentice Hall: Englewood-Cliffs, NJ.

Sommer R. (1983) *Social Design: Creating Building with People in Mind*, Prentice-Hall: Englewood-Cliffs, NJ.

Spelman W. (1995) 'Once bitten, then what? Cross-sectional and time-course explanations of repeat victimisation', *British Journal of Criminology*, 35, 366–83.

Spelman W. and Eck J. (1989) 'Sitting ducks, ravenous wolves, and helping hands: New approaches to urban policing', *Public Affairs Comment*, 35, 2, 1–9.

Stokes M. (1996) *Designing Out Crime*, Proceedings of the Town and Country Planning Summer School, Royal Town Planning Institute: London, p. 83.

Taylor I., Evans K. and Fraser P. (1996) *A Tale of Two Cities*, Routledge: London.

Taylor R. B. (1988) *Human Territorial Functioning*, Cambridge University Press: Cambridge.

Taylor R. B. (1997) *Crime at Small Scale Places: What We Know, What We Can Prevent and What Else We Need To Know*, Conference on Criminal Justice and Evaluation, National Institute of Justice, http://www.ncjrs.org.

Taylor R. B. (1999) *Crime, Grime, Fear and Decline: a Longitudinal Look*, US Department of Justice, Office of Justice Programs, National Institute of Justice: Washington, D.C.

Taylor R. B. and Harrell A. V. (1996) *Physical Environment and Crime*, US Department of Justice, Office of Justice Programs, National Institute of Justice: Washington, D.C.

Tempe Police Department (1997) *Tempe Crime Prevention Through Environmental Design*, Tempe Police Department: Tempe, AZ.

Thompson A. H. (1975) *Military Architecture in Medieval England*, EP Publishing Limited: East Ardsley, Wakefield.

Tien J. M., O'Donnell V. F., Barnett A. and Mirchandani P. B. (1979) *Phase I Report: Street Lighting Projects*, Government Printing Office: Washington, D.C.

Tilley N. (1992) *Safer Cities and Community Safety Strategies*, Crime Prevention Unit Series, Paper 38, Police Research Group, Home Office: London.

Titus R. (1999) 'Personal opinion: Declining residential burglary rates in the USA', *Security Journal*, 12, 4, 59–63.

Topping P. and Pascoe T. (2000) 'Countering household burglary through the secured by design scheme: Does it work? An assessment of the evidence, 1989–1999', *Security Journal*, 13, 4, 71–8.

UN Commission on Crime Prevention and Criminal Justice (1999) *Strategies for Crime Prevention: Discussion Paper on the Theme of the Eighth Session of the Commission on Crime Prevention and Criminal Justice*, United Nations, Economic and Social Council: Vienna.

UN Commission on Environment and Development (1987) *Executive Summary: Our Common Future*, Oxford University Press: Oxford.

United States Conference of Mayors (1998) *Crime Prevention Through Environmental Design in American Cities: Report of a Survey of Mayors on Uses of CPTED as a Crime Prevention Strategy*, National Institute of Justice: Washington, D.C.

United States Conference of Mayors (2001). http://www.usmayors.org/.

United States Congress, National Commission on Urban Problems (Douglas Commission) (1968) *Building the American City*, report to the Congress and to the President of the United States, 91st Congress, 1st Session, 12 December.

United States Department of Housing and Urban Development (2001) http://www.hud.gov/library.

University of South Florida Urban Design Group (1990) *Gateway 2000: North Tamiami Trail*, University of South Florida: Tampa, FL.

Urban Task Force (1999) *Towards an Urban Renaissance*, Spon: London.

US Department of Justice (2000) *Criminal Victimization in United States, 1998; Statistical Tables*, US Department of Justice, Office of Justice Programs, Bureau of Justice Statistics: Washington, D.C.

Vale L. J. (1995) 'Transforming public housing: The social and physical redevelopment of Boston's West Broadway development', *Journal of Architectural and Planning Research*, 12, 3, 278–305.

Valentine G. (1991) 'Women's fear and the design of public space', *Built Environment*, 16, 4, 288–303.

Van Dijk J. J. M. (1997) 'Toward a research-based crime reduction policy, crime prevention as a cost effective policy option', *European Journal on Criminal Policy and Research*, 5, 3.

Velasco M. and Boba R. (2000) 'Tactical crime analysis and geographic information systems: Concepts and examples', *Crime Mapping News*, 2, 2.

Wagner F. W., Joder T. E. and Mumphrey A. J. (1995) *Urban Revitalization: Policies and Programs*, Sage: Thousand Oaks, CA.

Walker J. (1997) *Estimates of the Costs of Crime in Australia in 1996*, Australian Institute of Criminology, Paper Number 72, http://www.aic.gov.au.

Walker M. A. (1995) *Interpreting Crime Statistics*, Clarendon Press: Oxford.

Waller M. (2000) *1700 Scenes from London Life*, Four Walls Eight Windows: N.Y.

Wallis A. and Ford D. (1980) *Crime Prevention Through Environmental Design: The Commercial Demonstration in Portland, Oregon*, US Department of Justice, National Institute of Justice: Washington, D.C.

Wekerle G. R. and Whitzman C. (1995) *Safe Cities: Guidelines for Planning Design, and Management*, Van Nostrand: NY.

Whyte W. H. (1980) *The Social Life of Small Urban Places*, The Conservation Foundation: Washington, D.C.

Wilson E. O. (1980) *Sociobiology*, Belknap Press: Cambridge, MA.

Wilson J. Q. (1975) *Thinking About Crime*, Basic Books: NY.

Wilson J. Q and Kelling G. L. (1982) 'Broken windows', *The Atlantic Monthly*, 211, March, 29–38.

Wong C. (1997) 'Crime risk in urban neighbourhoods: The use of insurance data to analyse changing spatial forms', *Area*, 29, 3, 228–40.

Wood E. (1961) *Housing Design: A Social Theory*, New York Citizens' Housing and Planning Council: NY.

Wood E. (1967) *Social Aspect of Housing and Urban Development*, United Nations, Number 67.IV.12, NY.

Zahm D. (1998) 'Why protecting the public health, safety, and general welfare won't protect us from crime', in Felson M. and Peiser R. B. (eds), *Reducing Crime Through Real Estate Development and Management*, Urban Land Institute: Washington, D.C., pp. 71–89.

INDEX